CW00925981

THE BADGER

Also by William Fotheringham

Put Me Back on My Bike: In Search of Tom Simpson

Roule Britannia: Great Britain and the Tour de France

Fallen Angel: The Passion of Fausto Coppi

Cyclopedia: It's All About the Bike

A Century of Cycling

Fotheringham's Sporting Trivia

Fotheringham's Sporting Trivia: The Greatest Sporting Trivia Book Ever II

Merckx: Half Man, Half Bike

Racing Hard: 20 Tumultuous Years in Cycling

THE BADGER

THE LIFE OF **BERNARD HINAULT** AND THE
LEGACY OF FRENCH CYCLING

WILLIAM FOTHERINGHAM

CHICAGO
REVIEW
PRESS

Copyright © 2015 by William Fotheringham

First published in Great Britain in 2015 as *Bernard Hinault and the Fall and Rise of French Cycling* by Yellow Jersey Press, Random House, 20 Vauxhall Bridge Road, London SW1V 2SA

This edition published in 2015 by Chicago Review Press, Incorporated

All rights reserved

Chicago Review Press, Incorporated
814 North Franklin Street
Chicago, Illinois 60610
ISBN 978-1-61373-418-6

Cover design: John Yates at Stealworks.com
Cover photo: John Coles—PhotoSport Int/REX

Printed in the United States of America
5 4 3 2 1

For Andy Walker, Robert Vogt and his late wife Ginette,
for that golden summer of 1984.

CONTENTS

LIST OF ILLUSTRATIONS

1. Bernard Hinault, Brittany, 1977 (Offside).
2. Robert Le Roux (archives Le Télégramme); Cyrille Guimard, 1977 (Offside); Hinault at the Montreal track world championship, 1974 (Offside).
3. Climbing out of the ravine during the 1977 Dauphiné Libéré (Offside); being helped on his way during the 1977 Dauphiné Libéré (Offside).
4. Rendez-vous chez Hinault, 1977 (*Paris Match*/ Getty Images).
5. Hinault and family outside a house in Yffiniac, 1977 (*Paris Match*/Getty Images); in Yffiniac, 1977 (Offside).
6. At the riders strike, Valence, d'Agen, 1978 (Offside); being congratulated on winning the 1978 Tour de France (Getty Images).
7. Leading during the 1979 Tour de France (Getty Images); winning on the Champs Élysées from Joop Zoetemelk, 1979 (Corbis).
8. Cyclocross (Offside); in the snow at Liège–Bastogne–Liège, 1980 (Offside).
9. On horseback, Nevada, 1981 (Offside).

ACKNOWLEDGEMENTS

While this book draws on interviews going back over the last twenty-five years, specific thanks are due to the following for giving up time for me in 2014: Bernard Hinault, Robert Millar, Marc Madiot, Jean-Francois Bernard, Warren Barguil, Sean Kelly, Sean Yates, René Hinault, Sam Abt, Philippe Bouvet, Patrick Lefevere, Joop Zoetemelk, Stephen Roche, Philippe Crepel, Daniel Gisiger, Phil Edwards.

Thanks are due to my brother Alasdair for interviewing Andrés Gandarias, Julián Gorospe and Pedro Delgado on my behalf, and to Philippe Bouvet for supplying telephone numbers, back copies of *l'Équipe* and inspiration.

Thanks are also due to my agent John Pawsey and the team at Yellow Jersey Press for all their support and hard work: my eternally patient editor Matt Phillips, copy-editor Justine Taylor, designer Kris Potter, production Phil Brown and Bethan Jones for publicity.

The most valuable contribution however has come from my wife Caroline and children Patrick and Miranda, who offer priceless affection and patience as the stresses and strains mount as each book is written.

'The Mole had long wanted to make the acquaintance of the Badger. He seemed by all accounts to be such an important personage.'

– Kenneth Grahame, *The Wind in the Willows*

CHAPTER 1

THE BADGER IN A TRAP

*'Everything you do is a permanent challenge. You have to
be on top of it all the time but treat it as a game.'*

– Bernard Hinault

Bernard Hinault was stuck. Crammed into the front pas-
senger seat of the car in a backstreet of the Norman town
of Lisieux, there was nowhere for him to go. The door
wouldn't open; the crowd was too densely packed.
Winding down the window was a no-no; too many bodies
were pressed up against it. It was a balmy midsummer
evening, the sun was setting, the fans had turned out in
force and they had been waiting for a good while. Old,
young, men, women, each wanted to get a sight of him,
touch him, ask him for an autograph.

Hinault had arrived fashionably late for the start of the
Lisieux criterium on 23 July 1985, and through the evening
the crowd had swelled in anticipation of his arrival. They
had started out looking for prime spots on the circuit,
then had moved as if by osmosis, filling the pavement in

front of the building where the riders were to get changed. The crush was understandable: two days earlier, Hinault had won the Tour de France for the fifth time, joining Eddy Merckx and Jacques Anquetil in the record books. Here he was, in the flesh.

I can't remember how Hinault eventually got out of the car and made it to the door of the changing rooms. What I do remember is that while the script called for a bit of badger-type aggression – a snarl, at least, if not a swipe of the claws – there was none of that. He sat calmly and waited for the organisers to find some muscle and give him the space to emerge. He looked slight – he is one of those cyclists who looks larger on his bike than off it – and not unreasonably he looked a little tired. He didn't win. That privilege was reserved for the 'regional' Thierry Marie, a first-year professional who had just finished his debut Tour.

I wasn't in the throng around the car containing the man in the yellow jersey. Ironically enough, I hadn't come to see Hinault. The history-making and the drama of the 1985 Tour were not to be denied, but for a large group of us, the interest was more parochial. Along with a gaggle of teammates from the Etoile Sportive Livarotaise – a club based in a cheese-and-cider-making village ten miles to the south – I'd come to watch Thierry, our club-mate of the year before. Thierry was one of three Livarotais in the big race that evening: with him were François Lemarchand, another first-year pro who had just finished the Tour, and Alain Percy, a first-category amateur who had been selected for the Norman 'regional' team. They were the guys we trained, yarned and joked with. They were our conduit to the world of Hinault and company. That put the Badger well within six degrees of separation.

The little world that had bred Hinault, Maurice Le Guilloux, Vincent Barteau, Laurent Fignon and countless French professionals since the war was also our world. It was a world in which there were races by the score every weekend, and a fair few during the week. At some time in the year, almost every centre of population in Normandy and Brittany had its *Prix du Comité des Fêtes* or *Prix du Cyclisme*, no matter how isolated the village or how small the hamlet. Some had two or three in a summer. Hinault and the others we were watching had all started in those races. They had moved up to the bigger events, regional semi-Classics run with pride by clubs like ours, and thence into the stratosphere. Hence the connection. For Livarot, a small-town club from deepest rural France, fielding two riders in the same Tour was an unlikely feat – at least since the days of 'regional' teams came to an end in the 1950s. It was like a backwoods football team fielding two players in an FA Cup final. For our boss, Robert Vogt, it didn't get much better than this.

The point of the post-Tour criterium is – was – that you see your heroes in the flesh. It adds an extra, personal dimension to the photographs and the stories. Hinault had been a key part of my cycling life since it had begun in 1978, and now here he was. Stuck in a car, emerging to be lost in a sea of bodies, then whizzing past in the high-speed string backlit by the setting sun. It was Hinault's curly hair, hedge-thick eyebrows and bared teeth that had filled the covers of the copies of *Miroir du Cyclisme* that I devoured as a teenager. I would lose myself in his world to the point that in physics lessons the teacher would return me abruptly to a land of equations and Bunsen burners with a coolly targeted lump of chalk. Hinault's Tours and Classics were the ones my late father and I listened to on long-wave French radio stations, brought to us by Jean-Rene Godart and Jean-Paul Brouchon.

I had no particular passion for Hinault in spite of his obvious status as the top dog in the sport. What appealed was the fantastically clandestine nature of cycling: the process of discovering a culture few knew about or had an interest in, a journey guided by a language few people spoke and media that weren't readily available. The magazines had to be bought in a shop in Soho; the radio had to be tuned to the right station at the right time. But Hinault always cropped up at the memorable moments, and their scarcity made them all the more notable.

On school exchange in Brittany in the 1979 Easter holidays, I pestered my hosts to let me watch Paris–Roubaix and Liège–Bastogne–Liège, where Hinault was among the impotent chasers behind a dominant Didi Thurau. Somehow, I found a radio on which to listen to the finish of the Ballon d'Alsace stage of the 1979 Tour – Hinault's epic, now largely forgotten duel with Joop

Zoetemelk – as my school form picnicked on a hillside in Devon during an outing when French exchange students returned that July. Hinault's 1980 Sallanches world championship I watched in episodes one afternoon on a visit to our twin village in Normandy, with the race split up by a long lunch and a drive between houses, during which my brother sicked up his Camembert.

Inspired by the knowledge that Hinault had broken away early at Sallanches in the rain to avoid confusion in the bunch, I tried something similar a year later at the Devon and Cornwall junior divisional championships, only to realise that it might have worked for him, but wouldn't for me. By 1982 I was wearing the John McEnroe-style sweatband in Renault-Elf's yellow and black, popularised by Hinault and Laurent Fignon. If the Badger and the Professor were happily flying in the face of practicality and good taste, I had no qualms about doing the same.

The 1984 Tour, Hinault against Fignon, was the first I lived in full, in France. I didn't appreciate it at the time: this would come to be the way that I experienced most Tours from 1990 onwards as a journalist, through French television and the newspaper *L'Équipe*. Every afternoon in that baking hot July – racing and training permitting – I trekked religiously up the hill in Livarot to M. and Mme Vogt's house, where the curtains would be drawn against the sun so that we could watch Hinault's drawn-out defeat and Fignon's utter triumph. We couldn't avoid feeling smug, given that we knew that the following season our Thierry would be riding with Fignon and Guimard at

the all-conquering Renault-Elf team. With hindsight, it's
amusing to recall the Schadenfreude we felt in the knowledge that Hinault had quit Guimard the previous autumn.
Now he was getting a kicking, and our boy was going to
be among those putting the boot into the Badger in 1985.
That July, no one expected Hinault to bite back.

The best part of thirty years later, I was again looking at
the figure of Hinault squashed up in a car, but this time
there were no crowds to get in the way, and I was in the
car too. It was one of the red Skoda Superb saloons,
emblazoned with logos and festooned with radio aerials
that are driven by the Tour de France's top brass and we
were sitting on the top of Holme Moss. The Yorkshire
moorland was deserted, as you would expect in midweek
at the end of March, and it was bone-achingly cold in a
wind that seemed to come a long way from the east.

A national institution transposed to foreign territory
made entertaining watching on that spring day in 2014.
Hinault was contracted to visit Yorkshire to publicise the
Grand Départ of the Tour in Leeds the coming July, and
to that end he had begun with a ceremonial visit in the
red Skoda to the Robin Hood pub in Cragg Vale. He'd
had a rapid pie and pint in the bar – the photograph by
Simon Wilkinson made many of the papers. He'd run
through a load of questions for the local press, then slipped
into cycling kit for a spin to the top of what purported
to be the longest continuous ascent on English soil with
a group of local cyclists. He had signed anything and

everything from posters and T-shirts to the bunting which the locals were going to run up the telegraph poles when the Tour visited on 5 July.

Hinault had moved on from his years as the angry man of French cycling. He was no longer the guy who once said that he wished he had a jacket with tacks on it, to ward off the back slappers who would hassle him after stages. *Le Blaireau* had mellowed into an authoritative father figure, like the Badger Kenneth Grahame described in *The Wind in the Willows*. He jumped through the media and marketing hoops with the same professionalism that was his hallmark on the bike: he had signed up for it, so he got on with the job, with no second thoughts.

We drove from Cragg Vale over the Moss and up and down the plethora of little climbs that made stage 2 of the Tour into Sheffield one of the toughest opening-weekend stages in recent Tours. He waxed lyrical about the stone walls – 'imagine the skill, the hours of work that's gone into those' – speculated about what wine you might drink if you shot and cooked one of the pheasants in the moorland fields, discussed terriers, and enjoyed the comparison between Yorkshiremen and the famously tough and insular Bretons. He clearly relished the succession of tight little descents on narrow roads and the gritty little climbs that peppered the end of the Sheffield stage. 'The riders won't enjoy this, especially if it rains,' he said smugly. 'I'd probably have complained but I'd have had a bit of fun here.'

*

You could argue that the notion of professional cycling as fun died on the day that Hinault symbolically hung his bike on a hook after his farewell race in November 1986. The phrase *se faire plaisir* – have fun, take pleasure, enjoy yourself – crops up all the time when you talk cycling with him. It might seem curious to use the term about something that demands as much pain and sacrifice as professional cycling, but Hinault was not alone: it was Fignon's philosophy as well. In twenty-five years on the Tour, the only winner I've heard describe racing as fun was Lance Armstrong, but that's a different story.

Hinault's career neatly bridged two eras. He started out in 1975, when the sport had barely changed in its essentials since the Second World War – better bikes and kit, better roads but not much else – and when he hung up his wheels cycling had begun to resemble its twenty-first-century incarnation. By his retirement in 1986 it was a much bigger, far more business-oriented, fully international sport with more cash on the table and more sponsors. In Hinault's first Tour, 1978, the field comprised a mere eleven teams, with bike manufacturers dominating as sponsors and co-sponsors. Six of the teams were French. The Italians didn't even bother to turn up; a Swede, an Irishman and a brace of Britons (Barry Hoban and Paul Sherwen) were the only riders from outside the European heartland. By 1986, Hinault's last, the race had twenty-one teams, including two from Colombia and one from the USA, with a diverse mix of multinational sponsors, and riders from Australia, Norway, Canada and

Mexico, as well as the obvious Europeans and a plethora of North and South Americans.

When I followed Hinault's win in the 1985 Tour – in front of the same French television set as I'd watched him on in 1984 – the race was well into its transition from being a French event with a smattering of international entrants to an international sporting event which took place – largely – on French soil. It had gone global in just a few years. Some historians locate the turning point as 1981, when the Australian Phil Anderson shook Hinault by clinging on to his wheel at the Pla d'Adet finish in the Pyrenees and briefly wore the yellow jersey. Anderson was the first non-European to lead the race, and that prompted Jacques Goddet to write his keynote editorial on globalising cycling in *L'Équipe*, *'un Tour mondialisé'*. The American Greg LeMond's victory in Hinault's last Tour was the first for a non-European; for veteran *L'Équipe* writer Pierre Chany, the presence of four nations in the top five overall represented the 'complete internationalisation of the Tour'. Chany reminded his readers that a few years earlier, it would have been unimaginable for the *maillot jaune* to come from outside Europe and looked forward to a time when no nation would dominate cycling – which is where we have arrived in the twenty-first century.

Hinault played his part in the transition in the 1980s. After his mentor Cyrille Guimard signed LeMond, he and Hinault took a celebrated trip to the US, marked by the 'cowboy togs' photo shoot, where Hinault, LeMond and the Renault manager posed in Old West outfits. This now looks like a key turning point. Hinault's later transfer to La Vie Claire exemplified the change in cycling: Renault was the state-owned car maker, with all the emotional baggage that went with that, while La Vie Claire was a chain of health-food stores run by a charismatic if roguish capitalist Bernard Tapie. It had a Mondrian-inspired racing jersey that summed up its modernity. And in drawing Tapie to cycling, Hinault brought in the big money.

Hinault is rightly hailed as cycling's last champion in another way. Since his time, no Tour de France winner – and barely any other riders at all – have raced an entire season with the goal of winning everything on offer. 'The last of his kind perhaps, racing from spring to autumn, triumphing on all terrains, piling one exploit on another, forging the second greatest record of cycling history behind Eddy Merckx,' wrote Olivier Margot in the introduction to *L'Équipe's* centenary celebration book of the Tour in 2003.

Fignon echoed Margot, pointing out that the reductive approach to targeting just the Tour de France has in its turn reduced the stature of the champions who adopt it: 'When Hinault was on song he would wipe out everyone; he would win everything he could from the start of the season to the end. Back then, cycling champions didn't do things in a small way. When the Badger won, he won big-time.'

'Hinault just did things, like falling off in the [1977] Dauphiné and winning, dominating [the 1980] Liège–Bastogne–Liège in the snow,' recalls Sam Abt, a journalist who covered the era for the *Herald Tribune*. 'They were extraordinary demonstrations of strength.'

There was another, broader change. In 1978, the American writer Felix Magowan could claim that 'In the Latin countries, cycling is a sport practised mainly by the socially disadvantaged, those who might otherwise go into boxing . . . For the most part, the cyclists are the children of peasants, either landless day-labourers or small farm holders. In France they are more apt than not to be from Brittany, the one province where cycling enjoys a following akin to that in Belgium.' That had gone by the late 1980s, partly because the international mix of the professional peloton meant potential racers came from far beyond cycling's traditional industrial and agricultural base, but also because economic change across Europe meant there were fewer peasant farmers and industrial workers who needed cycling as a means of escape. Cycling changed its sociological mix in Hinault's time, enough for Margot to describe him as 'one of the last, symbolic representatives of a suffering working class'.

Most famously, however, Hinault was the last of the sport's *patrons*, a series of authoritative figures going back to the founding days. They were the men with the hardest characters and the strongest legs, who could dictate the pace of the racing, and could exert influence with organisers and other teams. Their whims could affect their fellow professionals' chances in other races, their influence could dictate what appearance money their inferiors earned. The *patrons* – Merckx, Rik Van Looy, Hinault,

Anquetil – were a blend of union leader and mafia boss, but they had this in common: they ruled the sport through muscle and mouth. Hinault's status as a *patron* was established early on when he took on the organisers of the Tour de France in 1978, and he continued to dominate his fellows to the end of his career. After which, the *patron* went the way of the dodo.

Hinault was the last man standing in another way. In 1985, France's dominance in the Tour could be taken for granted, purely because of recent history. The notion that no Frenchman was going to win the Tour for at least thirty years was completely outlandish, more outlandish than the notion the race might one day start in the British county of Yorkshire. On the grass verges around the criterium circuit in Lisieux in 1985, either suggestion would have drawn derision, but the idea that the French would still be waiting for another home Tour winner in 2015 would have been unthinkable. The French won lots of stages in the Tour, and they won lots of Tours. Between Eddy Merckx's last win in 1974 and Hinault's last in 1985, the French nailed nine Tour wins out of a possible eleven, five for Hinault and two apiece for Fignon and Bernard Thévenet. The eight years between Thévenet in 1975 and Roger Pingeon in 1967 looked like a big gap, but it also seemed an aberration – down to the exceptional ability of Merckx – given that the late 1950s and 1960s had seen French victories aplenty

As French sportsmen love to say, the truth of today is

not that of tomorrow. Things change fast. By 1990, the first Tour I reported on as a journalist, home dominance was already looking shaky: Fignon had been bedevilled by injury, but his near-miss in 1989 meant he was still to be included in a list of Tour contenders, and there was no one else of his stature in France. From then on, the decline was so rapid that by the 2000s, French stage wins became exceptional events.

The Festina doping scandal in 1998 rocked the sport in France to its core; the top team in the country led by the national darling Richard Virenque was proven, humiliatingly, to be founded on institutionalised doping and a swath of other squads and riders were implicated. Amid the uncertainty, tales of the decline of cycling at the grassroots in France abounded, from bike-shop owners who complained that no youngsters raced bikes any more to race organisers – from the area of Normandy where the calendar had been so prolific when I raced there only twenty years earlier – standing by the Tour de France route brandishing placards complaining that the national federation had no interest in local events. Understandably, there were pessimists who felt that cycling in France was in long-term, permanent decline. The leading commentator at *L'Équipe*, Philippe Brunel, and the writer Jacques Marchand were among those who claimed that the French public would desert cycling in the same way they had quit boxing since the days of Marcel Cerdan and Jean-Claude Bouttier.

Cycling in France clearly isn't dying out and probably

never will, but French cycling's tortured search for
Hinault's successor – not a five-times Tour champion,
merely a one-time Tour winner – is far from over. That in
turn means that Hinault's story is not yet quite complete.
Hinault's succession matters, and not merely in France.
Why? Because in what is now cycling's showcase event,
'the France question' is a key part of the plot and by the
2000s it was disturbing outsiders as well as locals. That's
partly because, unlike the great stadium events, cycling's
showcase is largely defined by its location. Whatever brief
excursions it makes beyond the borders, the Tour can only
take place in France, but that backdrop in turn impacts
on the race to an extent that say, the location of Wimbledon
or Roland Garros does not. The race travels through
Brittany so the fans and media look for Bretons. Because
the Tour is rooted permanently in France, French success
enhances it, bringing out fans, bringing in sponsors, oiling
the wheels of officialdom. People from outside France are
drawn to the Tour because of its quintessentially French
qualities, and having French cyclists performing well is
part of that picture.

Back in France, the national soul-searching is understandable. Success or lack of it in the Tour has implications
right down the cycling food chain to the Livarot cycling
club, the Lisieux criterium and the smallest races. But
more broadly, there is what the British referred to – pre-
Andy Murray – as Wimbledon syndrome: the frustrating
sense that a nation has created a great international sporting event but can't succeed in it. The Tour's media profile

and duration means that for thirty years, that absence has been rammed home for thirty days a year. So while Belgium has moved on from the post-Merckx succession crisis with a gradual realisation that there won't be a second Cannibal, France is still desperately seeking its second Badger.

The crowd in Lisieux on that balmy evening thirty years ago hadn't come to see a throwback to the golden age of French cycling, the last champion from the 'amateur' era, or a champion who epitomised a sport in full transition from parochial backwater to international mainstream, or *le dernier patron*. Not even the most pessimistic would have come to watch a French Tour winner on the basis that it wasn't going to happen again for a very long time. We took Hinault on his merits as a champion, and they were many.

By 1985 his record was largely complete: those five Tour wins, plus three in the Giro d'Italia, two in the Vuelta a España, the brace of Giro–Tour doubles and the 1980 world championship. The welter of major one-day victories, sometimes several in a season, now largely forgotten amid the obsessive interest in the Tour: Giro di Lombardia, Liège–Bastogne–Liège, Paris–Roubaix, Amstel Gold, Gent–Wevelgem, Flèche Wallonne, the Grand Prix des Nations.

Beyond the bare results – not as extensive as those of Eddy Merckx – was the manner of some of those wins: the epic Liège win in the snow of 1980, the three-week duel with Joop Zoetemelk in the 1979 Tour, and of course the clinical brutality of the world title at Sallanches. Some of Hinault's results were simply eccentric because of their utter recklessness: a bunch sprint win on the Champs-Élysées in 1982; an outlandish attack with Zoetemelk to sprint it out man for man on the Champs at the end of the 1979 Tour; a cycling version of who could piss highest up the wall with Francesco Moser that got out of hand in the 1979 Lombardy.

For the French, Hinault was more than a mere cyclist. He was also a symbol of *'La France qui gagne'* – a Winning France – in an era when France lived through all sorts of doubts outside the sporting world. The Badger was part of a golden generation of French sportsmen, all of whose careers ran roughly parallel through the late 1970s and early 1980s: Michel Platini between 1976–87 including the World Cups of 1978, '82 and '86; Alain Prost, who broke through in 1979 and would win his last Grand Prix in 1990; Yannick Noah, who turned professional in 1977, and won the French Open in 1983 and Wimbledon in 1985; Jean-Pierre Rives, the blond, blood-spattered rugby rebel who reigned from 1975–84 and who received his Legion d'Honneur from François Mitterrand at the same time as Hinault.

Such success came at a difficult time for France, believes Sam Abt. 'From the late 1970s through the '80s there was a crisis of confidence – a big flight of capital, no one was sure what France's place in the world was or what the socialists would do. When I moved here in 1971, it was a second-world country – my concierge didn't have a refrigerator and put milk outside to keep cool. Not many had cars. So someone who was a true champion stood out so much. Hinault was Teflon-coated; nothing stopped him.'

Hinault's mentor Cyrille Guimard was not a Merckx fan – the pair never really hit it off – and he places both Anquetil and Hinault above the Cannibal, and believes Coppi would be above him as well. Those who competed with Hinault also placed him on a pedestal, by virtue of what he inflicted on them on the road. 'Merckx was the greatest, but Bernard was the most impressive,' reckoned Lucien Van Impe, who contested victory in the Tour with both the Cannibal and the Badger. 'I've never seen inner anger like his. He had the ability to take command of a situation in a fraction of a second.'

'Physically superior to Merckx', was the verdict of Joop Zoetemelk, another rider who contested the Tour with both men. 'Eddy wanted to win everything – criteriums, small races, six days – but Bernard was more reasonable, started the season more steadily, but anything Bernard wanted to win, he could. Bernard wouldn't want to win eight stages in the Tour; Eddy would want everything – stages, green jersey, mountains. He was *trop gourmand* for my taste.'

'He had a totally different character to the riders who came after him – Miguel Indurain, Pedro Delgado, LeMond,' said Robert Millar who saw Lance Armstrong in his early years, and Hinault in his prime. 'They didn't race the way he raced. Hinault either cared or he didn't. When he didn't care about winning he'd bumble round and hurt you now and again just to remind you he was there – you wouldn't know Greg or Miguel were in some races, but Hinault, you always knew. He was the most impressive of all the guys I raced against, even Lance,' believed Millar. 'Lance had the aggression but Hinault had the edge in physical ability. He'd probably have found a weakness in Lance and beaten him.'

Hinault only gained true popularity by the time I saw him in Lisieux, after he had been through the mill of a potentially career-ending injury and that 1984 defeat. Early in the 1980s, he was in a state of cold war with the French media, one of whom described the Tours of 1978–82 – which included Hinault's first four victories – as 'the most boring of the entire post-war period'. He was pilloried at times for failing to play the media game, for adopting the role of the anti-champion, downplaying what he did, 'reducing international cycling to the dimensions of a medium-sized provincial business', according to the writer Olivier Dazat.

Guimard's belief is that the greatness of a sportsman depends on the way he or she plays on the emotions of those who look on; his case is that Hinault stimulated a greater emotional response than Merckx, which may well be true among the French. 'Sporting logic doesn't create heroes. From a certain level upwards, when you want to be loved, the volume of victories and the value of those victories cease to count, but what matters is the emotions that they evoke, the way the plot pans out and the side you choose to take.' If the true gauge of greatness in sport is whether or not you are talked about years after you stop competing, Hinault qualifies by virtue of his part in perhaps the most talked about Tour of all time: 1986, his 'fratricidal' battle with LeMond.

That race followed a pattern: throughout Hinault's career there were times when he would put logic to one side and let emotion take over. He would bin the plan and race for the sheer hell of it, as amateurs do. Sometimes, he looked to have the unalloyed joy of the fat man sprinting with his teenage son for a road sign; to that, all cycling fans could relate. It transcended statistics.

'Standing at a machine with the same piece of metal in front of me, doing the same thing to it, that was work. What we do – you as well as me – is a game,' he told me in 2014. 'Cycling is a game. *C'est du bonheur*. Competing for me was always a game. It can be painful, but it hurts because I want to hurt myself, that's all. If I don't want to do it, I don't do it.

'If you play poker, that can get serious, because there can end up being a significant financial side to it, but for the rest, it's *du bonheur, du plaisir*. Even when it doesn't work. When it doesn't work, you analyse why it hasn't worked. Why didn't I win today? Because I did something stupid, because I raced poorly, because I didn't train enough. It's down to you, not to other people. I never blamed any defeat on anyone else. It would be down to me. Even when I was a schoolboy, a junior, I always had that pleasure.'

Asked if that joy stayed with him, Hinault just says, '*tout le temps*', adding, 'The game is winning, as well. It's about demonstrating that you are capable of doing something different.' It is different, he maintains, from the absolute need to win that – most notably – drove Eddy Merckx. 'I didn't see things in precisely the same way. Eddy wanted to win everything. For me, I would give myself four or five objectives in the year and that would be enough. And then, if I didn't hit those objectives, I wouldn't be very happy. I would ask myself questions: why didn't you win? What mistakes did you make? I won a lot of races outside [those objectives] because I wanted to have fun.' His point is that what counted was the enjoyment of what he was doing, not winning per se. 'You are in the race, you are with your rivals, you're keeping an eye on them, left, right, all round. If someone isn't placed right, bang, you attack and eliminate him. The victory is what comes at the end of the day.'

'What motivated Hinault wasn't his *palmarès*, but turning a situation around, fighting with an adversary,' believes Philippe Bouvet, who reported on the Hinault years for *L'Équipe*. That's why he could fairly be called 'the last cyclist with real ardour', as Philippe Bordas wrote in the book *Forcenés*. 'The paradigm of larger-than-life. The last to justify cycling as a way to be different.' And that is why Bordas concluded: 'Cycling history ends with Hinault.'

CHAPTER 2

ON THE EDGE

*'Tout champion d'exception porte la croix ou l'étendard de
sa marginalité' – 'All exceptional champions are outsiders;
it's a burden and a badge of honour'*

– Cyrille Guimard

In Goscinny and Uderzo's Asterix books, the village of
the indomitable Gauls is drawn in the far west of France,
in Brittany. There is the faintest hint of huts gathered
behind timber-stake walls as Bernard Hinault's cousin
René joins up the dots on a sketch map of the outskirts
of the Breton village of Yffiniac, near Saint-Brieuc on the
northern coast. 'Lucie and Joseph Hinault lived in this
cottage with Bernard and his brothers and sister; Joseph's
parents were here, Lucie's sister – she was a Guernion
– and her ten children were in this house, and another
Guernion sister, my mother, was here.'

The four cottages on the outskirts of the village of
Yffiniac – La Clôture, La Tenue, La Rivière and Levauriou
– stood cheek by jowl, spread across 500 metres on a

shallow hillside or so; a hamlet called la Fraiche. Between them, in the 1950s and 1960s, they housed some twenty children from the four branches of the Hinault–Guernion clan. It was a small community of its own, where everyone knew what everyone else was up to, where various members of the family – the children in particular – would help out their relatives at harvest time, and where the children lived in and out of each other's houses. La Clôture, home to Joseph and Lucie Hinault and their four children – of whom Bernard was the second oldest – was relatively new. Joseph had the house built not long after Bernard was born in November 1954, prior to which the family had shared La Tenue with Joseph's parents and an uncle.

The holdings were small – the largest, Lavouriou, was only about thirty hectares, substantial enough for Brittany at the time, but not large – and the plots of land were all mingled with each other. There was a constant tug of war between the requirement for hands to work the land, and the need the youngsters felt to forge their own identity away from the village and learn a trade before coming back, perhaps. 'If you were strong as a teenager, you were put to work early on. All our parents had to count their pennies,' says René Hinault, who had to leave school at fourteen to work the land so that his juniors could gain their education in their turn.

They were a close-knit group. As often happened, Bernard's parents had met at a family wedding, that of René's parents, where they were bridesmaid and usher;

tradition dictated that they should also be godparents to the firstborn, and the rest was history. 'We are all *un peu tête de cons*,' says René. 'A bit pig-headed. When we make our minds up, it takes a hell of a lot for us to change them.' In his various memoirs, Hinault makes much of his rebellious youth even if at times he verges on self-parody. 'I was the most terrible scoundrel that Yffiniac has ever known ...' he said. 'Donkey, Mr Angry, Little Stubborn Breton – there were plenty of nicknames during the first twelve years of my life as I piled one prank on another, big and little, with an insouciance and an hyperactive nature that I didn't try to conceal.' Bernard and his three siblings rarely sat still – there are few photographs of them, because, as he observed, they weren't the kind to wait and 'watch the birdie'.

Bernard was the most hyperactive of these four live-wires. 'He was more disruptive [as a child] than any I ever knew,' his mother Lucie told the writer Jacky Hardy. 'I often called him, "little hooligan". He wasn't bad, he just wouldn't stay in one place.' Young Bernard's favourite game was letting the chickens out – and, one writer claims, killing one with a stick if he could manage it – but the beatings and tellings-off that ensued didn't leave him cowed or bitter. They were part of the deal. 'He didn't hold grudges,' said his mother. 'You'd stop scolding him and he'd leap into your arms.'

Letting out the hens meant trouble, because in the economy of *La France Profonde*, every egg mattered, and Hinault's was a classic rural upbringing. Joseph and Lucie had moved around in search of a living: first they quit Brittany for Normandy, where they worked on a farm before they became aware that agriculture wasn't going to pay. That realisation took the couple to the outskirts of Paris where Joseph earned the professional qualification to become a platelayer for the national rail company SNCF, before returning to Yffiniac.

The country lad who seeks a career on two wheels rather than till the soil has been a constant theme in cycling since people began racing bikes in the nineteenth century, right up to the last five-times Tour de France winner, Miguel Indurain, a few years after Hinault. Both Hinault and his mentor Cyrille Guimard emphasised their rural roots, in particular the way they made a man strong-willed and independent, attached to the earth and its values. Like most rural working-class families, the Hinaults had a big garden with hens and rabbits, and – typically for Brittany – an onion patch to raise a few extra francs.

'Simple people,' wrote Guimard. 'Everywhere, from morning to night, one fixed idea obsessed the entire family: work, work first, work always. My family could kill pigs, grow potatoes, gather corn and build walls. No more. And no less.' As a teenager, Hinault liked to work in the field with his father, digging, planting, weeding, harvesting the beans and onions. There were years when their plot yielded a ton of beans, ten tons of the onions that went to the cooperative and 'made the ends of the month a little easier'. This background gave Hinault more in common with Fausto Coppi, Raymond Poulidor or Jacques

Anquetil, than with Eddy Merckx, whose family emerged from peasant roots to lead a relatively well-off existence above a suburban grocer's shop.

According to Guimard, Joseph kept himself to himself. 'He was discreet, almost hidden from view. His wife [Lucie] was more happy-go-lucky, but without ever getting involved, never interrupting or leading discussions among the family.' Young Bernard confessed that he was fascinated by his father's job, 'involving what I felt must be huge responsibilities and insane risks'. 'A sort of hero,' he once said. Platelaying was a tough manual job, not highly paid, 'like a convict breaking stones', in the words of one French writer. There was no comparison with the life of an athlete in terms of the responsibility, but in the danger, the physical effort, and in the eyes of a teenage son, a certain degree of glamour, there were resonances at least. This was blue-collar rural life and indeed, Hinault speaks of his father's classic *celeste* railwayman's overalls, typical of senior *paysans* at the time, which he wore every day apart from Sunday morning when he changed for mass. His father was quietly spoken, a disciplinarian with a firm hand, which meant Bernard's siblings tried to keep to the straight and narrow. Their second-born brother, on the other hand, just kept letting the chickens out.

Hinault was a combative youth, nicknamed Cerdan after the legendary French boxer of the 1950s. '*Un bagarreur*, a brawler,' says René. This is another thing that Hinault makes much of, fitting as it does the reputation he subsequently acquired in cycling as the Badger. 'At school, even with the bigger lads, I put myself about,' he told Philippe Bouvet. 'I got a bit back, but I dished out a bit too.' There was an undercurrent of violence in his boyhood: blows on the head with a wooden ruler to correct any errors in the morning dictation at school; the fights on the way home which Hinault said in his memoirs that he relished, when the boys from rival establishments would meet in a narrow lane. 'There were plenty of other ways home but I liked fighting too much to choose another route. I would go that way as a challenge. Every evening my fear and my courage were put to the test and I wasn't impressed either by the age or the size of my opponents ...I wonder if I wasn't happy to go to school because of the potential it offered for measuring myself each evening against the other pupils.' Deep down, he wrote, he liked a bit of 'argy bargy'. In one fight, he wrote of being 'close to strangling' a pupil from that other school.

Hinault wasn't a happy scholar. He had a good memory but a short attention span. In class, early on, he would hide himself behind the vast stove in the schoolroom and look out of the window. But he would tell his mother, 'If I don't work at school, it's because I don't like it. And when I find what I like I will put in twice the effort and be the best at it.' He seemed to devote a lot of energy to fighting the system, in spite of the consequences. He played truant with friends; his father would always find out and he'd get a slap. He and his fellow pupils would burn the ruler their schoolmaster used to beat them; he dodged two years of catechism by taking communion at the same time as his brother, who was two years older; later, at college, he recalled an episode when he and his fellow trainee engineers had a teacher who liked to lean back in his chair on the two rear legs – or he liked it, until they put a broken chair behind his desk, and he fell on his back. Hinault was an independent soul, so keen to start work at fourteen that he gave the owner of a garage on the nearby Route Nationale 12 the impression that he was sixteen – the legal minimum age – so he could start work as a pump attendant.

A last-minute surge of study meant he passed the *certificate d'etude primaire* at fifteen and went to technical college in Saint-Brieuc, where he started an engineering apprenticeship; woodwork would have been his first choice but the course was full. Here the brief flirtation with athletics began, when he came under the wing of a PE teacher, Daniel Carfentan, 'the first guy who gave me an athlete's body'. He joined the athletics section of *Club Olympique Briochine*, and Carfentan trained him up: cross-country running in winter, 1,500m and 3,000m in summer. From 1969 to 1971, young Hinault was a runner, improving steadily year on year, and strong enough to finish tenth in the French junior cross-country championship at Compiegne.

At the same time, cycling was getting its hooks into him. It had always been there in the background. The Hinault family watched the Tour de France on television at 4 o'clock every July afternoon, although the job at the service station put paid to that. In that small community, Bernard and the others would have known about the weekend races their cousin René rode, and they set up mock events of their own, using a red bike that had originally been intended for the oldest, Gilbert. Because everything they had was shared among the four of them, each had a go; at his first attempt, Bernard went into a tree but soon became the most devoted user of the bike, even though it was too big for him and he had to use a brick as a mounting block.

He would return home from riding the bike covered in cuts and bruises, and his mother would implore him to take it just a little bit steadier. But he was an impatient youth who liked to court danger. He moved on from letting the hens out to setting vast fishing lines at low tide in the nearby Saint-Brieuc bay with his cousins. Once or twice he came close to grief when the rising tide caught him out as he waded through one of the channels in the vast expanse of sandbanks. Suddenly he was up to his neck and swimming hard. 'I thought I would never cover the four hundred metres to the edge.' But it didn't stop him going back, across the sandbanks in the middle of the night, by the light of a pocket torch.

He fell precipitately into cycling. His years spent running round an athletics track meant there was no lengthy induction, although there were ways in which he prepared for bike racing without knowing it. He had been bought a bike at fifteen as a reward for passing his exams; he rode it daily into Saint-Brieuc to technical college, to avoid the two-kilometre walk from the bus station in Saint-Brieuc. The trip was ten kilometres; on the way in, to save five or ten minutes, young Bernard would try to tailgate one of the trucks that ground up the long hill from Yffiniac. 'It was a dangerous exercise: you had to calculate it right on the corner at the bottom of the hill and get enough momentum so that you could keep the right pedal speed up the hill. I liked it. I would get as close as possible, and it was a matter of honour not to get tailed off. Catching the trucks was a game. It was fun: at the same time a challenge, laughing at danger, and sustaining an intense effort. I liked the challenge.' On the descent homewards, it was the same process in reverse; trying to go as fast as the cars speeding down the hill.

Not surprisingly, he didn't struggle when he began cycling with René, who was eight years older and had been racing since 1965, between spells working on the farmland, which tended to put paid to his form in summer at harvest time. René held a second-category licence, placing him midway up the amateur hierarchy. The key period was a couple of weeks in late April and early May 1971. Towards the end of April, young Bernard went out on his old bike for a training ride with René, 'his first real outing', his cousin recalls: 75-80km with the inevitable hills. 'I was going well, I ended up racing seventeen days that May – that was just the ones I finished – I was a second cat, I was winning races, and there I was with a sixteen-year-old, who was hurting my legs on the hills. To stay with him I was having to use a gear two teeth smaller than he was.' In other words, the sixteen-year-old was spinning his legs so easily that the mature rider alongside him was having to push himself in a considerably higher gear in order to keep up the same speed. According to René, every training ride with Bernard developed into a competition.

The most common version of Bernard Hinault's snap decision to begin racing is that he watched René win one particularly dramatic local event on 25 April, and was inspired to take out his first racing licence two days later. But as René recalls, Bernard had already decided to begin racing before that inspirational event, which was at Plédran, the next village to the south-west of Yffiniac. 'He was supposed to race on 25 April, because there was a *cadet* race.' This was an event for the under-17 category, to which Bernard belonged, which would be run alongside the senior event in which René would ride. 'I had said over the winter that I would win the race at Plédran, because it was the closest circuit to Yffiniac that suited me, a circuit that went right over to Yffiniac. So I got Bernard to put it back a week.'

René duly won at Plédran – a good win, in which he bridged to an early break, attacked them, couldn't get away, but still won the sprint – and presumably that at least strengthened Bernard's desire to race. The older rider wanted his young cousin to build up to his racing debut, to acquire at least a few skills beforehand, but he was just too impatient to wait. By sheer good luck, Hinault's brother Gilbert had a racing bike, which he wasn't massively attached to; Bernard commandeered it. He had his racing licence from Club Olympique Briochin, which had just come to an agreement with René's club, Union Cycliste Briochine, that young riders would attend the *école de cyclisme* – structured activities run by most French clubs to bring on youngsters prior to racing – at COB, then transfer to UCB when they got older.[1]

On 2 May, the next Sunday, he rode that first race at Planguenoual, four kilometres from Yffiniac, north-east up the coast road towards Cap Frehel. He rode the *cadet* event; René was to ride the senior race later in the day. The advice of Robert Le Roux, who ran the COB *école de cyclisme*, was that Bernard should simply try to hang on to the bunch; instead, he won.

It could all have gone horribly wrong that morning. Later, Hinault was brutally honest about the fact that he had no idea how to ride in a bunch – but why would he when all he had done before then was running and slip-streaming lorries? 'Sweeping from left to right across the road, I devoted all my time and attention to avoiding riding in the bunch for fear of falling off. If anyone rode too close to me, I instantly imagined that we were going to collide. I would let myself slip off the back, then go straight to the front, then end up in the gutter.' Sometimes he rode on the verge. Time after time he was close to falling off.

---

[1] The story goes that the agreement rapidly foundered when the officials who ran COB realised how successful the young Hinault was going to be, and changed their policy so that they could keep him in the club.

'It was windy there, it was always windy on the coast, and he was always in the wind, because he didn't know how to find shelter among the others in the bunch,' says René. The end was pure Hollywood: the debutant escaped midway through the race, but that didn't concern the local favourite, Jean-Yves Ollivier, who had won his last four races, and was far more experienced than Bernard. He knew René, who had let slip beforehand that his cousin had not raced before. Even so, he took the trouble of bridging to the newcomer with a counter-attack, then shadowed him towards the finish. 'The finish was up a long drag into the middle of the village,' recalled René. 'I stood at the bottom of the climb, and when I saw Bernard there with Jean-Yves on his wheel, I thought, "Well, at least he will get second."' Jean-Yves thought the same, but could not believe his eyes when young Bernard opened up his sprint three hundred metres from the line. He had no answer.

'They opened champagne when they got home, and ate crêpes,' recalled Lucie Hinault. 'Bernard was happy, but no more than that. It seemed natural to him that he had won.'

He won his first five races, lost the sixth because of a collision with a spectator, then hit a run of poor form, one explanation being that his fitness was affected by having to work on the farm. Even so, by the end of the year he had won twelve of the twenty races he had started. He realised that he was spreading himself too thin, what with the petrol station and his studies, so cycling had to take priority. 'I had to choose quickly: mechanic, or cyclist. I chose cycling and put everything into it. Too bad for everything else.'

Carfentan wanted him to continue running, and even now, Hinault is pressed to say exactly what it was that made him choose cycling instead. '... *la compétition*, going with my cousin to the bike races. I thought I could be better than him. I liked running but was more attracted to cycling, and I was better at cycling.' For an impatient young man, the attractions were clear. The correlation between work and reward was far more immediate compared to the slow build-up required for athletics events, so too the adrenalin fix for a youth who liked to take risks. So many bike races to be ridden every weekend, on his doorstep. So many chances to win.

Bernard Hinault's choice to focus on cycling rather than on his part-time job or his studies was made so early that it caught his family by surprise. In July 1971 he briefly left the family home after an altercation with his father. 'It happened when I came home from training,' he wrote in his autobiography *Le Peloton des Souvenirs*, adding that this was not long after he had stopped working in the garage, to give him time to race his bike, and ironically enough, after he had returned to helping his father in the vegetable plot as he had done in his younger days. 'My father was waiting for me on the threshold. All of a sudden, he told me that I was doing nothing, that I was worth nothing, and asked me, "What are you up to?" I leaned my bike against the wall and looked at him. He didn't look at me but called me an idle so-and-so before going back into the house.'

Now, Hinault explains, 'He didn't want me to be a cyclist, he wanted me to find a job and so on'. The youth upped sticks and left, taking refuge with his cousins down the road – the family of ten at La Rivière where he had gone so often to play – sleeping among the straw in the barn, roaming the countryside by day, for three days resisting his brother's attempts to make him return. When he did go back home, it was to tell his father that he would give up the racing and get a job. 'My father lowered his head. "No, go on bike riding,"' and the question was never raised again. The episode was not a one-off spat, René says; 'with [Bernard's] father, it was a constant head-to-head. There was no issue with his actually riding the races, the problem was the training. The assumption was that if you went out on your bike and you weren't racing, just training or just riding, you were just out for leisure.'

It left Hinault no option but to succeed in his chosen course. His pride would not permit any other way. 'I was the only one [of the family] to make a decision like that,' he told me. 'Maybe I'm just pig-headed. The others didn't have the same choice to make – they went into a profession and got on with it. I had the choice: either I went into a factory or I became a cyclist. And my father, who had fed me, didn't really understand that you could earn a living on a bike as well as in a factory. I felt I could [do that]. I said to him: "It's for me to choose, it's not your decision." But from the moment when you have made that decision you can't pretend any more.'

Hinault wasn't escaping anything, he says now. He wasn't attempting to rise out of poverty; he wasn't trying to be different. The dispute with his father arose because he felt he had no option but to persist on the road he had said he would take, because as he saw it, the investment he had made came from him and him alone. 'I had everything I needed. I had enough to eat and clothes to wear. I was fine. As for the rest: if you want to compete, you get your kit, you pay for it. And that's what makes you want to win. It's your kit. You've invested in it. You want something, you have to go and get it. And then it's yours.'

Hinault's transformation into a bike racer was not a matter of being inspired by a star, of being led, or driven, or dreaming. 'Bernard Hinault did not see himself as a cyclist, but as an engineer, for the simple reason that the fact that he had to earn a living had been drummed into him,' wrote Benoît Heimerman in *L'Équipe*. But Hinault did not have to see himself as a cyclist, because from his early incursions into the hen-run he had treated life as a challenge: fishing in the bay was a battle against the sea; the trip to college was a competition with the lorries; working at the garage, he got round the rule which dictated he had to be sixteen. It was Bernard versus whichever part of the world he happened to be engaging with at a given time.

Now, he says, he can get the same satisfaction from seeing a good bike go over the counter at his son's bike shop. 'You sell something that's right for someone, with the correct kit on. That's pleasure. That's your work. Everything you do is a permanent challenge: competing in a sport, and daily life as well. You have to be on top, all the time, but it's a game. It's how you are. It's in you.'

CHAPTER 3

THE BRETON BOY

*Goude ma vezer skuizh ec'h aer c'hoazh pell – 'Tire your-
self out and you can still go far'*

– Breton proverb

The race which became known as 'Le Championnat des
Hinault' took place in July 1972, in the little village of
Hillion. René remembers it well: he broke away as soon
as the flag dropped, mopped up as many of the early
primes – lap prizes donated by the crowd – as he could
manage. Soon he was joined by Bernard, now a junior
and permitted to race with the over-18s. The gap was
already substantial and the pair eventually opened up a
three-minute lead over a chasing group that included
another cousin, Hubert, who finished fourth, while a
further three minutes back Michel – René's brother – won
the bunch sprint for sixth.

'Everyone was betting that Bernard would beat me,'
recalled René. 'He could have done, but I suggested we
cross the line together. It was a sentimental thing – you

imagine doing that with someone in your family – but the officials didn't like it, they said we hadn't raced together properly.' It should have been the perfect tribute to the cousins' dominance – the family's dominance – in the race, but the *commissaires* ruled that the pair shouldn't have the winners' bouquets, so there was no podium ceremony; they even tried to fine René and Bernard. The irony, as René points out, was that they had been 'flat out' all the way; 'There was no other way for Bernard to race.'

It's not surprising that René gets a little emotional when recalling 'Le Championnat des Hinault' and the battle that ensued with officialdom, but Bernard remembered it too, strongly enough to a give a full account in a television interview in 2013. It might seem surprising that a man with five victories in the Tour de France should recall the details of a small local race after forty years, but it was clearly an emotional afternoon for a seventeen-year-old; a couple of hours of unadulterated fun in front of a home crowd, followed by a final denouement which can only have prompted the feeling that 'no one likes us and we don't care'.

Drive north-east from Yffiniac up the coast towards Hillion, which is just four kilometres up the Baie de Saint-Brieuc, cast your mind back forty-odd years to the races that Bernard and René Hinault recall, and one thing strikes you: it all happened so close to home. Just as the Hinault houses clustered together on that hillside above Yffiniac, so the races rubbed shoulders as well: Plédran, Hillion, Planguenoual and the others. The starts would be so close that René, Bernard and the other Hinaults could ride there on their bikes with ease with clubmates and friends. The extended family could roll up and watch without expending too much time.

Bernard Hinault's brief amateur career came just over halfway through the golden age of local French amateur cycling, which extended through three decades from the 1950s to the late 1980s. The Hinaults' Brittany was the epicentre. The fearsome reputation of the Bretons still held strong a dozen years later when I was racing a little way to the east in Normandy, but the western province had been one of the earliest strongholds of cycle racing in France in the mid-nineteenth century, and the sport took off in earnest after the foundation of Paris–Brest–Paris in 1891.

Brittany had produced its share of Tour de France winners including Lucien Petit-Breton, Jean Robic and Louison Bobet, the first man to win a hat-trick of Tours – 1953–55 – a handsome brute with perfectly Brylcreemed hair, a baker's son from Saint-Méen-Le-Grand in the heart of Brittany. With his all-round ability, and his capacity to dominate the world stage – which he did in the era when Fausto Coppi's career began to fade – Bobet was the key figure of a golden age of Breton cycling, when the Tour de l'Ouest would draw crowds four or five deep and Bretons would lead both the Équipe de l'Ouest, and the Équipe de France, as was the case in the 1953 Tour.

The scale and breadth of Breton cycling in the 1960s and into the 1970s still astonishes. In 1960 there were

1,504 races in the region – more than one for every community, with a criterium circuit that was extensive enough for riders to earn a living without ever leaving Brittany, and of sufficient depth for intense local rivalries to burgeon. There was an entire track-racing circuit, with outdoor velodromes in not just the major cities but in tiny communities. Places with only a few thousand inhabitants such as Plouay, Callac and Chateaulin became known across France for their races.

The British journalist Jock Wadley wrote an evocative description of the *courses des pardons* – which he described as 'religious festivals observed with deep faith...following the ceremonies there are traditional fairs, dancing displays and other carnival novelties. In former days wrestling matches used to be the big draw but nowadays the chief secular attraction is the road race.' The tradition lives on today in the week of racing known as the Mi-Août Bretonne. The bike races would be combined with walking competitions, bowls matches, and often a full fairground. Some villages even went as far as building roads especially for their races. Along with Flanders and the Basque Country, Brittany still has one of the strongest regional identities within cycling and it is no surprise that, like Flanders, Brittany still has its own professional team bearing the region's name.

The clichéd picture of Brittany blends most facets of Great Britain's Celtic fringe: a threatened language, a visceral connection to cycling to match that of the Welsh

THE BRETON BOY   41

to rugby or the Scots to football. Like the Scots, the Bretons are 'thrawn', like all the Celtic 'edge' nations, they have a deep-rooted sense of identity; the *gwenn ha du* (black and white) flag is a constant sight, but with this nuance: it is no longer particularly associated with separatism, more with the identity of the region. '*La tête dure*' is the term many Bretons use for themselves.

This view of the Bretons is often conjoined with their cycling. In the (presumably ghostwritten) introduction to *l'Aventure du Cyclisme Breton*, Hinault writes of Breton cyclists who struggle to travel away from their own backyard, which was a well-known phenomenon – 'the secretive Breton, who could only flourish in his own soil, where he had his markers, his friends, his habits, his public and where he could follow his own footsteps'. But he also notes another type of Breton: the swashbuckling explorer, 'the conqueror of a new world'. One example outside cycling would be the legendary yachtsman Eric Tabarly, double winner of the Observer Single-Handed Trans-Atlantic Race and responsible in large part for the sport's popularity in France today.

Cyrille Guimard, who was to manage Hinault as a professional, relished their shared identity. 'As Bretons, we were made to understand each other,' he wrote. 'Hinault was the granite and the square hedges of the *bocage*.' Cycling's Bretons are men with intense attachment to their home. They fight pugnaciously and stubbornly for what they want, they are blunt of phrase – Hinault quotes Robic as telling his wife, as he left to win the Tour, 'You are poor now, but in three weeks you will be rich' – and they behave with dashing zeal when they take their talent abroad.

Dipping into the world of French provincial cycling as I did for a couple of years at the tail-end of the post-war boom, I can suggest what would draw a teenager into this milieu. As 'Le Championnat des Hinault' emphasises, cycling was often a family affair, brother following brother, sons and nephews following fathers and uncles. The Hinault clan was far from unique. My companion at races, Jean-Luc, had a little of the Hinault about him: plain talking, exuberant in life and racing, one of a big family from a small cottage, not a man who liked to be caged in. His elder brother raced, as had their father before them. In a world where so many competed, and where every village had an old-timer who had either taken part in the Tour or ridden against someone from the next village who had, there was nothing particularly intimidating about starting to race, and turning professional was not a drastic step. It was part of the fabric of rural life.

Bike racing held obvious attractions for a country boy. It took you away from the monotony of farm work to a milieu of adrenalin, ready cash, and recognition among family and friends. Compared to feeding cattle or repairing agricultural implements, it was pure glamour. Any event would draw roadside spectators on deckchairs; in those quiet parts a peloton of up to two hundred riders filling the road was always worth a look. Any race – Sunday afternoon *Prix du Comité des Fêtes* or Saturday evening demi-nocturne – would take over the village or small town, which would fill with riders changing in their cars on every pavement, pissing en masse in the hedgerows and gates. Cycling bound you to your fellows, marking you as one of a subgroup: *un coureur cycliste*. In local shops other cycling families would always do you a deal on ironmongery or vegetables. The club would meet on a midweek afternoon for *entrainement collectif*, with a team car in tow; you would pedal imperiously down the rural roads and thunder through quiet villages.

The race venues were mere pinpricks on the Michelin map. The format was always the same: a tractor and trailer for a grandstand, a makeshift sound system with ample feedback, well-used numbers handed out in the back of the Bar-Tabac on the main square, *primes* donated by local businesses, a programme which didn't list the riders' names – because you all entered on the day – but which made sure those cash sponsors were well advertised. The race would be on a small circuit. It was often hilly or dangerous or both, because there weren't many roads to choose from in the middle of the countryside; critically it would include a finish outside either the fairground or the local *mairie* to draw a crowd composed of locals who didn't look as if they ever got further from home than the nearest market town. No one wore crash hats although sometimes, if we felt the opening laps might be dodgy, we wore them then bunged them to a helper at half-distance. That in turn meant that the words *casque obligatoire* in the calendar pointed to a more than usually tricky circuit.

Bernard and René settled into a rhythm in this little world. In his first year, they would travel to a place that hosted both a senior race and a *cadet* event as support; Bernard would ride with the *cadets*, René the event for second categories. In Bernard's second season of racing – when he was a first-year junior – he was allowed to ride with the seniors, which must have simplified matters. 'I would tell him not to say always that he was going to win,' recalls René, 'and he would just reply that I had said I was going to win that race he watched at Plédran. But that wasn't the same. He told me, "If I say I'm going to win, I don't have the right to lose." In any case, it didn't make a lot of difference, pretty soon everyone expected him to win no matter what he said.'

It's easy to forget since the decline of the French amateur calendar that it was possible to compete three or four days a week. There were so many races to win that the most talented riders would learn how to take those victories in a wealth of different ways – Guimard, for example, landed forty wins in one year as an amateur. There were flipsides, however. With so many opportunities, a competitive rider's need to win could be sated long before he turned professional. There were many prolific French amateur winners who turned professional, didn't find success rapidly, then returned to the amateur ranks where they could get the winning feeling every week. This was particularly common in Brittany and Normandy.

Young Hinault needed one key element to help him make his way through this world: at sixteen and a half, up against infinitely more experienced teenagers, he was short of knowledge and he needed to acquire it quickly. René was the obvious source of information, but one key individual was at his disposal: Robert Le Roux. Bernard Hinault's enduring respect for the man who ran Club Olympique Briochine is easily measured: 'Everyone called him *Pépé* Le Roux – Granddad – but not Bernard,' recalled René Hinault. 'For him, he was Monsieur Le Roux.' To this day Hinault refers to his old mentor as M. Le Roux.

One story has it that the trainer was told by Bernard's future soigneur Joel Marteil that he really needed to look at him. '*Celui la, c'est un futur super*'; 'pppphhhh,' exhaled M. Le Roux, 'I'm shown twenty of those every year.' Hinault figures on the front cover of *Coureur Cycliste, Ce Que Tu Dois Savoir*, Monsieur Le Roux's exposition of his methods and his philosophy. He is on the back cover as well, along-side the writer; Hinault is slumped against the hoarding of a velodrome, with Le Roux kneeling alongside him, stopwatch around his neck, holding Hinault's hand while he takes his pulse after a training effort.

On the flyleaf of his book is a picture of another pro-tégé – a slender, quicksilver English youth who, when the book was written in 1975, was the biggest star Le Roux had helped to forge. When Hinault teamed up with Le Roux it was only twelve years since *le regretté* Tom Simpson had made a lightning passage through Saint-Brieuc and the COB; before his premature death in 1967, he had won a world road race title, taken Classics and worn yellow in the Tour de France. When Hinault and Le Roux met, Major Tom was fresh in local memories, and the coach would have been known as the man who helped the future world champion at a formative stage.

Hinault does not dish out praise lightly, but he still waxes lyrical about Le Roux, maintains he was the only real influence on his cycling career in his early years, and he still has his own copy of the book. Le Roux oversaw Hinault's lightning career as an amateur – two years as a junior, one as a senior – and his influence lasted far longer. 'He looked after me until I was eighteen, maybe a bit later, and when I turned professional I realised he'd told me a lot of things, and I seemed to have forgotten them,' Hinault says now. '[As a youth] I had physical force enough to win even if I made stupid mistakes, but when I arrived at the highest level, I made the same mistakes, but I didn't win. And I would say to myself, "What did Monsieur Le Roux tell you? Think. Ride with your head, not with your physical strength." And that would get me on my way again.'

The blurb on the book is fulsome: 'A born educator – in all the meanings of the term – [Le Roux] has forged an ideal which he pursues and transmits to his pupils by inculcating them, with his paternal authority, willpower in the face of suffering, faith in effort, righteousness and a love of justice. That's the Le Roux miracle: forming men through sport and arming them against the vicissitudes and setbacks of life.' The 'paternal authority' was key: Le Roux was as single-minded as his greatest protégé. He was a man who stuck to his guns, who had a dictatorial side, and could be possessive about his charges. In that sense at least, it was a meeting of minds.

Le Roux's Club Olympic Briochine was an umbrella body for a number of sports including basketball, athletics, boxing and judo. Le Roux ran the cycling section, which was based at the Beaufeuillage velodrome on the north-east side of Saint-Brieuc – just up the hill from Yffiniac by happy coincidence – and when they first met in spring 1971, Hinault was a runner, with little other than his determination and his physique to recommend him.

Le Roux was in his sixties; he had been a French champion in artistic gymnastics, and was now a teacher of physical education. 'A fantastic guy with young people,' says Hinault. 'He never had any children of his own, because he never married. We were a bit like his children. He looked after football players, cyclists, runners, organ-ised training camps in the mountains in summer. He was really devoted to the cause of young people in sport. Perhaps he never found the woman he wanted to, so all that emotion was invested towards young people in sport – and quite a lot of his money I think. He invested [in us] out of his own pocket.

'[M. Le Roux] was the kind of person you would like to have in every cycling club,' adds Hinault. 'He wanted his riders to be multidisciplinary – try out cyclo-cross, track, road. And there was something [he said] that I still say to young cyclists: you mustn't restrict yourself to one sport.' Forty years later, Le Roux's theory was backed up more formally in David Epstein's groundbreaking *The*

Sports Gene. Hinault continues: 'You need to take part in a number of different sports to find the one that you like the most, experience different environments, because every sport has its own ambience, different demands, different champions. It's not always about your physical qualities, but it can be about your dexterity, your vision of a sport.'

Le Roux was religious, attending mass every weekend, and there is an element of muscular Christianity in the imprecation to the parents of budding cyclists which opens the book. 'Your ambition is, above all, to make your child a man; so make him into a sportsman, right now.' The introduction ends with this message: 'As an assessor alongside the judge of the Youth Tribunal at Saint-Brieuc, how many times have I heard the judge or the head of probation say to parents: "If he had done sport, he would not have ended up here."' The tone of the book is not merely one of moral mission; Le Roux closes the volume with a manifesto for change in French cycling to benefit young athletes. But Hinault wasn't drawn to the trainer because of his idea of mission or because of any broader sense of what he did. The youth needed to be guided by someone as strong-minded as he was; his headstrong nature needed to be channelled. That called for a man with an equally strong sense of self, although on occasion Le Roux would have to call on René to call his cousin to order. M. Le Roux was, '*Assez directif*, pretty bossy,' says René. 'A man who liked things done his way, who wanted to impose his will.'

The book is largely practical, divided up into bite-sized nuggets of information interspersed with practical philosophy. Le Roux has certain principles: most crucially, 'in daily life, always think about your race on Sunday and be aware of the sacrifices that you have to make to get to the start in the best possible condition. It's hard. All the things you will have to do take a will of iron...every day.' There are sample training programmes for cyclists of all ages, brief nutrition guides, and instructions that have a Boy Scout ring to them: a section headed *sommeil*, sleep, states that bedroom temperature should be eighteen degrees, and you shouldn't keep on the same underwear you have worn during the day. Some of the content smacks of old-wives' tales – don't shower immediately after a meal, footbaths as a way of preventing colds – while some is now standard training lore, for example, paying close attention to dental hygiene. There's a mystical, ritual tone to some sections: tubular tyres should be bought eight months before needed, covered in talcum powder and stored in paper, away from sun or moonlight. The chain should be soaked in fat; no part of the saddle or seat post should be aluminium.

As might be expected from a PE teacher and former gymnast, there is a lengthy programme of calisthenics, with similar sketch diagrams used to illustrate how to ride in the peloton depending on the wind direction. Le Roux advises his charges to learn swimming, partly because, in small doses, it's useful for cycling, but also because it's handy if you fall into a river. The key quote, however, which Bernard Hinault would repeat time and again, was this: 'If you want to win bike races, you will make money. If you want to make money, you won't win bike races.'

Hinault packed his early life in cycling into just three seasons. In early May 1971, he could barely stay upright in the bunch. A year later, in his second season racing, he notched up nineteen wins. Outside northern Brittany, eyebrows were raised first in mid-May 1972 – just over a year after that hesitant debut – when he came from nowhere in the Premier Pas Dunlop, which incorporated the national junior title. The race was held near Arras, which meant a two-day excursion from Brittany; Hinault was one of fifteen juniors from the region who travelled in a minibus. Jean-Marie Leblanc, from 1989 to 2006 the director of the Tour de France, but in 1972 a newly retired ex-cyclist starting a career in journalism, reported the race for his paper, *La Voix du Nord*, and described Hinault 'with his long hair, his slightly overweight look, socks halfway up his calves, using a big gear . . . he dropped everyone on the hill at Pas en Artois'.

Hinault was up against riders a year older than him, among them the two strongest juniors in France. One was Bernard Vallet, who already had ninety-nine wins to his name and would go on to a more-than-decent professional career, including winning the polka-dot King of the Mountains jersey at the 1982 Tour. The other, Jacques Osmont, had a decent amateur career, but never made the grade as a professional. Vallet recalled that he simply could not hold Hinault's wheel when he turned the wick up; the young Breton rode the last fifty-seven kilometres alone.

M. Le Roux was not entirely delighted, however. René had had Bernard's bike tuned up by a local mechanic before the race – his cousin paid for it, as money was still short – and had got the mechanic to fix a 13-sprocket on the bike, giving Bernard a gear which was higher than he would usually ride. 'I'd checked the course, it was flat, and I knew if it was windy and he got away he'd have his legs round his ears; he'd be pedalling so fast on a lower gear,' explained his cousin. Afterwards, Bernard sang the praises of the 13-sprocket, and M. Le Roux was not best pleased, because it went straight against one of his key precepts: that a young cyclist should focus on leg speed, not big-gear power. The section of *Coureur Cycliste, Ce Que Tu Dois Savoir*, adjacent to a table of gear sizes, reads, 'Don't look for a 13-tooth sprocket in this table, it's not there. Only professionals are capable of using it firstly because they are stronger than you and secondly because they know how to use it in an appropriate way...using it would lead you into making huge blunders because you would use it too often.'[2]

The other significant win came at the end of the season in the Grand Elan Breton, a time trial over sixty kilometres

---

[2] The belief that using big gears was damaging was quite widespread in the 1970s; as late as 1978, one French *directeur sportif* still forbade his professional team to use *la 13-dents* until April, preferring them to develop leg speed even if it meant not winning races.

open to all categories, which Hinault won at an average speed of 41.7km ahead of the Irish cyclist John Mangan. Mangan was then in the first flush of youth, and his career among the amateurs in Brittany would last into the 1980s; for his even younger rival, this result at the age of seventeen meant one thing: he had a huge engine.

Le Roux advised Hinault to get his obligatory year of military service out of the way at as young an age as possible, on the basis that the transition to racing as a senior was going to be tough regardless. He would have to take twelve months off his bike in any case, and the earlier he did so, the less it would harm his career. Most waited until they were twenty; Hinault went at eighteen. Usually, promising young French athletes served at the Bataillon de Joinville,[3] which had been founded in the 1950s to enable the best French sportsmen to avoid damaging their potential. Hinault did not qualify, having only taken up cycling the year before, and instead he enrolled on the tank artillery course. Although he pulled out on the final day because he had no interest in gaining the qualification, he took typical pleasure in learning a new trade: 'I wasn't a bad gunner, on manoeuvres I put twenty-eight shells out of thirty-two on target and managed to blow up an oil drum at five hundred metres range.'

---

[3] The Bataillon was dissolved in 2002 when obligatory military service came to an end. Its successor, in cycling, is the Armee de Terre professional team.

He returned to Brittany in December 1973 many kilo-grams heavier after his year without racing – ten or twelve depending on which version you read – then went back to work at a heating engineers. A forty-kilometre ride to work and days spent unloading radiators from thirty-tonne lorries took off enough of the weight for him to win his first race of 1974. Having never raced as a senior, and having missed his second year as a junior, he started again at the bottom of the amateur ladder as a fourth category. This was to be his only season as a senior amateur. Early that season, his future teammate Maurice Le Guilloux spotted him at a third and fourth-category race – one of the bread-and-butter events that make up the lower end of the French amateur calendar – in the village of Tramain; he had been worried about Hinault's reputation, but his fears disappeared: 'He weighed at least seventy-three kilo-grams and I said to myself that with a physique like that he would never make a professional.'

At the end of the season, however, Le Guilloux saw Hinault race again, this time in Yffiniac, in a race for first, second and third categories – close to the top of the amateur tree – and watched him get rid of four of the strongest local racers with a kilometre to go. 'He had long hair, red-white-and-blue socks, looked a right Fred, not like a bike racer. His bike was knackered, a real old gate. Today's riders would bung it in the bin.' Le Guilloux ini-tially assumed that Hinault had been 'permitted' to win because he was racing at home, but learned later from one of the four also-rans that the quartet had formed an alliance against the youngster, but he had responded to all their attacks, turn and turn about – then had jumped away himself. 'We were thinking we'd seen plenty of young champions turn up here and there, but Hinault just sat on the front raking in all the *primes*. There were several of them ganging up on him but he just burned them off his wheel, one by one.'

In 1974, Hinault also returned to the track, winning the Breton pursuit and kilometre champs, and earning selection for the national pursuit championship. Here he won the gold medal, thanks to the loan of some light wheels from the multi-Olympic champion Daniel Morelon – a reminder now that Hinault was still getting along without the best kit. He was clearly not intimidated: before the final, he told the crowd, 'Bet 10,000 francs on me' – old francs, so about £10 at the time – 'and you won't lose.' The French national team took him to the world track championships in Montreal that August, where he was eliminated in qualifying, ten seconds slower than he needed to make the cut.

With sponsorship from a local bike maker and distributor, Juaneda – who also backed a small pro team, Magiglace-Juaneda – his appearances on the road made more impact. In the Route de France, the most important amateur stage race in the country, he finished second overall to Michel Laurent – another future professional, albeit one who never fulfilled his potential – while still riding on a third-category licence, as he had won enough races to be promoted from fourth category to second but the Breton Federation had yet to supply him with a new licence. His stage win at Vichy came after a break of eighty-six kilometres, just a few yards in front of a frantically chasing peloton. Then he returned to racing with his third-category licence, winning two races. The second and third finishers protested, as he was technically a second category, and he was disqualified.

The critical race was the Étoile des Espoirs, a week-long event run by the Paris–Nice organiser Jean Leulliot in early October, to bring together promising amateurs and young professionals. This was Hinault's only outing in the French national team jersey as an amateur on the road – he suspected it was because some more highly rated riders were not available so late in the season – and he made a massive impression for a relative unknown. On the time-trial stage, he finished second to Roy Schuiten. That would have raised eyebrows: the Dutchman, who died in 2006, was one of the best time triallists of the 1970s and the reigning world professional pursuit champion. Hinault ended up fifth overall, just behind a fellow Breton who was facing the end of his career due to persistent knee problems: Cyrille Guimard. The race included an episode of pure farce when he escaped early on one stage – as he was used to doing in third and fourth-category races – overshot a corner, ran straight on into a farmyard, and smashed into a cart. More seriously, it proved Hinault's ability to race with the professionals.

He had known that as early as May that year. The Route de France should have been daunting for a rider with his level of experience, as it was the toughest amateur stage race in France where the elite of amateur racing showed their worth with their eyes on professional contracts. At the race, Hinault was being courted by Jean 'Mickey' Wiegant, the director of France's leading amateur club, Athlétique Club de Boulogne Billancourt. Wiegant warned Hinault that if he didn't join his team, ACBB, his riders would make a point of preventing him winning whenever they saw him at a race. Mickey was one of the most imposing figures in French amateur cycling, an austere man who liked to be called monsieur, and who had managed Jacques Anquetil, Shay Elliott, Jean Stablinski and André Darrigade. His team acted as a feeder for the powerful Peugeot squad, the richest in France. He was a legendary talent spotter; les petits gris, as ACBB were known, inspired fear whenever they turned up at a race. None of that mattered to Hinault, who replied, 'Whatever. I don't give a monkey's. I'll be a professional next year.'

CHAPTER 4

RIPPING UP THE SCRIPT: RISE AND FALL

'A provocative figure, but in some ways astonishingly mature.'

— Philippe Bouvet on the young Hinault

Newcomers to the world of professional cycling in the mid-1970s were expected to behave in a set way. Conventions that went back a generation and more dictated that they should keep their voices down and do as their elders and betters told them. There was a hierarchy and it had to be respected. New professionals were at the bottom of the heap when it came to getting appearance contacts and finding openings in races.

The pecking order mattered most at the criteriums which made up so much of the Breton calendar, and where professionals made most of their money. The unwritten rule was that the crowd had come to see the big names, and they had come to watch them race. The stars couldn't compete at their physical limit day after day, so the races had to be 'managed'. A group of senior racers would dictate the 'order of play': who would attack early on, who would contest the *primes*, who would win in the end, and who would come second. There was every incentive to adhere to the script: it wasn't just that any rebels would attract abuse from their colleagues; more importantly, the senior pros, and the agents who paid them, could influence which of the junior riders rode which criteriums. That meant that a youth whose face didn't fit wouldn't earn a living.

This was how the 'heads' of the peloton – Rik Van Looy, Fausto Coppi, Jacques Anquetil and their ilk – had always run things. It wasn't unheard of for riders to rebel. 'Foreigners' such as Tom Simpson, Barry Hoban and Shay Elliott had been known to disobey, particularly when they felt they had been left out of whatever deals were done, but it was rare, which explains why the events of Easter 1975 turned heads. There were two important professional criteriums in Brittany over the weekend: Camors, on the southern side of the peninsula between Lorient and Vannes, which was a relatively recent addition to the calendar, and Ploërdut,[4] forty kilometres to the north-west, which had been run since 1948. The Grand Old Man of

---

[4] The Camors criterium, also known as the Ronde des Korrigans, is still run, but in late July, as part of the après-Tour de France circuit. Ploërdut was organised annually until 1981, with a final one-off edition in 1992.

French Cycling, Raymond Poulidor, was racing at Camors for the first time and he was supposed to win, according to Maurice Le Guilloux, Hinault's training partner and neighbour at the time. 'That was no problem, that was the tradition. Hinault was a young pro, he wasn't part of the deal, so he went flat out, mopping up all the *primes* with the rest of us chasing fifty metres behind. It was insane.'

Two senior riders, teammates of Poulidor, Jean-Pierre Genet and Barry Hoban, were delegated to ask Hinault to calm down. After the finish, Cyrille Guimard, the senior Breton rider present, informed Hinault that he would receive no money because he had 'wound up' all and sundry. Guimard told Hinault that the next day, at Ploërdut, he didn't want him to show his face anywhere in the race; he was not to go off the front, and he wasn't to finish in the first ten. According to Le Guilloux's account, Hinault was not impressed: 'He spent the whole race at Ploërdut on the back of the string and the organiser, who wasn't happy about it, cut his money by half. Hinault wasn't happy either.'

Annoying his elders was a pattern in the early Hinault years. In August 1975, there was a similar episode at the Circuit de l'Aulne criterium at Châteaulin, a key fixture on the Breton calendar, and another race that is still going today. The race – now run as the Boucles de l'Aulne – had a history going back to the 1930s and the spectator count could nudge six figures, but its USP was its date: the evening after the world road race championships, with the new world champion flown in to appear in his rainbow stripes.

On this particular evening, the veteran French sprinter Jacques Esclassan was in charge of dividing up the cash; only those who had been at the world championships – the senior riders – were in on the deal. They would split their winnings, including the *primes*. Before the start, Esclassan approached the rider who had travelled down with Hinault, Raymond Martin, and asked him to join the 'pool'; Martin declined, having shared his costs with Hinault, unless the youngster was included. His request was turned down. Martin told Hinault, who smiled 'a carnivorous smile' and said, 'Watch me.' As at Camors, Hinault went for the *primes*, winning the first three from Merckx, making a derogatory gesture as he did so. It was Merckx who told Charly Rouxel – a teammate of Hinault's on the Gitane squad – to calm down his young teammate as he would now be 'in on the deal'. But accommodating Hinault wasn't the way to calm him down: he took the fourth *prime* just to make his point.

'That was how Bernard Hinault joined the cycling elite,' wrote the cycling historian Benjo Maso, but the truth is more convoluted. Robert Le Roux had advised Hinault to turn professional as soon as possible, working on the principle that the best racers had little to learn from riding amateur events. Moreover, the 1976 Olympic Games were on the horizon and the French Cycling Federation were determined that their best amateurs would be available for the national team. If Hinault was not professional by the start of 1975, he would probably be prevented from taking out a professional licence before September 1976 to ensure that he rode for France in Montreal.

He and Le Roux were not going to wait until the Olympics were over. Times were lean, however, with the withdrawal of two major sponsors in Bic – once the backers of Jacques Anquetil and Luis Ocaña – and the television company Sonolor, who had financed a team run by the former world champion Jean Stablinski and supplied by the Gitane cycle company. When Hinault joined Stablinski in January 1975 – the team's sponsors having been reduced to Gitane and their component supplier Campagnolo – he was paid only 2,500 francs per month, the SMIC – the French legal minimum wage. That was understandable: the team had lost its main sponsor, and Bic's demise meant managers were enjoying a buyer's market. Half of Hinault's first month's salary went on paying the expenses for his first team training camp, as was the custom until the 1980s; even without that, his wage was not enough to support him and his family.

He had married in early December 1974. He had encountered his future wife Martine at a wedding, between one of his many cousins and one of her neighbours, in the spring of 1973, the year of his military service. They met as the bridesmaids and relatives processed from the *mairie* to the church; famously, he wrote in his memoirs, 'at first sight, I didn't find her that remarkable; at the end of the day, I didn't think that at all. We had spent a lot of time together, talked a lot, barely been apart.' They moved into a small apartment in Rue de l'Eglise in Yffiniac, opposite the local cycle shop. By the time Hinault left for his first professional races, she was pregnant, but to make up for his small salary, she kept her job as a secretary at the local milk producers' cooperative.

The contract with Stablinski had come about through Hinault's club sponsor of 1972 and 1974, Tertre, an electronics retailer, who worked closely with Sonolor, Stablinski's former sponsor. In addition, Hinault had caught the eye of the Gitane sprinter Willy Teirlinck during some of his mad-dog moments at the Étoile des Espoirs. There was a local connection of a kind: the bike manufacturer Gitane was based in western France, founded at Machecoul in Loire-Atlantique in 1930. The state-owned car company Renault had bought 30 per cent of Gitane's holding company Micmo in 1974; backing the team was part of their push into the French domestic cycle market in competition primarily with Peugeot but also with two smaller bike makers, Lejeune and Mercier.[5]

At the end of January 1975, Hinault received a telegram telling him where the team training camp was held – Saint-Paul de Vence in the South of France – and

---

[5] Gitane is now part of Cycleurope, owned by Swedish conglomerate Grimaldi Industri AB, while production has been moved to Romilly-sur-Seine, to the east of Paris.

as was typical for the time, this was his only contact with the team over the winter once his contract had been signed, so he had to set off at once. There was only one issue, beyond finding the train fare: he didn't have a suitcase, and had to borrow one from his mother-in-law. Driving south was out of the question, as he had yet to take his test. Later, he would share lifts with Maurice Le Guilloux, who recalls him turning up at his house on a blue *vélomoteur*, with his father's leather SNCF backpack on his back and his race kit in a pannier. In the south, he began racing as soon as the training camp was over, starting with the Étoile de Bessèges in early February.

For a new professional aged only twenty, and just a single season as a senior amateur behind him, Hinault's initial results were impressive. In Paris–Nice, riding with the likes of Guimard and Merckx, he finished seventh. He gave a radio reporter a quote of the kind that would become familiar to Hinault watchers – 'Merckx has two legs, the same as me' – and showed potential climbing ability by hanging on to the leaders on Mont Ventoux. That led *L'Équipe* to mark his cards, together with Michel Laurent, as a prospect for the future. In April 1975, he won the Circuit de la Sarthe, an 'open' event where the top 'amateurs' from the Eastern bloc – full-time bike riders supported by the state – rubbed shoulders with young professionals. Later on, he finished second in Paris–Bourges, sixth in the Grand Prix des Nations and, at the end of the year, he was the winner of the Promotion

Pernod, a season-long award for the best new professional in France.[6]

Those results happened against a background that was less than propitious. Hinault was a brash youth, who had been thrown into a milieu far more demanding than racing under the wing of M. Le Roux at Saint-Brieuc. He had just married; his and Martine's son Mickael was expected in June. He was only twenty, young for a professional, in a team under pressure due to the early loss of their leader, Alain Santy, who broke his wrist in Paris–Nice.

It was not a forgiving environment and the man guiding him through it was not best suited for the role. Stablinski, who died in 2007, was a sharp-faced man, pleasant and incisive in manner, but with a hint of the Godfather about him. When I interviewed him in 2001, he came across as a man with a firm sense of his own rightness – understandably so given the way he had dragged himself out of a coal mine and into a rainbow jersey. Stablinski had been one of the leading characters in French cycling in the 1960s, alongside his teammate Jacques Anquetil. He was a ruthless, clever racer, who had showed no compunction when buying off riders to help him overcome one of his best friends, Shay Elliott, on his way to the world title in 1962.

---

[6] The trio of season-long Pernod prizes – Promotion (for new French professionals), Prestige (for best French pro) and the international Super Prestige Pernod – were awarded through points scored in major races. They ran from 1958 until 1987, when a French law on alcohol promotion brought the sponsorship to an end.

Hinault was no shrinking violet: the first thing his new teammates had observed was that the young Breton was 'not afraid of anyone and he speaks his mind, loudly'. He was a young man who did things his way. Maurice Le Guilloux recalled one of their first races together, early in 1975: they drove together to the Tour de l'Oise, and on the way, Hinault insisted they stop to eat.[7] He devoured a vast steak and ordered a bottle of red wine. Le Guilloux, knowing they had a prologue time trial to ride that evening, drank a glass, expecting to see Hinault struggle later in the day. He finished third; Le Guilloux thirty-eighth. 'Later on, he came and said, "See how dumb you were, you should have finished the bottle."'

Conflict was inevitable. In the past Hinault has described Stab as 'a gentleman who seemed to have no knowledge whatsoever of cycling', but now he is gentler. 'We weren't on the same wavelength at all,' is his summary. 'You shouldn't throw stones at him – things have moved on, that's all.' Stablinski's philosophy was that of his time: race often, do what you are told, and if that doesn't work, find another job. Long-term career development was not part of cycling then; short-term team interests were paramount. Hinault puts it this way: '[His attitude was] OK, go and ride, we'll see what you are made of, you are a good little lemon, and when the juice has all gone – in the bin you go.' To give Stablinski his due, this was still the modus operandi for some team directors until recently.

---

[7] The Tour de l'Oise was renamed the Tour de Picardie in 2000.

'He was concerned about the guys, but had no sense of planning, training or setting out a racing programme,' said Le Guilloux. 'With him, whether you were young or old, you followed the same rules. No favours, no short-cuts, you sweat and you don't argue.'

'He put me into virtually every race that the team did,' said Hinault. 'It was madness and it wore me out rapidly.' Stablinski didn't dislike Hinault – he was happy to give him extra kit when asked – but he had no idea what he needed or how to handle him.

Stablinski's contention was that he made Hinault race often in order for him to learn his trade, but it wasn't that simple, given the youth's tendency to race like a mad dog. Maurice Le Guilloux recalled Hinault's first race in Belgium: 'He had absolutely no idea what he was doing. He attacked from the gun and spent the first hundred and fifty kilometres off the front.' The older riders had been asked to show the youngster how to race in the wind. Hinault 'saw none of it; he was several minutes up the road'.

Stablinski answered the criticisms in his biography, *Les Secrets du Sorcier*. 'Hinault began on a small wage, but our best-paid rider was only earning four thousand francs a month. We didn't ask him to win, just to learn a profession of which he only knew the basics. That's why I took him to Belgium so often, but instead of staying in the peloton to learn its workings – how to ride close, how to ride in the wind – he would attack. I never had any falling out with Bernard, it was all through the people in the middle, like Le Roux. He insisted that we give him the details of Bernard's programme, but amateur racing bears no resemblance to the professional world.'

Stablinski said it himself, his approach brought him into conflict with the two key people in Hinault's life: Le Roux, and – implicitly – Martine Hinault. The understanding with Le Roux had been that the progress of his protégé would be carefully managed, there would be no rush. That clearly didn't happen, and – not surprisingly given his background and character – Stablinski didn't see why he should take the views of a Breton schoolteacher into account. Le Roux was proprietorial about his charges and he was still helping Hinault, who he assisted in the run-up to the French professional pursuit title on the track, which the young man won.

Like many Breton cyclists, Hinault did not like being away from home. On his way north to race in Belgium following the training camp in the Midi early in the season, Hinault took a long detour to the west, to visit Martine, without telling the team. 'I wasn't supposed to go home but I needed to go back. Just for one brief night. It was important for me. I was young, I didn't just think about cycling; there were emotional needs that were worth a secret detour.' Martine had not seen a cycle race when she first met Hinault, and she said much later that it took her until 1978 to realise what a cyclist's life truly entailed. That, too, may explain why her husband struggled to adapt to life under Stablinski.

The final straw came in early June, on the final day of the Dauphiné Libéré when Stablinski told Hinault he would race through the month in the Midi Libre and Tour de l'Aude. There was mention of a start in the 1975 Tour de France; he knew that Hinault – with his no-holds-barred style of racing – would make headlines by livening up the early stages 'even if he's falling apart', as Stablinski said. Hinault recalled that when he was told his programme, 'I decided that very evening to leave Stablinski. In the Dauphiné, my goal was to show my *directeur sportif* that I wasn't capable of riding the Tour. It wasn't difficult.' Stablinski subsequently denied that he wanted Hinault in that Tour, pointing his finger at the sponsors.

It was a major dispute, Hinault said. 'I wasn't too bothered that he was going to show me the door because I was about to put him through the window.'

Hinault finished the race, and caught the first train home from Avignon to be with Martine as she prepared to give birth to their son Mickael. The period of time around the birth coincided with a massive low, due to the emotion of the event and his poor relationship with Stablinski. His manager was outraged at his disobedience; Hinault came close to giving up. 'Mentally, I was broken. I was no good for anything and particularly no good for riding a bike,' said Hinault.

He raced the French national championship, shortly after Mickael's birth, on zero training; he continued to the Étoile des Espoirs, where he rode less well than the previous autumn, and fell on the final corner of the time trial, injuring his knee. At the Grand Prix des Nations, the knee was injected and he rode through the pain to finish sixth, moving ahead of Raymond Poulidor and into fourth place in the Prestige Pernod, the season-long points competition that rewarded the best French professional.

With the benefit of thirty years' hindsight, Hinault was milder in his explanation of what happened. 'I got on OK with [Stablinski], but we didn't see eye to eye. He wanted to see how I got on in all the races, because I was going well, but I didn't want that. I can't say I knew Stab well, because we were only together a year; all I know is that he made the mistake of believing that all cyclists were made in his image. He wanted immediate results, and I was thinking of the future.'

It was a classic impasse. Hinault could go no further with Stablinski, but where could he move to? He had made contact with the GAN team – sponsored by Groupe Assurance Nationale – led by Poulidor but they were rigidly structured around the veteran. Came the moment – the final Classic of the French season, Tours–Paris – came the man: Cyrille Guimard, the fiery sprinter with the ropey knees who had called Hinault to order at the criterium in Camors. Guimard was on the point of retirement at just twenty-eight, and had been asked to take over at Gitane, which in turn had just been bought out by Renault. He wanted Hinault. 'He said, "If I was to take over the reins at Gitane, would you stay?" "If it's you, yes, if it's Stab, no." He said it was likely he would take over. I had raced with him, had a bit of an idea of him, understood how he saw things. That interested me a bit – he began talking about a career plan.'

Guimard was not to everyone's taste. He was not universally liked in French cycling, he was not particularly close to his fellow *directeurs sportifs* – Sean Kelly, for example, recalls that he did not get on with Jean de Gribaldy, a fixture on the circuit until the mid-'80s – and his uncompromising views always made him something of an outsider. They still can. He remains a faintly distant figure, somewhat aloof, given to slightly portentous turns of phrase. As a rider, Guimard was aggressive, and inventive, but his body was not up to the task. One rival recalled, 'We used to call him "the little rat" because he was so sharp, and clever; he wasn't that much physically but he could do a lot with not much. And then he put that brain to work for Hinault.' Joop Zoetemelk, who raced with Guimard, concurs: 'Small in physical potential but he got the maximum from what he had.'

Guimard had several key qualities that enabled him to build a relationship with Hinault. He was a fellow Breton. He had begun his career with a similar lack of respect for the established order. He had an innovative way of thinking and he was highly ambitious. Like Robert Le Roux, he had a character as strong as Hinault's. He was rightly nicknamed Napoleon or Le Petit Chef [the little boss]; in self-belief, he was the match of his young protégé. His deal as *directeur sportif* of Gitane included some unconventional clauses: he would be paid the minimum wage for his first year, as he had no idea whether he would be a success, and he would start work after the world cyclo-cross championship in early 1976, where he ended his racing career with fourth place, having won the French championship two weeks before.

He was determined to have Hinault in the team. 'You have the future Tour winner [but] you need his signature fast,' Guimard told his bosses as they negotiated. 'With him, anything is possible, but it won't be easy if he's racing against us in years to come.' He had spotted Hinault long before he thought of becoming a team manager; he had watched him dominate an amateur track meeting at Saint-Brieuc, and had seen his 'mad-dog' attacks at first-hand in races like the Étoile des Espoirs and Paris–Nice. Guimard saw in Hinault the same quality that had earlier led him to harass Merckx mercilessly from the moment he turned professional – 'an absence of any complexes', as they both always put it.

'It was obvious. Hinault was a great of the future,' said Guimard. 'I knew it. I was certain of it. I'd raced the Étoile des Espoirs with him and I'd already seen and understood. I remember going up alongside him to ask him to calm down, to tell him that if he kept wasting energy by going in every move, he would blow his lid. He was aggressive, too much so. He was a thoroughbred such as I had never seen before. It would just take a little time to tune him up.'

At just twenty-eight, Guimard was one of the youngest team managers cycling had ever seen, younger than most of his riders and the exception among *directeurs sportifs*. Like his fellows, he was an ex-rider who had moved into management, but he had been forced to stop while still relatively young. His ambitions as a rider had been thwarted by his troubled knees and it could be argued that that meant he had a point to prove. His objective, he said in his memoirs, was to provide his riders with the support he would have wanted when racing himself. He didn't want to be a laissez-faire manager, because 'since the dawn of time the cyclist has been a fragile being – more fragile than many believe – who needs to be supported, advised, reassured, guided and above all else, incorporated into the life of a team'. Hinault describes Guimard's position in the early days as neither a mate nor a boss, but another rider, rather like a *capitaine de route*, a senior pro who dished out advice but who happened to be driving the team car.

Guimard was careful in his recruitment – possible signings would be invited to a training camp, then he would listen to the views of the team on them. If the rider's face didn't fit, he was dropped, no matter how impressive his physical ability. 'Very clever,' was Greg LeMond's view; 'A man with the Alex Ferguson touch,' said David Millar, one of his late recruits. Guimard had his eccentric, portentous side, as Fignon recalled in an episode from later in his career. 'During the first training camp, Guimard took the floor in front of the whole team. He was even more solemn than usual. The silence was impressive. The boss was about to say something. He came up with this jaw-dropping pronouncement: "Anyone caught with a bird in their room will be kicked out, *tout de suite*." We quickly worked out that he had never actually sacked anyone because they had been found with a girl in their room. He was just firing a warning shot.'

'He was the young guy with the best brain at the time,' says the French writer Jeff Quénet. 'He was the first *directeur sportif* to introduce periodisation. Before it was "train and race as much as I want you to" but he reduced the days of racing and got his riders to work towards real goals.'

'A very good trainer, and I'd say he's still among the best,' says Hinault now. 'He taught me a lot about racing. When Cyrille started out he was twenty-eight, M. Le Roux was seventy-ish; that was the difference. There was good in both of them. The vision of M. Le Roux was excellent as long as you were an amateur, but his views weren't that bad in any case. The difference between the two was that with M. Le Roux it was about doing sport [in general], with Cyrille it was about competing.'

For two men with such reputations – which they clearly both enjoyed and made much of – as 'pig-headed' Bretons, Guimard and Hinault were surprisingly tolerant of each other in their early years together. Hinault could appear immature but he showed patience beyond his years in adhering to the plan put to him by his new team manager. He was to target lesser races in 1976 – mainly medium-scale events on the French calendar such as Paris–Camembert and the Tour de l'Aude, keeping clear of major events such as the Dauphiné Libéré. At the same time, he would start the one-day Classics to gain some knowledge of their routes; in 1977 he was to move up a grade, and would target these, plus the Dauphiné and the Grand Prix des Nations. In 1978 he would tackle the Vuelta and Tour de France – to win. Compared with the scattergun approach of Stablinski, this was radical.

Guimard showed patience too, with a young man who was finding his feet. The Gitane squad travelled to training camp in early 1976 just after he had taken over the reins; Hinault was twelve kilograms overweight after letting himself go through the winter – by his own admission he had spent the off-season feeding Mickael, gardening and chopping wood. Guimard had just retired but was in tip-top condition from the cyclo-cross season and was able to ride with his new charges when they trained. He made a point of dropping Hinault on the climbs, usually with a sarky smile and a mickey-taking remark or gesture – for example, puffing out his cheeks hamster style – as the podgy youth slid backwards. It was classic psychology based on Hinault's combative character: Guimard didn't berate his rider, merely challenged him, in the knowledge that he would respond. 'If he had taken it badly, I might have chucked the whole thing: I might have given up the bike,' Hinault said later.

Hinault was late coming down for the first training ride, Guimard ticked him off and Hinault grumbled, 'This isn't the army.' Again, the *directeur sportif* didn't push the point, he merely gave an explanation: if the boot was on the other foot, and it was a teammate making Hinault wait, he would be unhappy. He was told: if it happened again, he would be training on his own. This set the tone for their early relationship; Guimard would tend to dictate what had to be done, Hinault would usually give way, sometimes unhappily. However, often he would find that Guimard was right, as at that year's Grand Prix des Nations where he insisted on his protégé doing an eighty-kilometre warm-up the morning of the race. Hinault didn't want to do it but it worked, and became part of his routine.

Gitane evolved slowly as a team in 1976, because Guimard was still using the riders who had been hired by Stablinski. Fortunately for Hinault, among them was the Belgian Lucien Van Impe, who was in his seventh season at the team. Van Impe was the opposite of the young Frenchman, a conservative rider who would opt for guaranteed successes such as climbing prizes and stage wins rather than gamble on spectacular mountain attacks. His unwillingness to take risks meant that Guimard virtually had to threaten him into making the winning attack in the 1976 Tour, but his presence in the team meant Guimard could afford to keep Hinault under wraps for the long-term.

As when he began his partnership with Robert Le Roux, Hinault's physical energy and combative attitude had to be channelled; he took a mischievous pleasure in attacking when the senior riders wanted to take a breather, but it was Guimard who warned him against making moves merely for the sake of annoying his colleagues. 'Taking into account his youth, his attacking mindset, his personality, his intense willpower, I had to direct him carefully, targeting set objectives,' said Guimard. 'He taught me how to race,' said Hinault. 'I would jump on every rider who showed his face at the front, so I would be shattered at the end of a race after wasting energy on useless efforts. Cyrille quickly made me understand that it wasn't down to me to chase everything. "You wait for the right moment ... When you decide to attack you put in a huge effort rather than ten small ones, and you will get away, every time."'

That May, Hinault won three races in ten days: the Circuit de la Sarthe for the second year running, the one-day Paris–Camembert – a solo win in Vimoutiers after escaping on the Mur des Champeaux to hold off the chase group by just 12sec – and another stage race, the Tour d'Indre-et-Loire. His versatility was the equal of the young Eddy Merckx. He competed with Jacques Esclassan – France's best sprinter at the time – in the bunch gallops, usually getting in the top three. He won the time trial in the Tour d'Indre-et-Loire at an average of over 44kph, beating Roy Schuiten. Guimard kept him out of the Dauphiné; instead he finished third in Midi Libre, and won the Tour de l'Aude. Later in the season, he added the Tour du Limousin. These were second-tier events, but for a second-year professional he was prolific; it was enough to win him the Prestige Pernod, the first of seven successive wins. At twenty-one years old, he was anointed the best French professional of the year.

The relationship between Hinault and Guimard was not always smooth: both men liked to speak their minds;

Hinault was far from mature as a cyclist, while Guimard was learning the ropes as a *directeur sportif*. In 1977, his second year under Guimard, Hinault was still capable of taking French leave as he had done under Stablinski. He was one of three Gitane riders who disappeared from that year's Tour of Flanders because they didn't want to risk their necks on the *pavé* in the rain and the cold. One, Roland Berland, didn't even venture out of his hotel room; Hinault and the other, Jean Chassang, did at least turn up at the start on Sint-Niklaas's main square, but they did not take the trouble to change into their cycling shoes. Just two hundred metres after the start line, Hinault turned round, rode to his car and headed for Brittany, still wearing his race kit. Guimard – probably concerned by the fact that this was a revolt involving not one lone rider but three of his team – had no hesitation in sending Hinault a registered letter two days later containing a formal warning about his conduct.

If the letter was intended to provoke a reaction in Hinault – and it probably was given Guimard's abilities to press the right buttons – it had the desired effect nineteen days later. In Gent–Wevelgem, as at Vimoutiers the year before, Hinault took a solo win, using his time-trialling skills – and it came in spite of a mistake by his mechanic, who had not changed the gear from the pancake-flat Classic, Paris–Roubaix, which had taken place two days before. Hinault felt the bigger gear, but was experienced enough by now to sense the moment when the lead group began to hesitate thirty kilometres from the finish, each man unwilling to take the initiative. 'He attacked through Menen, down a dead straight road, went again when they got close to him and stayed clear when they started the sprint behind,' recalled Barry Hoban. The small group behind included experienced Classic riders such as Walter Godefroot and André Dierickx, and two future world champions in Gerrie Knetemann and Jan Raas, but they had no idea what the rider in front of them was capable of: he won by 1min 24sec from the Italian Vittorio Algeri.

For Hinault's home press, it was a significant win, because French Classic wins were – and still are – so rare. Only one Frenchman had won in Wevelgem before him, and that *francais* was no less than Jacques Anquetil. However, Hinault was not taken seriously by the Flemish, because the best Belgians of the day, Eddy Merckx, Freddy Maertens and Roger De Vlaeminck, had all been sitting out the midweek Classic. One Flemish newspaper ran the headline, 'In the land of the blind, the one-eyed man is king'. 'Imbeciles,' was Guimard's verdict. Five days later came a bigger breakthrough in Liège–Bastogne–Liège, where the big names all turned up: Merckx, Didi Thurau of Germany, Maertens, De Vlaeminck. It was a vile day: cold with constant showers of rain, and in the final hour, rain and wet snow heavy enough to pile up on the cars by the roadside. During the final run-in off the Ardennes into Liège, the sturdy, middle-ranking Classics specialist Dierickx attacked from a select lead group on the final hill, la Côte des Forges, with twelve kilometres to the finish; Hinault went with him.

Dierickx had won Flèche Wallonne twice and now he was expected to add Liège. Knowing Hinault's ability in an extended sprint, Guimard told him to lead out Dierickx at the finish, briefly cut off his effort, then push on again. At the finish, the race did a U-turn alongside the river Meuse on the Boulevard de la Sauvenière before coming back in the opposite direction to the chequered flag; Guimard parked his car a hundred metres from the line on the other side of the central reservation and – with the chasing group in sight behind – he shouted at his rider when to make his move. 'I led out as Cyrille told me to do,' Hinault recalled. 'By making the first move, I gained a couple of lengths on Dierickx; I knew he was in a bigger gear than me.[8] When he came back to me I went again, without being too aware of where the finish line was.' Fifty metres out, Dierickx had pushed his front wheel just ahead of Hinault's, but by the line he was several lengths behind. 'He had completely underestimated Hinault's ability to withstand six and a half hours of intense competition and then have enough guile and strength to win the sprint,' wrote the British journalist Peter Duker in *International Cycle Sport*.

Winning in Belgium was all very well, but the point in time when Hinault truly entered the French national consciousness is clearly defined: the afternoon of 4 June 1977, as he descended the Col de Porte on the penultimate day

---

[8] According to one report, Hinault was not using a 13-tooth sprocket, but a 14, while Dierickx had a 13. M. Le Roux would have been proud of him.

of the Dauphiné Libéré. This was his first attempt to win a major stage race in the high mountains; the Porte came at the end of a stage from Romans-en-Isère to Grenoble over two other cols, Granier and Coq, and after the Porte it concluded with the steep climb up Grenoble's Bastille to the fortress built by Vauban. The field included the cream of the mid-1970s crop: Merckx, Thévenet, Poulidor, Hennie Kuiper, Joaquim Agostinho. There was also Hinault's erstwhile leader Van Impe, who had left the previous winter after asking Guimard for a massive salary increase, which Guimard knew he could refuse, because he had Hinault knocking on the door.

The race had begun on the Col du Coq, where Thévenet attacked; Hinault joined the leaders on the descent, then attacked in his turn on the Col de Porte. At the summit he was 1min 30sec up on Thévenet and Van Impe: 'I wanted more and more, I devoured the first three hairpins of the descent and at the fourth, boomph.' He looked over the edge for a second, 'and it was as if a giant hand had grabbed my neck. I hit the corner too fast, braked, landed in the gravel, braked again and completely locked the wheels up.' Over the plunging precipice he went, with the television commentator shouting 'ooh-la-la', no doubt fearing for Hinault's life as he disappeared from view. Lives can be lost, careers ended through this kind of incident, but miraculously a tree broke his fall; Guimard climbed down and hauled him out on his shoulders. 'The pair showed a miraculous sangfroid and promptness, giving the impression that this had been rehearsed,' wrote Olivier Dazat.

René Hinault had grabbed the spare bike off the roof rack and his cousin was still in the lead when he hit the Bastille – the hulking fortress which sits a thousand feet above Grenoble on the other side of the Isère from the city centre – after being cheered through the streets by people who had seen the crash live on television and come out of their houses to watch him go past. The Bastille is a four-mile climb, between 13.5 per cent and 15 per cent average – mostly, people go up there by cable car nowadays. Five hundred metres from the top, the young Hinault's nerves gave way. He was still traumatised by his near-death experience, and he climbed off his bike, walking about twenty metres before remounting to win the stage with Van Impe 1min 20sec behind. That evening, Guimard collected his bike from the ravine. The team mechanic had to go down on a rope; it was in bits, thirty metres below the road.

The writer Philippe Bordas drew a parallel between the moment when Hinault emerges from the ravine, and 'a violent birth'. The whole drama took place live on prime-time Saturday afternoon television with millions watching. From then on, Hinault was a national figure, and expected to win the Tour de France. After that, Merckx designated the young Frenchman as his successor – the Cannibal's way of passing the baton was to help Hinault after a crisis on the final day on the Col de la Forclaz, where he was in massive pain from the crash. 'My right thigh was killing me; I couldn't pull on the bars, I couldn't breathe and mentally I was worn out.' The chase behind a break led by Thévenet was intense, Hinault finished 1min 44sec back and retained the jersey by just 17sec.

The final time-trial stage went to Thévenet, by just 8sec. Hinault had defeated the 1975 Tour winner, and he had out-climbed the 1976 winner, Van Impe. Thévenet was to go on and take his second Tour in a few weeks' time, but he knew what was coming in the longer term. 'Next year,' he said, 'Hinault will be untouchable.'

CHAPTER 5

THE SLOW WALK TO THE TOP

'He marched forward like Napoleon.'

– Paul Sherwen

On 18 May 1978, at just after 4 p.m., Eddy Merckx read out a prepared statement for a large crowd of reporters who had been summoned the day before to the Brussels International Press Centre. He was to retire from racing forthwith. He repeated the statement in Flemish, French and English for the benefit of radio reporters. He took no questions. He blamed mental fatigue for the decision, the stress of having to spend the winter looking for a sponsor for his team, for the group of riders and staff who depended upon him for a living. Thus ended the Merckx era, the decade of 'Cannibal' domination that had begun at the end of 1967.

The two-year build-up to that teatime announcement in Brussels had formed the background to the races

Bernard Hinault rode in 1976 and 1977, and the plans that he and Cyrille Guimard laid. From the spring of 1976 it had been clear that Merckx was a shadow of his former self and his succession would soon become a live issue: the only question was when? The Cannibal's competitive drive was as strong as ever, but his body no longer responded as it once did. Merckx remained a major factor in most of the races he contested, but only one among several. The trajectory of his results through 1976 and 1977 was a constant downward curve. His impending departure was a matter of common knowledge through the spring of 1978.

Merckx stopped racing six months after two other key figures retired. Raymond Poulidor, France's most popular cyclist of the post-war years, hung up his wheels after the Grand Prix des Nations in September 1977 at the age of forty-one. With the 1973 Tour winner Luis Ocaña disappearing as well, that marked the end of the generation that had dominated cycling in the late 1960s through to the mid-'70s. Ocaña had been consistently inconsistent but Poulidor had been a firm fixture at the top of world cycling since his epic battle with Jacques Anquetil in the 1964 Tour de France; Anquetil's retirement in 1969 had left the field open for Poulidor to have first claim on the hearts of the French public. Although Bernard Thévenet managed three major achievements that always eluded 'PouPou' – wearing the yellow jersey, winning the Tour, and defeating Merckx – 'Nanard' had never had quite the same appeal. The upshot was that in the spring of 1978,

world cycling was looking for a new master, while French
cycling needed a fresh national hero. The goal was wide
open: Hinault had only to keep his eyes on the ball.

The incident that marked Hinault out as the new leader
of world cycling in the post-Merckx era was not a race
victory, but a stand-off on the main street of a small town
in the south-west of France on 12 July 1978. This should
have been a festive day for Valence d'Agen and its young
mayor, Jean-Michel Baylet. Valence had only five thousand
inhabitants and this was probably the biggest peacetime
event to happen to the sleepy community best known as
a stop-off on the Canal du Midi. But instead of a colourful,
spectacular sprint finish on the Boulevard Victor Guilhem
– the spectacle that Baylet's council had paid about
$20,000 to host – what they saw was without precedent
in the Tour. The peloton was walking slowly down the
road, clicking towards the finish line on their stiff-soled,
metal-plated shoes, pushing their bikes before them. The
procession lasted several minutes and the man at the front
was Hinault, 'marching forward like Napoleon', as Paul
Sherwen, one of the riders in the second row, told me.
Alongside the young Briton was Sean Kelly. 'Hinault was
in the front, with the crowd booing and throwing things.
He had his bottom jaw locked and was glaring at them.'
Pictures show Hinault standing in the front row, resplendent in the red, white and blue jersey of French national
champion, with his jaw jutting forward and his chest out,
the look on his face like that of a boxer at weighing-in.

To make the disappointment all the more acute, the crowd had had to wait overtime in the blazing heat – many of them covering their heads with folded newspapers – to see this bizarre spectacle. The riders were two hours behind schedule having covered the 160 kilometres from Tarbes at cyclo-tourist pace. Accounts of the crowd's reaction vary, but what is certain is the reaction of the mayor: M Baylet was outraged, and strode forward in his fawn-coloured suit to square up to Hinault, who had been pushed forward to represent the riders. The man pointing his chin at the cyclist – who looked him in the eyes like Clint Eastwood staring down the bad guy in a spaghetti western – was the scion of a local dynasty that combined radical left-wing politics with running a large publishing business centred on the *Dépêche du Midi* newspaper. Power was M Baylet's birthright – he had been appointed mayor of Valence the year before, succeeding his mother Evelyne,[9] who had represented the town for the previous nineteen years. From his family's south-western base, Jean-Michel would go on to a successful career in French national politics, thanks to the lengthy left-wing presidency of François Mitterrand, becoming a secretary of state in 1984, a minister from 1990 to 1993 and representing Tarn et Garonne in the senate from 1995 to 2014.

---

[9] Evelyne Baylet née Isaac was mayor of Valence from 1959 to 1977, president of the Tarn et Garonne general council from 1970 to 1982 and head of the Depeche du Midi publishing group from 1959 to 1995. She died in November 2014 aged 101.

Baylet expected his administration – and the people he represented – to get their money's worth, and as a rising young politician with his eyes on the national stage, he needed the Tour's visit to be a visible success. Hence his confrontational attitude, hence his criticism of the strike as 'a moral fraud' and hence his disgust at the conduct of athletes who he said had refused to honour a contract. In this, he echoed the Tour organiser Jacques Goddet, who felt that in entering the Tour the riders had implicitly accepted the rules, route and race conditions, and that this amounted to a moral contract. Others shared his views: Raphaël Geminiani and Jacques Anquetil in particular. Ironically – in view of Baylet and his family's left-wing politics – the socialist press supported the riders' stance on the ground that they were workers subject to exploitation.

When the race left Tarbes that morning, the organisers knew something was pending: they had offered a special prize of some 8,000 francs (£800) – about three months' salary – for the most aggressive rider. But instead of racing, the riders pretended to snooze under trees, staged mock crashes, ran up the verges with their bikes on their shoulders, cyclo-cross style, then walked across the line painted on the road at the first hot spot of the day, in the town of Fleurance. The mood was good-humoured, with Hinault squirting water from his feeding bottle at a television cameraman. Jacques Goddet and Félix Lévitan then suspended the day's prize money – as they had done after a previous go-slow in 1952 – invoking an obscure rule that a minimum average speed had to be respected.

The grounds for the strike were straightforward: the riders could take no more. They had finished the previous day's mountain stage at the Pla d'Adet ski station, taken the ski lift down to Saint-Lary, then piled into buses laid on by the Tour organisers for a fifty-five-mile transfer through the traffic jam of fans' vehicles and the race convoy, arriving at their hotels late into the evening. That morning they had to be up at 4.30 a.m. for a 7.30 a.m. start to the two 'split stages', the first of which finished at Valence, after which the riders would have two hours for lunch before racing again, 96km to Toulouse. The direct route was 190km, the total they would race was 254km. The next day there was a two-hour train transfer in the early morning for the stage start at Figeac. It wasn't the first issue of this kind. At Paris–Nice the previous year the riders had protested against a similar combination of transfers and multiple stages in the same day. Not all the riders were wholeheartedly behind the strike, recalls Joop Zoetemelk, who made a point of not being in the front row. 'Personally I'm not a striker, I believe you get the *parcours* of a Tour well beforehand and the time to change it is not during the race. But all the riders were in favour of doing something – it was extreme, long stages and transfers, not just for the riders but soigneurs and mechanics, everyone.'

Split stages were lucrative for the organisers. Félix Lévitan, who was in charge of the commercial side of the Tour, had realised the race could double the money it made on certain days by selling two stage finishes to the various town councils rather than the usual one. On the other hand, such stages entailed twelve- or fourteen-hour days for the riders. 'Conditions were primitive,' recalls Kelly. 'Lévitan had made the Tour a commercial success but the conditions for the riders had not improved. Nor had the prize money.' Sometimes the riders slept in dormitories. Meals were provided by the organisers but were 'always green beans', Kelly noted. 'We understand the financial imperatives of the organisers but we are not circus animals to be exhibited from town to town,' said Hinault's teammate André Chalmel, the head of the riders' union. 'We are not asking for more money, only for a little more consideration.' 'Our patience was stretched to breaking point,' said Kelly.

'Everyone was knackered, it was a hot day and someone said, "Let's have a strike," and it just escalated,' recalled Sherwen. 'Everyone was too tired to race. The word came down from the "heads" that we would stop at two hundred metres to go and just walk across the line. Everyone waited, then the big guys got into the front line. Kelly and I didn't believe there would be a strike. We were in the second line because a lot of guys didn't believe it would happen and thought they might get a chance for the stage win. Kelly said, "If anyone moves we're going for it." We didn't undo our straps until the last minute. We couldn't believe that no one broke ranks.'

Accounts of the crowd's reaction and the altercations that followed vary. In his first autobiography, Hinault wrote: 'I tried to talk to the mayor, but he wouldn't listen. I wanted to explain the reasons behind our action.

He wouldn't let me speak. I said, "*M. Le Maire*, when someone speaks to you, you shut your mouth and afterwards you can reply!" Spectators began to throw tomatoes at us. I put down my bike and jumped over the barriers to fight them.' On the other hand, Felix Magowan wrote that the crowd were delighted to see history being made before their very eyes. Hinault would later tell M Baylet that the strike had at least put Valence on the map.

It wasn't a given that Hinault would take the lead among the riders. He was the French national champion, but he was young, in his first Tour. Others had better claims to prominence: Andre Chalmel was leader of the riders' union, Freddy Maertens the rider with the most substantial *palmarès*. Gerben Karstens, a pugnacious little Dutch sprinter – and Hinault's teammate at Gitane in 1975 – was apparently a prime mover, and one of those who guided him to the front as they came into Valence. 'I was pushed forwards by the others in spite of myself and almost found myself in the role of a trade-union delegate, a spokesman,' wrote Hinault later.

This was a collective protest, organised by the 'heads' of the peloton, but the stand-off with Baylet meant that Hinault came to be seen as both instigator and leader: 'He took all the responsibility, stood in the front line, was spat at by the crowd,' said Sherwen. He also took all the flak in the press. In one version, Hinault claimed he was 'furious' because he was blamed for the entire event. Whatever the details, the upshot could not be denied, as Felix Magowan wrote in *Tour de France, the Historic 1978*

Event: 'Before today's strike, people were asking if the Tour had a boss. Today that was answered. His name is Hinault.'

Hinault's leadership at Valence had to be seen in the context of his victories that season: had he not won the races he did, his sudden grasp of the reins would have had less impact. In 1978, his dominance on the road and his display of leadership off it made a far more potent combination than Merckx had achieved. Merckx's fearsome reputation had built up gradually, but it was based solely on his larger-than-life achievements on the road. Hinault, on the other hand, was thrust forwards by events on and off his bike.

At the end of April 1978, before the Tour of Spain, Pierre Chany of *L'Équipe* wrote that Hinault had a 90 per cent chance of winning. This might seem astonishing to say of a rider in his first major Tour, but Chany was one of the most seasoned observers of cycling and he wasn't sticking his neck out given the previous twelve months. At the end of 1977, after the Dauphiné, after his two Classic wins, Hinault had won the Grand Prix des Nations, the classic time trial which at that time had just moved from Angers in western France (where Hinault finished sixth in the 1975 and 1976 events) to a new course at Cannes, where it was to remain through the 1980s. Hinault expected to finish third behind the two big favourites, Joop Zoetemelk and Freddy Maertens, but instead came in 3min 15sec ahead of the Dutchman. That was a colossal margin.

He turned up slightly overweight for the start of the 1978 season – a mere five kilos – but ended up second in Paris–Nice without particularly meaning to. He then went on to win the Critérium National[10] although it wasn't an objective, starting the final afternoon's time trial two minutes behind his fellow Breton Raymond Martin after Zoetemelk and Bernard Thévenet had made him struggle on the morning's hilly stage. This was a typical instance of team management challenging Hinault to get a response from him on the road; Guinard's assistant Maurice Champion had told his leader that there was no chance of his taking more than two minutes out of Martin in just twenty-two kilometres – at between five and six seconds per kilometre that was true on paper – and the Renault *soigneur* had joined in. Hinault responded in his usual style.

Riding the Vuelta – then run at the end of April – was Guimard's way of easing his protégé into three-week stage racing while avoiding the intense pressure of the Tour. The Spanish Tour was still the poor relation among the three major Tours, with relatively little prize money – less than a quarter of that on offer in the Giro – and no live television coverage; the field was correspondingly weak, with only ten teams on the start line, only four of them Spanish. Apart from Hinault's Renault, the others were

---

[10] At this stage the Critérium National was limited to French teams – and their non-French members – only. In 1981 the restriction was dropped, and it became the Critérium International.

mainly second-string Belgian and Dutch squads. That year's was a classic 'spring' Vuelta, with snow in the high mountains and it hit some of the wilder extremes of stage racing. A key mountain stage through the Sierra de Madrid was cut back to forty-six kilometres due to a snowstorm, demonstrations from miners and Basque separatists caused the final stage to be cancelled, spectators threw missiles at the riders, and a Renault rider, Lucien Didier, was barged off his bike by another rider, Enrique Cima of KAS, on a high-speed descent, suffering serious injuries.

Hinault won the prologue time trial in Gijon, then for ten days, let the *amarillo* leader's jersey go to the twenty-five-year-old Belgian Ferdi Van den Haute, a Classics specialist who was never likely to hold the lead through the mountains. 'We kept asking ourselves whether he could keep it, we got to the Pyrenees, and bam! He was seven minutes back just like that,' said his teammate of the time, Patrick Lefevere. Hinault won stage 11b, a brief uphill time trial at Barcelona, then retrieved the race lead the next day on the stage to La Tossa de Montbu. On this stage Renault produced some classic team racing when a new Guimard acquisition, Jean-René Bernaudeau, made it into the early break, and Hinault bridged to them on the toughest climb of the stage, Can Massana, with Bernaudeau shepherding him to the finish ahead of the eventual runner-up, José Pesarrodona.

Hinault then worked hard picking up time bonuses at intermediate sprints to open his lead on the Spaniard; it was a stressful business, with Hinault coming close to a punch-up with the Spaniard Enrique Martinez-Heredia on one stage, before becoming involved in a pile-up when a teammate intervened. 'It wasn't easy for him with the Spanish,' says Lefevere. 'They had had Merckx win in 1973, Maertens had dominated the Vuelta a couple of years before, and suddenly here's this French kid.' A solo stage victory in the Basque Country on the penultimate stage from Bilbao to Amurrio sealed his first win in a major Tour. The Spaniard Jose Pesarrodona finished second at just over 3min, Bernaudeau third at 3min 47sec.

One protagonist on both the key mountain stages was Andrés Gandarias, a seasoned second-string racer in the final year of his career. A native Basque, he had targeted the Amurrio stage on his home roads. 'I attacked with about 100 kilometres to go, an Italian came with me; after the final climb [Orduña] with about twenty kilometres to go, Hinault caught up with us. I had gone up to Hinault before I broke away and said, "Can I go for it?" and he had said, "Sure, no problem," and I'd done a deal with the Italian, too, so I was pretty surprised when Hinault bridged to us.

'He said, "There was some teammate ahead of me on the Orduña and I was pissed off because he kept on attacking, so I went after him, but come with me and I'll let you win the stage." But he was going too fast for me. On a short climb after Vitoria, maybe third category, just 8 or 9 per cent, one you could get up on the big ring, Hinault was simply going so hard, he was using a 54x17 [gear] on a climb like that, and he dropped me. At the finish he said, "Hey, why didn't you follow me?" and I said, "You were going faster than the blooming race motorbikes, that's why!" I told the journalists, "This guy has made me suffer like a dog, he's tougher than Eddy Merckx!" He was just like Merckx, he had to win everything. When I first came across him, I thought he'd do even better than Eddy, in fact. It wasn't that we underestimated him, he might have been young, but he was so good.'

Hinault's Tour de France debut had been on the agenda since 1975, his first year as a professional. As well as Stablinski's abortive attempt to get him to start the race that year, the Breton starlet was asked about the Tour as early as spring 1975, when he won the Circuit de la Sarthe: he replied that he wouldn't ride in 1975, or 1976. After every win that Hinault achieved, he would be asked about the Tour: after winning at Liège in 1977, for example, he told the press that he would wait. 'I'm not mature enough, but when I do ride, I will come in through the front door.'

Following his Classic double and spectacular Dauphiné victory, Hinault and Guimard had to resist an intense media campaign to make the Gitane leader ride the 1977 Tour. With Bernard Thévenet back to his best, briefly, the organisers – the newspapers L'Équipe and Parisien Libéré – could see the potential for a 'franco–français' duel, with the consequent spike in sales, but the two Bretons stood firm. 'His priorities had been set down for a long while: the Classics and the Dauphiné,' recalled Guimard. 'There was no question, even if [Hinault] had achieved various exploits, of rewriting a programme which had been worked out to the last detail…He was on the verge of a great career if he was guided well, with patience, and without going too quickly.'

The question remains open: could Hinault have won the 1977 Tour and thus possibly become the first rider to win six Tours? It is certainly possible but it is equally likely that he might have been overstretched physically and would have paid the price later in his career. Hinault did complete the Tour in 1977 – but he did so riding most of the stages ahead of the peloton and then giving his impressions to television. It is estimated that he covered about three-quarters of the route, missing the rest due to bad weather and inconvenient road closures. Riding the last time trial in Dijon for fun, he covered the course in the same time as Thévenet did later the same day on the way to winning the race overall.

Very few riders win the Tour at their first attempt: Merckx, Fignon, Felice Gimondi and Fausto Coppi were the most notable exceptions. What set Hinault apart – and puts him in a class with Merckx and Coppi in particular – was that he was widely expected to win, that his debut had been talked about for so long beforehand. 'He was a wunderkind. Everyone knew who he was. I remember writing something like, "This is the man France expects to win the Tour de France,"' recalled Sam Abt, who reported the race for the *Herald Tribune*. 'He didn't sneak up on anyone. He had people, not so much intimidated, but everyone knew who he was and how strong he was and he began to assert his authority.'

As the first Tour de France of the post-Merckx era, the 1978 race was expected to be anarchic as the big names jostled for dominance, but instead it was tightly controlled by a small clique: Hinault, Joop Zoetemelk, Hennie Kuiper, Freddy Maertens, Michel Pollentier and their four teams: Renault, Miko-Mercier, TI-Raleigh and Flandria. In common with the 1977 Tour, the field wasn't the best quality. The Italians – Francesco Moser, Giuseppe Saronni, Gibi Baronchelli, Felice Gimondi – stayed away, meaning the field was small: just 110 riders in eleven teams of ten, fewer than the Giro's field of 130.

Hinault had not shown strongly at the Tour of Switzerland, but that was part of the programme he and Guimard had agreed, as it came after a long break from racing following the Vuelta. The French national championship at Sarrebourg in eastern France was a different matter: during a lengthy and ultimately sucessful escape – 73km in total, 55km on his own – he luxuriated in a 6min 10sec lead at the start of the final lap. Victory was in the bag, until he was hit by a massive attack of hypoglycaemia, because he had been 'in too much of a hurry to think about eating'. He crossed the line in a state of obvious distress, prompting Jean-Marie Leblanc to write in *L'Équipe* that, 'There is no more beautiful winner than an exhausted winner. It will remain a great moment in sport: the image of Bernard Hinault fighting more against the tension that gripped his entire body, the blurring of his vision and his leaden legs, than against his adversaries and the elements.' The biggest enemy for the young cyclist was his own urge to win.

Hinault put his cards on the table early on, pointing out that there were 190km of time trialling in the Tour, and, 'The time I will take there, the other guys will have to get back from me elsewhere.' His and Guimard's strategy was to become familiar: gain time against the watch and avoid losing it elsewhere, although they accepted that Renault would lose time in the first key stage, the insanely long 153km team time trial from Evreux to Caen. As Hinault said, there was no point wearing themselves out to gain twenty seconds on the other teams. In the event, their actual time loss of 5min 15sec to the winners TI-Raleigh was mitigated by the fact that, for the overall standings, the stage carried time bonuses rather than actual time, resulting in an ultimate loss of only two minutes.

If there was an early glitch, it came when a Renault rider, Jacques Bossis, briefly took the yellow jersey after infiltrating a significant escape on stage 3 – Guimard wanted his riders to remain as unobtrusive as possible – but with the team time trial the next day, his tenure was happily brief. The first key stage for Renault was the long time trial on stage 8 over sixty kilometres in the Bordeaux hinterland between Saint-Emilion and Saint-Foy-la-Grande, billed as *l'Etape des Vins*. What impresses here, in hindsight, is not so much the fact of Hinault's victory as the attention to detail that went into it, down to his use of three-year-old tyres matured in his cellar. He tested his time trial bike during the previous day's road stage, and the following morning he moved into the farm owned by his teammate Pierre-Raymond Villemiane, twenty minutes from the stage start. By now, he and Guimard had developed a set routine that would serve them well: riding the course in the morning at 35–40kph, selecting his gears and wheels after that. Next came a meal and a nap – 'I knew how I would go from how I slept, if it was soundly, I'd go well' – then he would wake up one hour before his start time for a twenty to thirty-minute spell behind the car on the time-trial bike before going straight to the start.

Pacing was key in the Saint-Foy-la-Grande time trial, where Hinault rode an extremely strong final third, over-taking Maertens who had been fastest for the entire early phase; by the finish he gained 34sec on Jos Bruyère – appointed leader of the Belgian C&A team after Merckx's retirement – and 59sec on Zoetemelk. Equally important, both the previous winners, Bernard Thévenet and Lucien Van Impe, finished so far behind they were now out of the race for the overall. 'I wouldn't be surprised if he was fifteen minutes ahead in Paris,' said one team manager. It was, wrote Goddet in *L'Équipe*, the moment when the champion was born.

In the Pyrenees he fought off attacks from Pollentier and Zoetemelk by riding in the controlling style perfected by Anquetil and other time triallists, permitting the climb-ers to gain a little time, but riding steadily to limit his losses. Here, he became confident that he could climb with the best in the Tour; on the Col de Peyresourde, Thévenet abandoned, making the generational shift from the Merckx era almost complete. Then came Valence d'Agen, and the strike, which ended up causing Hinault's only wobble of the three weeks. Under pressure from the organisers and the media, he had trouble sleeping and was caught out the following day on a tough stage through the Massif Central when Renault missed an escape including Bruyère's teammate Jos De Schoenmaeker – another former lieutenant to Merckx – and were forced into a long chase on hilly roads.

That clearly left Hinault weakened for the next key stage, the time trial finishing on the Puy de Dôme climb, where he had planned to win the yellow jersey. Instead, Zoetemelk found wings to gain 1min 40sec, with both Pollentier and Bruyère gaining time. The Guimard–Le Roux tactic book stated that after a setback, a team leader needed to make an immediate statement, so the very next morning, en route to Saint-Étienne, their protégé made two early attacks with Hennie Kuiper. Better was to come: by the finish, the hills had whittled the field down to about forty. The stage had been whittled down as well, with 27.5km knocked off at the start in response to the Valence strike. Kelly had been appointed to lead out Maertens, and he duly began his sprint at 500m to go on the Grand Boulevard, having glanced down to make sure there was a wheel following him, Maertens' wheel he assumed. The picture of the finish tells it all: Kelly is looking to his right, aghast, as he realises that he has just led out Hinault instead of his sprinter. 'It's a slightly uphill finish, not all the big sprinters were there, and when

Hinault gets his head on, when he's in that mood, that aggressive Breton mood…As for me, I was pissed off – you don't get those legs every day.'

Events were coming thick and fast: the next day saw a key twist in the plot at l'Alpe d'Huez, where Pollentier dominated the final kilometres and – briefly – took the race lead only to be disqualified for an attempt to defraud the anti-doping control. From a three-man race, with the Belgian, Hinault and Zoetemelk within eighteen seconds of each other, it suddenly came down to Hinault and the Dutchman, who was awarded the yellow jersey four hours after the finish. Zoetemelk was a quiet, willowy all-rounder who had made his name as one of the many high-quality racers who had been unable to match Merckx in the mid-1970s. He was still recovering from the consequences of a severe crash in 1974, which had left him with a fractured skull and meningitis; he says now that he didn't find his very best form again until 1979. For several years, the crash deprived him of the ability to race strongly for the full three weeks of a Grand Tour; he would go downhill in the final week. In any case, he believed he needed two minutes in hand if he was to hold the lead all the way to Paris. With another time trial to come, fourteen seconds was never going to be enough.

The Dutchman barely hung on to Hinault when he put him under pressure on the final mountain stage into Morzine and that left the Breton perfectly poised going into the final *contre la montre* from Metz to Nancy.

Zoetemelk was suffering from bronchitis; Hinault had taken over three minutes out of him in the Grand Prix des Nations the year before. On paper he stood no chance over the seventy-two kilometres, a distance that would now be seen as way too long, and could be seen as the organisers' way of helping to ensure a Hinault win if possible. Even so, before the start, Guimard was pale and nervous; his protégé, however, was perfectly confident. Fifteen minutes before the start, he climbed into the back of the team car, put his feet up on the seat in front, pulled his *casquette* over his eyes and went to sleep. When the rider ahead of Hinault, Joaquim Agostinho of Portugal, was called to the start, Guimard and a *soigneur* came to wake their leader up. By the time he reached the outskirts of Metz, Hinault had already overturned his fourteen-second deficit; on the outskirts of Nancy, he overhauled Agostinho, who had started three minutes ahead of him. At the finish, Zoetemelk was over four minutes behind. That gave Hinault the Tour by 3min 56sec.

There were images everywhere on that Tour of Hinault's *prise de pouvoir*, including a podgy-faced Merckx shouting at his riders, Bruyère and Lucien Van Impe, from the C&A team car, but for the French, Bernard Thévenet's struggle on the Col de Marie Blanque in the Pyrenees had particular significance. A photomontage of his agonised, unsuccessful attempt to remain in the race was given a double-page spread in the *Miroir du Cyclisme* Tour review, headlined, '*La brume se lève*' (the mist clears).

Thévenet had struggled in 1976 with poor form as well, and his eclipse in 1978 was the end of him as a force. The man who had toppled Merckx in 1975, and enjoyed brief national fame in France as a result, was never the same cyclist again; he eventually cited excessive use of corticosteroids as a factor in his precipitate decline.

Thévenet was already yesterday's Bernard. After a disappointing fifth in the world championships on the Nürburgring, Hinault's season ended with victory in the Grand Prix des Nations at Cannes, with the Breton in a completely different role compared to the previous year. Then he had been an outsider, twelve months on he was the favourite, in French eyes at least, if not in the mind of the Italian Francesco Moser, winner that April of Paris–Roubaix. Asked about France's new hero, 'Cecco' answered, 'Hinault? Never heard of him.' With the victory under his belt, fifty-six seconds ahead of the Italian, Hinault responded, 'Moser? I hope he knows who I am now.'

For Guimard and Hinault, there had been no surprise in that year's events: 'He was supposed to win the Tour and he did,' recalled Guimard. 'There was no random factor in it at all, there were no fortuitous circumstances. For him, experiencing this massive event was almost normal, ordinary. It was the logical conclusion of a road he had no option but to take.' 'When you win the first time, it's the outcome of seven or eight months' work, so it wasn't a surprise for us,' said Hinault unemotionally. Others, like the Briton Paul Sherwen, were more impressed:

'We'd be on the little ring going uphill and he looked like he was in 53x14. We'd think, "Jeez, he looks strong." He seemed to ride the whole Tour on the big chain ring.' This was to become a familiar sight for the next eight years.

CHAPTER 6

THE GUIMARD SYSTEM

'You either love Guimard or you hate him.'

– Bernard Hinault

Bernard Hinault didn't rise to the top of cycling in isolation. The year 1978 marked the beginning of a lengthy spell when stage races, if not one-day events, were ruled by a mighty trinity: Hinault, Renault, Guimard; rider, team, manager. The Gitane squad had morphed into Renault-Gitane-Campagnolo following the national car maker's takeover of its cycle subsidiary; under Guimard's tutelage, and with Hinault the driving force, they would be a major player in cycling until the start of 1985. In 1978 the jersey changed from Gitane's blue and red, to yellow with black and white bars. 'The wasp-striped jerseys were awe-inspiring,' wrote Laurent Fignon, whose early cycling years coincided with the hegemony of the big three.

Guimard is largely overlooked outside France now, but in terms of Tour de France results, he has the best hit rate of any *directeur sportif* in cycling history: through Van Impe, Hinault and the late Laurent Fignon, he won seven Tours in nine years, 1976–84. If you factor in riders formed in his stable but who had moved on to other teams, his protégé Greg LeMond won three Tours between 1986 and 1990 while Hinault took another; Guimard's tally could be said to be eleven Tours in fifteen years.

Guimard felt that Renault bridged the gap between cycling's golden age in the 1950s and 1970s and the new age at the end of the 1980s. '[The sport was] going through a moment of transition...the Bernard Hinault of the end of the 1970s was caught between two periods. There was the period of the "giants of the road" – the likes of Coppi, Bartali, Gaul, Anquetil and Merckx, an era I would term "artisanal", empirical. Soon [came] the era of technology, of programmed champions, not to say "robotic", and worst of all, of scientific doping.'

Renault was not on a par with the armadas that Molteni and Faema built around Merckx, believes one rider who raced with both. 'Eddy had a big team, and there were times when he would simply set the team to work, they might go through a *ravitaillement* at a hundred kilometres per hour, for example. But Eddy had big riders in his teams, who he had persuaded to ride for him – Jos Bruyère, Herman Van Springel, Roger Swerts – so Hinault's teams were less strong. Bernard was more of an individual on the road. And Renault were more programmed than Molteni or Faema – they only went for it in the races Hinault had targeted.'

Then again, the opposition was tougher than that which Merckx faced, believed one Renault team member, Jean-René Bernaudeau. 'This isn't the Merckx era when all the riders considered it was a victory if they finished second or third,' he said in 1980. 'That gives Bernard's victories greater value because he finds it much harder to win races. The other riders contest everything and he has to demonstrate constantly that he is the strongest.'

Central to the changes Guimard wrought in his team was his refusal to accept the sport's core belief that could be traced back to its origins: that cycling was an individual sport which happened to be team-based. For him cycling was a team sport where each member – rider or staff – was a link in a chain. 'If a rider wins he has taken the best advantage of everyone's work, beginning with his own,' he wrote. Renault was to be completely oriented around Hinault, but with the proviso that the other riders had to be winners when the boss was not up for it. 'We were team riders but ambitious ones,' said Fignon. 'We knew we were going to win, but it was on one condition. Hinault would have to decide he didn't want to put his arms in the air that day, because if he was going for the win, we would be nowhere.'

There were many factors that worked against team unity: the riders' homes were spread across an entire country, so a lack of communication made it hard for team members to know what their teammates or protégés were doing – and it was easy for them to be dishonest with one another. Under the old-school system, smaller races served as informal selection events for bigger races, which rewarded short-term thinking, making it almost impossible to forge a unified team. The riders were reliant on performance-based criterium contracts for a third of their income, which also worked against team unity, as the criterium managers would favour winners over workers. Why should anyone help a possible rival, even if they wore the same jersey and rode the same bike?

Guimard's solution was to index his riders' salaries according to the team's results, taking into account the contribution they had made. When any one rider won a race, the other riders' salaries would increase the following year, according to a formula determined by the importance of the race, meaning that each rider felt involved in the team from the first to the last day of the year. The system also depended on the status of the rider relative to the race: Hinault's salary wouldn't increase if he won a minor event, but it would if a teammate won, which was intended to encourage him to help his *domestiques* win smaller events. That in turn would make them more willing to help him in the major races.

Another Guimard goal was to make his cyclists' careers more stable. So he made his riders full-time employees of Gitane, rather than hiring them from January to October, as was the convention at other teams. That move brought him into conflict with the two most powerful agents in the sport, Daniel Dousset and Roger Piel. Piel and Dousset sold *plateaux* of riders to the criterium organisers, which meant they effectively decided the riders' schedules for August and September when the criteriums were in full swing. That was the way the system had worked since the 1950s, but Guimard felt that if he was paying the riders twelve months a year, he had the right to dictate when and what they raced. After a two-year wait to ensure that Gitane were strong enough to guarantee that the criterium organisers wouldn't want to run their races without them, he persuaded his riders to bypass the agents, and took control of who raced where through the summer.

There were other moves that ultimately turned Renault and its leader into a force to be reckoned with. The size of the team was cut from the usual twenty to twenty-five riders to between fifteen and twenty, with the extra money spent on support personnel such as an administrator to direct the team's finances including outside contracts such as product endorsements and criterium contracts. That in turn meant Guimard was the only team head who could devote his time solely to preparing and managing the team, rather than juggling a multitude of minor tasks as *directeurs sportifs* tended to do at the time.

Another radical move was to forge links with the main hospital in Nantes in conjunction with a professor of sports medicine. Renault were also the first team to move beyond transporting the riders between hotels and race starts and finishes in team cars – they had a small bus with fifteen seats up front, which could be converted into couchettes and a space in the back for the mechanics' kit and the team bikes. And Renault was one of the first handful of teams to have a clause in their rider contract stating that a positive test for banned drugs would render the contract void.[11]

The company saw its cycling team as a test bed in the same way that the Formula One and rally-driving teams were for their cars. The car company's desire to innovate explained why they had gone against the obvious course and hired a youthful but open-minded *directeur sportif*. Guimard would benefit from partnership with the bio-mechanic and wind-tunnel service at Renault; Renault's work on aerodynamics and biomechanics, plus the way that the team's doctors looked after the riders all year round, were novelties in cycling, pointing the way ahead from the era when riders were left to their own devices for much of the season.

Equally revolutionary was the work Renault carried out on position and ergonomics, rather than merely giving the rider a bike: Guimard believed that if a rider was com-fortable and happy on his bike, he would train better and thus race better. In 1977, work began with help of Maurice Menard, director of the aerodynamics institute at Saint-Cyr-l'École – still used for wind-tunnel studies in the automotive industry today – and Hinault recalled that by 1978 Renault's engineers had re-evaluated his position and calculated that they had gained about two seconds per kilometre. Over a long time trial, such as the stages

---

[11] Others in the 1978 Tour with this clause included TI-Raleigh and Fiat-La France.

in the Tour at the time or the Grand Prix des Nations, that was a significant saving.

Ultimately, Renault and Guimard would evolve a position with the same broad lines for all Guimard's riders – using long cranks, and a massive stem to get the rider as stretched out as possible. Crucially – and again, radically – this was for all the team, not just for the leaders. In 1979 Renault and Gitane produced the Profil, the first road-racing bike with aerodynamic features such as concealed cables, front brake hidden behind the fork, and flattened tubes, which are now common across the industry.

Below the professional team, Gitane had already forged links with amateur clubs to provide a throughput of young riders into the team, but Guimard was a shrewd recruiter, moving faster than the biggest team in France, Peugeot, when it came to discovering riders like the Madiot brothers Marc and Yvon. 'Peugeot had its talent ladder and then there was *une filière* Gitane,' recalled Marc. 'I was in the Gitane *filière*, with Didier Louis, a bike dealer in Flers. It was like being in a family, based on local riders and local shops, small amounts of local help with sponsorship through the cycle makers. Guimard was quicker than the other [teams], looked at us younger, and made us progress quicker. With ACBB there was a delay of four to five years. Guimard recruited quickly, then there was a mould that you fitted into.' Hinault's former trainer Robert Le Roux believed, however, that if Guimard had provided Hinault with a really strong team of *domestiques* such as Merckx employed – rather than relying on a constant throughput of young riders – the Badger would have won more.

If the Renault cycling team was to develop immense resonance among the French public, that was not just down to Hinault and company, nor to its Formula One team starring René Arnoux and – in its final and most successful phase – Alain Prost. With popular products such as the utilitarian Renault 4 and the tractors that could be seen in fields everywhere, the publicly owned motor company was part of the fabric of French society, 'part of the flesh and blood of French life', Fignon wrote. And by extension, so was its professional cycling team. 'The company's status as a national institution enhanced Hinault's exploits and made Guimard's aura still more magisterial,' believed Fignon.

While Hinault's victories and *coups de gueule* dominated the headlines, in parallel Guimard's innovations were quietly transforming his team and influencing the way cycling would develop in the next fifteen years. Fignon notes Guimard's meticulous attention to detail: 'Even the slightest defect would be corrected. He knew how to ensure we all had the best equipment on the market: made-to-measure bikes, the newest gadgets.' By the time Fignon arrived at Renault in 1982, being in the team was, he said, 'the cycling equivalent of a degree at Oxford or Cambridge'. Coming up through Guimard's stable gave a rider such a strong identity that, Madiot says now, it was 'like having a tattoo'.

*

The Champs-Elysées has never seen anything quite like the Tour de France finish on the afternoon of 22 July 1979. It was unprecedented: the first- and second-placed riders overall – Bernard Hinault and Joop Zoetemelk – riding up and down the Champs together with the peleton split to pieces behind, then fighting out a sprint finish between them. 'A funny old day,' was the verdict of Paul Sherwen who finished fifth. Hinault won, making him the first Tour winner to win a road-race stage on the final day since 1935; his second overall victory at just twenty-four made him the youngest-ever double-winner.

Nowadays, the he final stage of the Tour has its traditions – apart from when it is a time trial as in 1968 or 1989 – and they are well known. The final classification from the previous afternoon is taken as set in stone. The riders promenade early on as they savour the imminent end of three weeks' racing. The race leader's team lead the field on to the Champs-Elysées circuit, and the peloton speeds up and down for the ultimate exhibition race, albeit one where the sprint finish is intensely contested.

The touch of madness Hinault and Zoetemelk showed that day was worthy of two amateurs, in the best sense of the word. Hinault had never been one to respect a script, and when the two riders contesting third place overall – Hennie Kuiper and Joaquim Agostinho – began attacking early on the stage, he wanted to join in the game. Zoetemelk, for his part, had told his teammates that he would attack Hinault on every one of the little hills that peppered the early part of the route. *'Le jeu de la competition,*' Hinault calls it – competing as pure play. 'Someone must have started sprinting for a sign and Hinault got pissed off, put the hammer down and rode through the Chevreuse valley like ten men,' recalled Sherwen. Sprinting for signs – didn't we all do that when we were kids on bikes?

'It was an incredible sight – two little guys on their bikes on this massive avenue,' Hinault told me. The escape began, he explained, because, 'Agostinho and Kuiper were attacking on every climb, turn and turn about. On the Cote de l'Homme Mort, I got out of the saddle and went for it; at the top you get to a roundabout where everyone slowed down – I really pushed it hard there, took the roundabout quicker than the peloton, got fifty metres' lead. I was enjoying myself. I got a minute, I thought it wasn't possible, that they were just letting me go. I heard that Joop had attacked and no one was chasing – so I waited at the top of the Pavé des Gardes.'

'I'd said to the team I'd attack on all the small climbs,' says Zoetemelk, who still laughs at the memory. 'I said, "I have nothing to lose, I'm only three minutes behind." So I would gain a few metres on every climb, and Hinault would then come back to me. On the last climb, he counter-attacked, and I don't know how long it took for me to catch him, I was riding, riding, but I couldn't let him go. When I got to him, the car with Guimard was already behind him, and Guimard said, "You've got such a big lead, you have to go on now." Bernard said, "No, no, no," but Guimard said, "No, on you go." My *directeur sportif*, Jean-Pierre

Danguillaume, came up and said the same. On the last lap, I said to Bernard, "You've won the Tour, perhaps in the finish you don't have to go flat out so I can win the stage." He looked at me like that' – here he does a passable imitation of a Badger glare – 'and it wasn't a photo finish.'

'Hinault had won the bunch sprint with a day to go so [this] added insult to injury,' said Sherwen. 'The bunch were all over the place. I was in the second group of thirty-five' – a decisive 2min 18sec behind – 'and the next group was seven minutes back.' It was a surreal sight, the promenade replaced by a one-day bike race, the script in tatters. Sam Abt recalled that an American television commentator watching the race on the Champs 'began shouting that Zoetemelk was trying to steal the Tour but Hinault wasn't letting him. He had absolutely no idea what was going on.' The American would have been new to the Tour, as this was the first year the race was televised in the US, but his confusion was understandable: this was unprecedented, and impossible to explain. It had no strategic logic. In that sense, it was akin to Eddy Merckx's legendary escape to Mourenx in the 1969 Tour de France, an *acte gratuite*, performed simply because Hinault could. 'No one had ever seen a *maillot jaune* do that before,' says Hinault now. 'What it showed was that nothing is written in advance in cycling.'

The Champs-Elysées escape was evidence of some-thing else: why Hinault worked so well with Guimard within Renault. It came down to this: his sense of himself and of the way he wanted to race was so strong that he had no inhibitions about bolting his own personal sense of how to race on to Guimard's system. Set against this, Guimard's great virtue was that in spite of the structure he built, as a *directeur sportif* he was flexible enough to accommodate the individual quirks of his leader, as long as he kept winning bike races, and as long as no serious rival to Hinault's status as No. 1 came along.

The 1979 Tour de France was the apogee of Hinault-Renault-Guimard's domination of the race, with the Renault leader winning seven stages, including the final two, and three of the last four. Not surprisingly, Hinault also took the points standings, while Renault added the team prize and the best young rider's white jersey with Bernaudeau. The breakaway on the Champs reflected the fact that Zoetemelk was the only rider within reach of the Frenchman when they reached Paris, with the third finisher, Agostinho almost twenty-seven minutes behind.[12]

It was a complete victory, with Hinault dominating every area over a field that was much bigger than in 1977 or '78 – 150 compared to 100 and 110. There was a decent showing from the Italians, who fielded three teams. It was as if all the opposition wanted to come and see what the new star was made of. In a nod to the riders' action at Valence d'Agen the previous year, there were no split stages,

---

[12] Zoetemelk is shown in the record books as finishing at 13min 07sec, but this includes a ten-minute penalty for a positive drugs test. The Dutchman's margin over Agostinho was so large that the penalty didn't affect his final placing overall.

but on the other hand, this was one of the last immensely long Tours: twenty-four stages and a prologue with a single rest day, on 14 July, from Wednesday 27 June to Sunday 22 July for a total distance of 3,950km, with back-to-back stage finishes up l'Alpe d'Huez and a gruesome leg across the cobbles of northern France nine days in.

It was also the high point of the duel between Hinault and Zoetemelk, the man who finished second to the Badger in three Tours: the Raymond Poulidor to Hinault's Jacques Anquetil. The Dutchman now lives in rural solitude to the east of Paris, in a wooded plot where his thirty fallow deer come and graze at the garden fence. He has a room over the garage filled with memorabilia from a career that began with a gold medal at the Mexico Olympics in 1968 and ended nineteen years later when he was still winning major one-day races at the age of forty. He is known, somewhat unfairly, as one of cycling's 'eternal seconds', a man who took six runner-up places in the Tour, three of them behind Hinault, but he was a prolific winner in his own right, with the 1980 Tour de France and a world title to his credit.

The duel between the pair had started in March at the Critérium International, which Zoetemelk – who had already taken Paris–Nice that spring – won after dominating the hill-climb stage. Hinault, typically, was not on form early on, but Guimard kept faith, as usual, and he was rewarded in April, when his leader took Flèche Wallonne in another result that surprised onlookers; the Italian Giuseppe Saronni – world champion three years later at

Goodwood – had escaped with the Swede Bernd Johansson and seemed set fair with a few kilometres to go. Hinault overhauled them just two kilometres from the finish, to their shock, and then bamboozled Saronni – by far the fastest on paper – by coming from the back in the sprint.

Zoetemelk was also hitting his peak, adding his first major Tour, the Vuelta, through late April and mid-May 1979, but in the Dauphiné that June, Hinault dominated, after losing the prologue to the Dutchman by a single second. He turned that round with four stage wins, including a time trial up the Bastille in Grenoble – site of the stage finish in 1977 after the legendary crash – and the toughest stage into Chambery where he and Holland's Henk Lubberding put two minutes into the peloton in a rainstorm; he added the final time trial in Annecy, extending his overall lead to 10min 27sec ahead of Lubberding. To complete the picture, Hinault took the points and mountains prizes, while Renault were crowned best team. Part of the Guimard philosophy was that the whole team should win; hence Hinault's willingness to help his Luxembourgeois teammate Lucien Didier take Renault's next race, Didier's home Tour in late June, and to assist the team's veteran, Roland Berland, in winning the French national title in Brittany.

The 1979 Tour was curiously structured, starting in south-west France with a prologue time trial at Fleurance, which in turn meant the race had to enter the Pyrenees almost immediately, before heading north and then east in a vast arc before hitting the Alps in the final week. Hinault

finished fourth in the prologue behind Gerrie Knetemann
– with Zoetemelk in exactly the same time – and fifth in
the first stage at Luchon. Here Bernaudeau took over the
yellow jersey, relinquishing it to his leader the next day in
the mountain time trial from Luchon to Superbagnères.
That went Hinault's way by 11sec from Joaquim Agostinho,
with Zoetemelk third at 53sec; wearing the yellow jersey,
the Breton added stage 3 into Pau. Then, the battle with
Zoetemelk began to build, as the Dutchman closed to just
12sec behind after Renault – aerodynamic bikes notwith-
standing – had an off day in stage 4's team time trial from
Captieux to Bordeaux, finishing fifth, but losing 41sec to
Zoetemelk's Mercier team. Two days later, the Tour crossed
Brittany to Saint-Brieuc, giving Hinault the chance to race
through Yffiniac in the yellow jersey; at the finish he came
second to the Belgian sprinter Jos Jacobs, and he made
sure to give a *maillot jaune* to M. Le Roux.

Renault's fine second place in another team time trial
extended Hinault's lead to 1min 18sec after stage 8, but
the picture of dominance was shattered on the cobbles
between Amiens to Roubaix the next day. In dry, dusty
conditions, Hinault punctured as the cobbles began 94km
into the stage, and had to commit to a 109km chase behind
an escape that included Zoetemelk, a raft of Classics
specialists – Didi Thurau, Ludo Delcroix, the stage winner,
an old rival in Andre Dierickx – and Michel Pollentier.
'The Ijsboerke team rode hard to produce a selection just
as the *pavé* began, and put three riders in the break,' says
Zoetemelk. 'I was lucky, I had my teammate Sven-Åke

Nilsson, we were going flat out just after the break formed when I punctured on the *pavé*. There was no team car with us, because we were less than a minute ahead; it was a front wheel, so he gave me his, and I got back to the break before the bunch caught me, but it wasn't easy.'

Behind, Hinault's teammates faded one by one, leaving him to chase alone for an eventual loss of 3min 45sec – not helped by another puncture late on – but in the eyes of one observer, Jacques Anquetil, he had at least salvaged his chance of winning the Tour. As Zoetemelk saw it, there were too many time-trial stages – a further three – still to come for him to have a chance of winning. What followed, however, was a race of attrition where Hinault took every chance to harass Zoetemelk and cut back the Dutchman's 2min 8sec lead. A 33km time-trial stage in Brussels gave him 36sec and the process continued over the Ballon d'Alsace – another 3sec – and southwards towards the Alps.

Hinault regained the yellow jersey in the 54km time trial from Evian to the mountaintop ski resort of Avoriaz but the battle was as good as won the previous day, when he took full advantage of a time bonus system so arcane that it could only have been dreamed up by the French bureaucratic mind.[13] 'There were four sprints with

---

[13] Stages 6, 12, 14, 20, 22 and 23 included a novel system for time bonuses. For each of the intermediate sprints in these stages, the first three cyclists received time bonuses of ten, six and three seconds. The bonus sprints also counted for a classification of their own; and the first three of this classification received extra time bonuses of twenty, ten and five seconds.

bonuses so I went for all of them – we started going for them five kilometres out, so there was no question of the sprinters getting involved. It was all with the goal of exhausting Joop because there was a tough time trial the next day. Did I risk tiring myself out? I don't think so.' It was the Merckx philosophy of total cycling: harass the adversary on every front. Hinault pulled back 40sec during the stage, and left Zoetemelk in no doubt as to the eventual outcome.

'After fourteen stages of constant harassment on every front available to the competitive cyclist, Bernard Hinault finally got to the meat of the matter, climbing Avoriaz at divine speed,' wrote Antoine Blondin. 'Only angels have wings, they say . . . Hinault had something of the archangel in him,' and with a pun that only Blondin could have made, he added, 'There was something of the Attila in Hinault, *dossard* [race number] *numero Hun*.' As at Saint Émilien the year before, he started conservatively and put his full strength into the second part of the course, up the mountain to Avoriaz; for Pierre Chany it was the moment when he 'entered the gallery of cycling monsters, rubbing shoulders with Coppi, Anquetil and Merckx'. After the time trial the third rider, Kuiper, was already 12min behind, and only Zoetemelk was in the picture, although few were betting on the Dutchman, now 1min 48sec behind.

Before Paris, there was a stage finish at Les Menuires, where Zoetemelk cracked for good, dropping another minute, then came the little matter of climbing l'Alpe d'Huez

twice in successive days. The second finish went to
Zoetemelk but it was a Pyrrhic victory, pegging Hinault
back by 47sec and creating just a soupçon of suspense
before the final time trial in Dijon, four days from the
finish in Paris. 'I hadn't won a stage, so I needed to win
one,' says Zoetemelk, 'but it wasn't going to make any
difference overall. By then, Hinault only had me to watch.
He could afford to let everyone else go.' At Dijon, Hinault
landed his fifth stage win, to increase his overall lead by
1min 9sec. That settled matters, but he wasn't done yet.
The penultimate day's bunch sprint to Nogent-sur-Marne
was slightly uphill, and Hinault was hungry enough to
win it from specialists such as Marc Demeyer, Guido Van
Calster, and Sean Kelly. Which left only the Champs-
Elysées, where Hinault was finally expected to take a back
seat. On paper at least.

Guimard was known as a strong-minded *directeur sportif*
but the 1979 Tour had proved that he was obliged to give
his leader a fairly loose rein. Once Hinault got the racing
urge, anything could happen and Guimard wouldn't always
be able to stop it. For a cycling fan, that was part of the
joy of the partnership. The Tour of Lombardy at the end
of that season typified the extent to which Hinault could
put his individual stamp on almost any event, whatever
Guimard's doubts.

The background to the race was a burgeoning rivalry
between Hinault and the leading Italians, primarily
Francesco Moser. Moser was – and remains – one of the

proudest cyclists in the game but physically he was only rarely a match for Hinault. Verbal sparring has always been part of the game for Italian cyclists and Hinault was always happy to respond, as the pair's exchange at the Grand Prix des Nations the previous season had shown.

At the end of 1978, Moser had managed to win the Super Prestige Pernod, with Hinault just a single point behind – thanks to his victory in the Tour of Lombardy where Hinault came third – but the rumour was that Moser had done so thanks in part to an alliance between the top Italians who had felt that their mutual interests would be better served by a victory for one of their own. In addition, Hinault was twice brought to the deck by the overenthusiastic Italian *tifosi*. So he was determined that there would be no repeat in 1979, particularly after he had destroyed Moser by 1min 45sec to win that year's Grand Prix des Nations. His closest rival, as it happened, was not Moser, but another Italian, the young prodigy Giuseppe Saronni, who had won the Giro and a host of other races in his twenty-second year. However, Saronni was far enough behind Hinault that he needed to win Lombardy in order to take the Super Prestige. On paper, he was as fast as Hinault in a sprint finish, leaving the Frenchman no option but to escape.

In his memoirs, Guimard related how Hinault and Moser set about each other early on, on the climb of l'Eco with 170km still to go. Cycling jargon calls it 'half-wheeling': you put your front wheel half a wheel-width ahead of your rival's, he responds by putting his half a wheel ahead of yours. The pace increases, and eventually one guy cracks. It's what amateurs do on Sunday club rides; it was what Hinault had done to his cousin René when they first went out training in 1971. 'They were in a world of their own, not even in the same race as the others, in a hand-to-hand fight to the death,' recalled Guimard. Hinault gained a metre, then another, as the rest of the field grovelled in their wake. At the top of the hill, to Guimard's surprise, the Frenchman was clear of the field – and he didn't sit up and wait, pressing on to gain a minute and a half on the field. 'I heard on the race radio, "Hinault alone in front." I said to myself, "What on earth is he up to now?"'

Moser and Saronni were a distant memory when Guimard drove up to his leader, wound down the window and said, 'OK, there are a hundred and fifty kilometres to go, now you've opened your lungs up a bit, are you going to throttle back?' Hinault insisted on continuing. A small group arrived from behind including his teammate Bernard Becaas and the promising young Italian Silvano Contini, together with his *compagno di squadra*, Tommy Prim of Denmark. 'Prim and Becaas did all the work as far as Como, then we turned left up the next climb and they went straight on to the finish,' recalled Hinault. From that group Hinault went on to win, with only Contini hanging on to him to the finish, and the next little group 3min 20sec behind. It was worthy of Merckx: Jean-Marie Leblanc wrote in *L'Équipe*, 'It was an incredible risk and it paid off.' Guimard was more succinct: 'a massacre'.

CHAPTER 7

CHEFS D'OEUVRE

*'One's prime is elusive...you must be on the alert to rec-
ognise your prime at whatever time of your life it may
occur. You must then live it to the full.'*

— Muriel Spark, *The Prime of Miss Jean Brodie*

20 April 1980. The peloton rode up out of Liège into the
Ardennes in a grim mood. The leaden skies and the cold
told them what was coming in the next eight hours as they
looped south through the hills to Bastogne and back: snow.
'It was cold and dry when we set off, nothing coming out
of the sky, but as we began climbing from the official *départ*,
the rain started coming down,' recalled Sean Kelly. 'I went
back to the team car for gloves, a long-sleeved jersey and
a rain jacket over it, and as I went back to the peloton the
snow began to fall.' Kelly spent the first twenty kilometres
of the race huddling at the very back of the long string of
cyclists as they sploshed through the bone-chilling puddles.
'I was always at the end of the line, and there were guys
coming back in the other direction all the time, riding back

to Liège, the ones who had been at the front of the bunch and had given up.'

The precise number of riders who abandoned early in that race is not known, and accounts vary: this is an epic that has lost nothing in the telling. What matters is that it was the bulk of the field, which is almost unknown in any race. 'Some of the guys had their families out to watch them, with their cars, and those guys were just stopping and getting in,' said Kelly. 'One of my teammates rode back to Liège after forty kilometres, straight to the hotel, but he couldn't get his clothes off because his fingers were so cold, so he just got in the bath with everything on. We were just riding in the tracks left by the race cars, because the snow was too thick [elsewhere] on the road.'

This was the Arctic environment in which Bernard Hinault won his second Liège–Bastogne–Liège. It rates, not unreasonably, among his finest victories. The resonances with insane feats of the past in extreme weather – Eddy Merckx most notably at Tre Cime di Lavaredo in 1968, Eugène Christophe in Milan–San Remo in 1910, Charly Gaul at Monte Bondone in 1956 – were obvious. There was no suspense once he had eluded what remained of the peloton, only twenty-one of whom even made it to the finish. It is a compelling image: the Badger splashing along the slushy channel in the snow cut by the car tyres, muffled up in woolly jerseys and thick racing hat, thick snow on the trees and verges. In some places there was barely a single spectator to cheer him on from the roadside, because anyone with any sense was sitting in front of a warm fire at home.

It was less a race than a fight for survival: the Belgians Ludo Peeters and Rudy Pevenage – later to become the German Tour de France winner Jan Ullrich's confidant – attacked not long after the race turned in Bastogne and headed back north across the Ardennes to Liège. When Hinault accelerated to pursue them both, with eighty-five kilometres remaining, there was no response from the bedraggled remnants of the field. The second man home, Hennie Kuiper, ended up 9min 27sec behind, while the last man, Jostein Wilmann of Norway, was a massive twenty-seven minutes adrift.

It took a certain amount of psychology on the part of Guimard and company to get Hinault to the point where his competitive instincts took over. He wasn't much happier than his fellows, close to crying as the ice crystals hit his eyeballs. He told Maurice Le Guilloux – the only other Renault rider to go any distance – that if the snow was still falling at the feed station at Vielsalm, on the way back north, he would stop. By some meteorological miracle – perhaps related to the fact that Vielsalm is on the southern side of the Ardennes – the snow had stopped temporarily before the survivors got to the feed. It was still cold, but these things are relative. Guimard had warmed up dry clothing for his leader, prepared two bottles of hot tea, and put him on a new bike, with an extra-low gear, to enable him to climb the hills with less risk of wheel spin on the slippery roads. A little later, he told

Hinault to take off his racing cape: to keep warm, the Renault leader began riding harder and realised the rest could not keep up.

After the race, Hinault was able to give a decent-length interview to Belgian television; the roads in Liège were dry, and the second man home, Kuiper, had even removed his arm warmers for the sprint. Hinault wasn't visibly distressed or shivering as he spoke to the cameras. Then he returned to a room in the Ramada hotel, just up from the finish line on the Boulevard de la Sauvenière. He got into a cold bath, because his body couldn't bear the pain of hot water. Exactly thirty-four years later, we sit on the terrace of a four-star hotel over a coffee and admire the view across the Meuse and the city shimmering in the sunshine. It could be summer. The story goes that Hinault's frost-nipped fingers still feel the effects of that day; I've always wondered whether it is true. 'I can still feel it in the second finger of both hands,' he says. 'They are still not right. When it's below four or five degrees and I have to work outside, I need to wear gloves.'

Among the memorable aphorisms produced by Hinault's mentor Robert Le Roux was this: 'Every race should be a personal masterpiece.' It doesn't mean blandly, 'Do your best.' What Le Roux appears to have meant was that the cyclist should attain a state of absorption and total concentration akin to that of an artist painting a great work, or a composer orchestrating a symphony. It is explained by a longer passage in *Coureur Cycliste, Ce Que Tu Dois*

Savoir, where Le Roux quotes the great Henri Pelissier's account of his state of mind as he approaches the finish of a race: 'I hear nothing, I feel nothing. I am in a world of my own. I have only one word written on a black plate in front of my eyes: WIN. You could say to me, "You will win, but you will die afterwards," I wouldn't stop, because I care about nothing. There is no question of fatigue, legs, muscles, pain. Only my head, the desire, the effort, the fantastic need to perform. I will do anything. I don't recognise anyone. I am speeding down a narrow corridor between two big walls.' If you wonder what makes a cyclist like Hinault or Merckx race as they do, part of the answer is in that quote. Part of their make-up is the ability to achieve such absolute focus day after day, year after year, in all environments.

For Hinault, having a point to prove always helped as well, and not everyone believed he would come good that spring. He made his usual slow start to the season after taking six weeks off at the end of 1979 then struggled in Paris–Nice – run off in appalling weather like most of the races at the start of the 1980 season – and failed to finish. That was enough to induce French television to run a programme announcing that he was over the hill. The twist was that the reporter who carried out the interview, Jean-Paul Ollivier, did not believe Hinault's best days were over – he was told by his boss that the storyline had to be Hinault's decline – and he set up the piece with the Badger's connivance, pre-warning him of the 'vicious' questions and getting him to prepare 'outraged' answers. The programme may have been hammed up, but Hinault would have noted the doubting voices. Of course, Ollivier was right. By the start of the Classics, Hinault was moving again: fifth in Amstel Gold, fourth in Paris–Roubaix, third in Flèche Wallonne.

The spell from spring 1979 to spring 1981 can be said to be Hinault's prime; 'Neige–Bastogne–Neige' in 1980 was the first of four 'masterpieces' produced by the Breton in the twelve months between late April 1980 and mid-April 1981. However, as is so often the case when a person is at their zenith, the first chinks appeared in the carapace as well, the first hints of weakness; Philippe Brunel, for one, traces the knee problems that haunted Hinault in later years back to the way he pushed his body through the snowy Ardennes. You look at the photographs, and as well as the big snowflakes on the gloves and hat, you notice something else: Hinault's knees have no protection against the elements.

During the spring of 1980, Hinault's Renault teammates gave Cyrille Guimard a gift: an Italian audio course on cassette tapes. By the time the team went to tackle the Giro d'Italia in May, Guimard was sufficiently proficient that when asked the Italian for 'badger' he could produce the word not only for Old Brock but also for shaving brush, to which the French word *blaireau* also refers.

The Italians knew what was coming their way. 'We'd seen Hinault in the Classics, but he wasn't a threat there like the Belgians were,' recalls Phil Edwards, the Bristolian who was Moser's chief lieutenant. 'In those days, the standard at the Tour was head and shoulders above the Giro. The Italians hadn't won the Tour in years, they were lucky to get a rider in the first six. There was a lot of exaggeration in Italy, everyone wanted an Italian to win, but we knew Hinault was the big favourite.' Guimard and Hinault knew the importance of conquering the Italian fans and media – the former through the latter. For all their love of cycling, the *tifosi* were quite capable of sabotaging a non-Italian who was attempting to win their biggest race. There was already history between Hinault and the two leading Italians, Francesco Moser and Giuseppe Saronni, but with the *tifosi* and the organ-ising newspaper *La Gazzetta dello Sport* on their side, winning the Giro would be easier. The Renault manager and his protégé hoped this would be the first step in conquering the triple that only Merckx had achieved: the Giro, the Tour de France, and the world championships, which that year would be held on a course in the French Alps made for a cyclist who uses a bludgeon rather than a rapier.

Guimard took his crash-course in Italian, and Hinault spent a long evening in the little village of Castellania just after he had finished fourth in the prologue time trial at Genova, where Moser pulled on the first pink jersey of the race. The trip to the former home of the *campio-nissimo* Fausto Coppi was an impromptu affair, organised by Ollivier. Hinault took a bunch of orange lilies bought for him outside the Renault hotel; he made sure to take a journalist from *La Gazzetta* with them. As Ollivier noted, 'The rider who intended to win the Giro–Tour double had come to pay his respects to the first man to achieve the feat'; Hinault also visited Coppi's brother Livio, who still lived in the village. The homage paid to their greatest cycling hero delighted the Italians.

Hinault took the pink jersey after the fifth stage, a time trial to Pisa – after which Moser announced that he and his rival Saronni should join forces against the Frenchman – but he and Guimard were both aware that their young Renault team would not manage to control the entire race. So Hinault relinquished the *maglia rosa* to Roberto Visentini. The tactics were questionable; while the young Italian was not a dangerman, Renault allowed two talented outsiders – Wladimiro Panizza and Giovanni Battaglin – to gain time along with him.

The French team then bided their time before making a first move on the fourteenth stage to Roccaraso. It was a masterly display of Guimard tactics; each day, the Renault sprinter Pierre-Raymond Villemiane had been contesting an intermediate sprint that carried points towards an overall classification with a Fiat Panda as first prize. So the peloton thought there was nothing untoward when the Renault team led their sprinter out for the line in the little town of Isernia, after which the road rose to the two climbs in the southern Abruzzo mountains that would decide the stage: Rionero Sannitico and Roccaraso. But two hundred metres after the line, as the peloton relaxed after the sprint, Hinault made his attack, catching the leading Italians unawares and winning the stage, with only the oldest rider in the race, Wladimiro Panizza, able to hang on. 'Sometimes those hilly stages in the south can be as damaging as the Dolomites,' recalls Edwards. 'I remember Hinault riding everyone off his wheel that day. It was pure strength.' Panizza relieved Visentini of the pink jersey, meaning Renault still did not have the task of controlling the race. The message was clear though. 'Everyone knew it was Hinault's race after that,' says Edwards. 'There was such a difference. It felt like racing with Merckx on those mega stages in the Tour. There was no point in having an alliance against him – you were only racing for second.'

Like its beginning, the race's end had resonances of Coppi. Three days from the finish in Milan, going into the toughest mountain stage of the race – westwards through the Dolomites from Cles to Sondrio – the early mountain stages had whittled the leaders down to a three-way battle; Panizza in the *maglia rosa*, Hinault 1min 5sec behind and a dangerman, Giovanni Battaglin, a few seconds further back. The race was clinched with an attack on the Stelvio Pass – the mountain indelibly associated for all Italian fans with Fausto Coppi – in another example of the Renault way: the French team put three riders ahead of the peloton, including Jean-René Bernaudeau, who was in the lead when Hinault attacked just before the toughest bit of the 24km ascent. After climbing through massive snow banks to the 2,757m summit, he caught Bernaudeau on the descent and the pair rode the 80km remaining to the finish together. There, Hinault let Bernaudeau win. The Italian press weren't entirely sure that this was good form – their stars, such as Moser and Coppi before him, tended not to indulge *domestiques* in this way – but Hinault explained that Bernaudeau had come to the race just after the death of his brother, had been close to abandoning due to his grief, and that the win would help him regain his feet a little. That effectively sealed the race: Panizza ended up 5min 43sec behind, Saronni seventh overall at almost 13min, while Moser had abandoned.

There is a memorable image in the French magazine *Miroir du Cyclisme*, which helps to explain the outcome of part two of Hinault and Guimard's plan for world domination in 1980. Hinault is on the start ramp of the prologue time trial in the Tour de France, in the German town of Frankfurt. His calf muscles are tensed – the photo is taken just as he makes his initial starting effort – and there seems to be barely a millimetre of fat on them. For the moment, that merely illustrated Hinault's near-perfect form after a Giro where he and Renault had never been pushed to the limit. His dominant performance in Frankfurt emphasised that: over the 7.6km, only Gerrie Knetemann finished within 17sec.

The Tour promised to be a tougher test than the Giro, for one reason: the perennial challenger, Joop Zoetemelk, had moved over the winter to the dominant team of the day, TI-Raleigh. That carried risks for Renault, because the British-backed squad were far more powerful than the Dutchman's previous squad, Miko-Mercier, and their speciality was winning team time trials in the Tour. There were two such stages in the 1980 race, and they would enable Hinault's biggest rival to offset his probable losses to the Frenchman in the solo time trials. So it proved on day two, when Raleigh put 44sec into Renault in the first *contre la montre par equipes*, cancelling out the time Zoetemelk – who started that Tour off form due to illness – had lost in the prologue.

Renault put Yvon Bertin in the yellow jersey the following day after a marathon 276km stage to Metz, where he and two others were given ten minutes' leeway; on the next day's even longer stage to Liège, Bertin gave way to one of his breakaway companions, Rudy Pevenage, who was to hold the jersey for the first half of the race. Hinault gained 1min 16sec on Zoetemelk in the time trial on the Francorchamps motor-racing circuit, then moved further ahead after another never-ending day in the saddle, from Liège to Lille, eight hours in pouring rain, with the final phase over the cobbles where Hinault had struggled the previous year.

It was 'a stage both sumptuous and sinister', Jean-Marie Leblanc wrote in *L'Équipe*. This was one more element in an insanely hard start to the Tour: a run of immensely long stages in appalling weather. 'Rain, rain every day, a week of rain and cold,' recalled Sean Kelly. The stage to Lille finished over an hour behind schedule due to a headwind and a go-slow pact among the riders, organised by Hinault. They finished in near-darkness.

This was the 'hell of the North' at its most infernal, with heavy rain creating vast puddles – most of the cobbled lanes are so old that they lie well below the level of the fields around them, making them natural conduits for any excess rainwater – so that it was impossible to read the surface. A puddle could hide a pothole up to a foot deep. You think of the wet, you think of the cold, you think of the impact on those incredibly lean legs, with so little fat on them: so little protection for those tendons against the wet and cold.

Hinault had organised a pact among the leading riders to neutralise as much of the stage as possible, but being Hinault, he had also decided to erase the memory of the previous year's defeat by dominating on the cobbles. 'Hinault was his usual self,' related Kelly. 'He was pissed off with the race organisers having so many cobbles, as he was many times. So it was, "I'll show these fuckers!"' When Jan Raas of Raleigh raised the pace – it is unlikely that the Dutchman intended to attack as his leader Zoetemelk was below par – it was inevitable Hinault would respond to what he saw as a challenge. Zoetemelk had started the Tour short of form after falling ill in the Tour of Switzerland a couple of weeks before the Tour started, so Hinault sensed the perfect chance to bury his biggest threat. He finished with only Hennie Kuiper on his heels, and the peloton including Zoetemelk over 2min back.

That pushed the Dutchman's deficit to 3min 43sec, well over the 3min 7sec he had dropped in the whole of the 1979 race. One week in, Hinault looked to have the

Tour sewn up. But the cobbles did for him, he reckoned years after. '[The *pavé*] stages were over two days, in dire weather and they were long. The first day everything was fine, the second I thought, "Damn, I've got a sore knee." The doctors explained that the shockwaves from the *pavé* had made little crystals form, as if tiny pebbles had appeared under the tendon. It got worse day by day from there.' Whether the pounding on the *pavé* was the cause of the tendinitis in his right knee will never be known; what is certain is that Hinault had a history of knee problems dating back to his amateur days as a track racer. The most recent issue had come earlier that year when he banged a knee after his gears slipped.

Fortuitously, the race organisers took out the worst of the cobbled sections in the first 20km the next day, but the day after there was no compromise: a 65km team time trial in the morning and a road-race stage in the afternoon. It was a day with those split stages Hinault hated so much. He lost some of his gains from the previous day in the team time trial, where Renault had no option but to wait for him due to his sore knee, and his teammates left him behind on the hills. 'His arrival in Beauvais was a new spectacle: bent over his machine, his face tortured with the pain, moaning, looking for a few kind words from anyone,' wrote Henri Quiqueré in *Miroir du Cyclisme*.

Soon it became obvious that it was more than a temporary upset. 'The point I realised was when we sprinted for a time bonus up a little hill somewhere in that first week,' said Zoetemelk. 'Normally Hinault wouldn't let me get anywhere, but on this one, I was well clear of him.' The whole race knew what was going on. 'He was really suffering on the stage to Nantes,' recalled Paul Sherwen. 'There were breaks going with riders like Sven-Åke Nilsson and Zoetemelk and he was really bawling his team out, yelling at them to get up and chase. "Where the hell are you all? Villemiane, I gave you the French championship and where are you now?"'

That image exemplified the six days of struggle which followed Lille, when 'the whole of France was walking with a stick', as Quiqueré put it. Hinault hoped that a rest day in his native Brittany might give him some respite before stage 10, the time trial from Damazan to Laplume. In normal circumstances Hinault would win here, and take the yellow jersey from Pevenage, whose ten-minute lead had been gradually whittled away. The *maillot jaune* was Hinault's, as expected, but the result was a surprise: Zoetemelk won, with Hinault 1min 39sec behind. 'It simply wasn't logical,' recalled the Dutchman. Hinault had been riding within himself to keep the knee intact for the mountains as best he could; he survived the next day, but 50km into the twelfth stage from Agen to Pau on 8 July, he understood that he would not make it through the Pyrenees.

It cannot be said that Hinault's departure was a dignified one, but it is hard to see how it could have been. After the Pau stage, he told the press that he would go on into the Pyrenees – 'I'm optimistic' – but in the lobby, he met his cousin René, who was working for Renault on the race. 'Come upstairs,' said Bernard. In the lift he told René, 'I'm not starting tomorrow.' 'He was about to meet a television crew who had a contract with the team, and he had no option but to make out he was still going on in the race, but he knew he was stopping.' At the dinner table, René noted, he told his teammates nothing. One teammate had been warned, however: Hubert Arbes, who lived forty kilometres away in Lourdes and who had abandoned the race earlier. At between 10.30 p.m. and 11 p.m. Hinault and Guimard met the race organisers Félix Lévitan and Jacques Goddet in the kitchen – in some accounts a back corridor – of the hotel Intercontinental, where they were dining with the Communist Party leader Georges Marchais. He broke the news to them, then he escaped through a back door and into a car to drive to Arbes' house, with René at the wheel.

'I could have continued from Pau, but if it was a matter of stopping on the first *col* and watching the peloton from behind, there was no chance of that,' he explained to the agency AFP the following morning. 'Without the *pavé* I don't think I would have had to abandon,' he told me. 'I'd won the prologue and two stages in six days, I had fantastic condition and I'd just won the Giro. After the Tour, I was aiming for the world championship. I was set fair for a full house.'

Hinault's departure did not go down well with the French press. In those days, breaking news rarely happened on the Tour. It rarely happened at the sacred hour when the press had finished tucking into a steak and red wine and were moving on to the cognac. Before Hinault, only eight riders had quit the Tour while wearing the yellow jersey. For France's biggest star, the defending winner and odds-on to win three in a row, to do so, and in the dead of night, was an immense event. Lévitan and Goddet, highly placed at *Le Parisien* and *L'Équipe* respectively, got the jump on their colleagues. Others were briefed by Guimard at 11.30 that night in the hotel lobby, then had to rewrite their stories as the presses rolled. Guimard looked ill at ease in the television interview he gave, and the slightly mocking tone he adopted can't have helped relations.

Several journalists, including Jean-Marie Leblanc of *L'Équipe*, were at a convivial evening organised by an informal grouping known as the 100 Kilos Club – formed of members of the Tour caravan who had a certain degree of embonpoint[14] – which included a meal 'which was not meant for thin people' and an accordionist called Mireille. The 100 Kilos Club had just got on to the singing phase, about midnight, when there was a knocking at the door: it was a motorcyclist, soaking wet, who announced that Hinault had left the race. 'Stop taking the piss, come and have a drink,' was the universal reaction; the motorcyclist persuaded the hacks, Mireille broke off mid-*chanson* and there was, according to Leblanc, a panicked rush for the nearest available telephones. Other journalists simply didn't know until the next morning.

---

[14] Leblanc makes it clear in his memoirs that he was actually only 93 kilos but had been invited as *un stagiaire*, 'an apprentice'.

The phone rang all night at the Arbes' house; as René and Bernard left to Saint-Brieuc the next day, Arlette Arbes presented them with a massive picnic basket, with food for the journey. The dimension of the affair meant they would be unable to eat anywhere public on the long drive home. 'We had to go incognito,' recalled René. 'I don't recall any drama, any visible suffering. You make the decision, then it's very pragmatic. He had made his mind up and had no option. The page was turned.'

Guimard's strategy was intended to limit the damage to his rider, but the fallout took years to settle. 'Hinault didn't feel he owed it to anyone to explain,' believes Sam Abt. 'I don't think he knew how to explain. There wasn't a word to anyone. Rather than face a barrage of questions he pulled out and there you were. He was a demigod – who was there to question him?' In the view of Philippe Bouvet, in the flight from Pau, 'He stirred up the long-term misunderstanding which came to characterise his relations with the press. He barely understood that people could be interested in him beyond the simple statement of a victory' [or by implication, a defeat]. At the time, Hinault's explanation was that he didn't have the courage to face a press conference. 'In the state of tension I was in, I wasn't sure I would be able to restrain myself. One question out of place and I was capable of being violent. There was enough bad stuff going on without having a load of people expressing their sympathy. I wanted to be alone.'

*

Asked about his identity as the Badger, Hinault has always been fond of saying that when it is in a tight corner, *le blaireau* retreats to its burrow then comes out fighting. The paradigm for this – and quite possibly the example in his mind – is the seven-week spell that followed the midnight flit. Hinault felt beset from all sides. When he and his family returned from Lourdes, the waiting journalists had tied a rope across the road outside their house, and parked a car in the way so that they had no option but to stop. He was not impressed. Immediately after dropping his wife and son at the house – they had been on the Tour in the days leading up to his departure – he set off for Lannion to see his doctor. The journalists followed in the cars; he took to a back lane and drove on the verge to raise so much dust that they would lose sight of him.

The doctors found nothing and prescribed a week's rest; if the pain returned after that, he would need surgery. The pain went. But the scars remained. There had been insinuations that the injury was due to the use of cortisone, a banned substance that helps the body overcome pain. In his first autobiography Hinault wrote that from crowds at criteriums came the shout 'cortisone user' (*cortisoné*). At the Tour of Germany a few weeks later, he confronted a journalist who had written 'we assume it's cortisone'; the journalist asked, 'How are you?' '*Comme un cortisoné!*' came the answer. 'I did not speak to the journalist again for a long while,' Hinault wrote.

The world championships on 30 August was more than a way of gaining revenge on the multitude of detractors, and the bad luck that had stalked him in the Tour, where Zoetemelk had ended up taking the only victory in his sixteen starts. The World's was a challenge that went back four years. Hinault had been circling the rainbow jersey with intent since 1976 when he was twenty-one and was selected for the France team in the professional road race for the first time. That year, Hinault had come in fresh from victory in the Tour du Limousin, but was – as a second-year pro – not designated as a leader in the French team, run by Jacques Anquetil and Colonel Richard Marillier. However, he did make it clear that he was approaching the race in his usual way, with no inhibitions about the bigger names, and that he would try to win. At a key moment late in the race when the eventual winner Freddy Maertens had escaped, Hinault asked the French team to chase; they were unable or unwilling to respond. He was furious; he still believes that had he been able to bridge to Maertens, the Belgian and his companion Francesco Moser would have paid him little attention, and he might have won.

After finishing sixth – just behind Eddy Merckx, who won the sprint for fifth place – he swore he would never race for France again. A year later at San Cristobal in Venezuela, however, he was designated the leader of the French team, but finished eighth behind Moser. In 1978 he started favourite after his Tour win, but was heavily marked by the Italians and the Dutch and ended up fifth, while the following year he had ridden twenty-three post-Tour criteriums by the time the World's came round; he still managed to figure in the main group, well behind the winner, Jan Raas.

It had been known for some years that the 1980 race at Sallanches would be one of the hardest world championships ever. The 13.4km triangular course lay at the centre of France's skiing heartland of Haute Savoie, with Mégève just to the south, Chamonix to the east. One side was the Domancy hill, with its views of Mont Blanc, 2.7km long, 10 per cent average gradient, rising as steep as 14 per cent in the final kilometre before the summit. There was a twisting descent and a brief flat portion before the next time up the climb. Domancy had to be tackled twenty times for a total of 4,400m of climbing – the equivalent of a high mountain stage in the Tour. The French team's *directeur sportif*, Jacques Anquetil, likened the race to climbing the Col du Tourmalet four times in one day.

Hinault had had the race in his mind for several years, and planning with Colonel Richard Marillier, the French national trainer, began in January. An August training camp was disrupted by Hinault's knee injury and his consequent need to race, to make up for missing half the Tour. He opted for the Tour of Limousin, but suffered from a stomach infection and pulled out. He left the race to ride the 90km from Tulle to Limoges with the team mechanic, a Breton named Jean-Pierre le Godec, who had raced at first-category level as an amateur. Hinault decided to turn the ride into a race against Le Godec; if he won, he would be fit for Sallanches. The day before the race, he was recommended to ride three hours with a couple of cols although the team complained this was too hard. One teammate, Bernard Bourreau returned to their hotel and made a sign with his hand as if he was using the accelerator on a motorbike.

On the day, Anquetil drove the team car, Marillier was in the stands, while Guimard watched the race on television; all three were linked by radio. On wet roads, the French team were ordered to make the race as hard as possible from the off, riders like the bespectacled, mournful faced Mariano Martinez, King of the Mountains in the 1978 Tour de France. 'He was monumental,' recalled Marillier. 'When Hinault understood that he couldn't go any further, he slipped back down the line on the hill to see how the rest were faring. "They are cooked," was his verdict.' Their leader made an experimental early escape with Johan de Muynck of Belgium; what followed was a war of attrition after that. By halfway only thirty riders remained in the lead group. Eighty kilometres from the finish, only Hinault, Michel Pollentier, Jørgen Marcussen, Gianbattista Baronchelli and the Scottish first-year professional Robert Millar were in contention.

Millar believes it was probably the most impressive single day's racing he experienced in his sixteen-year professional career, which included stints at the front in the Tour de France with Miguel Indurain, Pedro Delgado, Greg LeMond and Gianni Bugno as well as the Badger. 'It was the first time I saw Hinault in action, the first time I'd been there at the front when he was going for it,' recalls Millar. 'It was so hard that there were no attacks. You [would] go up steadily, without any accelerations, and the guys are struggling, and that's enough to make a selection. Every lap there were one or two dropping back. It was ten out of ten on the scale of hurting.

'I had never seen anything like that. I'd seen the top guys in the Classics come past on the hills, going much faster, but this was different,' continues Millar. 'You'd see the speed we were climbing, and Hinault was just cruising. As it went on it just seemed to get faster because we were getting more and more tired. Every time up the hill, the noise got louder and louder, it was a football match atmosphere. He seemed to feed off it and got more crazy. Five laps from the finish it was obvious no one was going to beat him. That was how he operated. It was just brutal. That was my introduction to the world of Bernard Hinault.'

The only rider who could hold Hinault towards the end was Baronchelli, but on the final lap, at the hardest part of the climb, Hinault noticed the Italian struggling with his gears – he clearly could not find the right one. He pressed harder on the pedals, opening a gap of two hundred metres by the top of the climb; it expanded to a minute in the eight kilometres to the finish, with the third rider, Juan Fernandez of Spain, at four minutes. Only fifteen of the 107 starters made it to the finish.

It had been eighteen years since a Frenchman had won the title; the last incumbent, ironically, was Hinault's former manager Jean Stablinski. 'In my eyes that day remains the Everest of his career,' wrote Bouvet on

Hinault's retirement in 1986, 'the day of complete fulfilment where everything was perfect, where there was no longer any rival at his level, no one to match his excesses.' Millar agrees: 'It was relentless. He just wore us down. He'd turn his head and he looked like he wanted to murder us. He just knocked the crap out of everyone.'

Hinault's aversion for the cobbled lanes of northern France is celebrated, as are his various diatribes against Paris–Roubaix and other races that used them. '*Je ne ferais jamais ta saloperie*' – 'I will never ride your disgusting race' – he once said to Albert Bouvet, the Breton great who had devised the current course at the end of the 1960s together with Jean Stablinski. In 1980, he won the sprint for fourth on the Roubaix velodrome, met the organiser Jacques Goddet on his way to the showers and said, 'You will never see me in this circus again. Call this a bike race? Don't make me laugh.' Now, he explains, 'I hated the *pavé*. It was the worry of having a bad crash, the fear of losing a whole season rather than fear in itself.'

Considering it was a race he openly disdained, Hinault was oddly and consistently strong in Paris–Roubaix, finishing the Classic every year from 1978 to 1982, with a lowest placing of thirteenth. One reason why this might be is suggested by *L'Équipe*'s Philippe Bouvet: 'They were made for each other. The *pavé* have character, so does Hinault. And he has power, brute strength coming from his lower back muscles, extreme endurance and love of a challenge.' In 1978, when Hinault described the Hell of the North as 'a really stupid race [*une course de cons*]', he added this key proviso: 'but I will make it mine. [*je vais me le faire*].' The personal challenge of doing something he hated added a new twist to the battle: Paris–Roubaix wasn't just a race between him and the other riders, but between him and one of cycling's great institutions. The key fact about Roubaix is that the cobbled lanes it uses are a throwback to cycling past. The precise point is that it is pointless, with no place in the modern world of cycling. The position Hinault had adopted left him in a cleft stick: if he didn't win it or at least come close, he would be accused of ducking the challenge.

The rainbow jersey he had won at Sallanches brought Hinault a new dimension; he described how the very next day, he rode a nocturne on the Norman–Breton border at Fougères, and particularly enjoyed the sensation of turning on the power in the string of riders while wearing the stripes. He didn't get to enjoy it for long in 1980, however, as his season ended prematurely with a crash in the motorbike-paced Critérium des As. That, however, didn't change his basic desire: to work harder over the winter than was his wont, and start the season at full throttle.

The rainbow jersey is sometimes said to be a curse; often in cycling history, its wearer has had a poor season after pulling it on the previous year. The greats of cycling tend to be exempt from this, suggesting that the 'curse' is likely to be as much down to a sudden excess of extra-curricular commitments leading to a disrupted winter as to the malign finger of fate. In 1981, with a winter's hard work behind him, Hinault was winning in February, with a stage in the Tour of the Mediterranean. At the end of March, he achieved something unprecedented: the clean sweep in the two-day Critérium International, taking all three stages.

In early April, he and Renault were compelled to ride the Amstel Gold Race, Holland's only Classic – they had wanted to compete on home roads in the Tour du Tarn, but professional cycling's governing body decided otherwise. Renault slouched unwillingly into Limburg with a scratch team of six riders, half of them 'ill or convalescent'. They took no more than basic kit with them, no track pump for their tyres, no drinking bottles, merely a couple of spare bikes and wheels; the race organisers had to lend them a team car. Amstel is a tough event, a constant succession of little hills and corners in the Limburg area of Holland; it was a foggy day, and Hinault and his teammates rode around 'like tourists' – although there was only grey mist to look at – until the final kilometre. Suddenly Hinault decided to race, 'just to amuse myself', he said later. He realised he had the legs to finish in the top ten, but knew he would have to lead out the sprint to make sure. As in other sprints, when he led out, no one came past him, although the four-times winner Jan Raas got his front wheel as far as Hinault's bottom bracket before giving up two hundred metres from the line.

Paris–Roubaix fell ten days later. That spring, it was Hinault's major objective, but it was far from the only thing on his mind: Martine was expecting their second child at Easter 1981. On race day, to make sure that he could remain abreast of any developments, the Renault leader arranged with the veteran radio journalist Jean-Paul Brouchon that Martine would be provided with a telephone number for a contact in Brouchon's office. If she went into labour, she would call the office, they would radio Brouchon, who would be at the head of the race on his motorbike, and would inform her husband. In the event, Alexandre arrived forty-eight hours later.

It was a dry Roubaix that year, but as challenging as might be expected. Hinault suffered two flat tyres and three crashes, one on a perfectly straight bit of tarmac. At one point he could be seen with his bike on his shoulder, cyclo-cross style, running through a field by the roadside – amusingly, most of the spectators blocking the verges didn't actually seem to notice him behind their backs. The usual plethora of punctures and pile-ups left only six in contention thirteen kilometres before the race reached the Roubaix velodrome. It was an elite group: Moser, who had won the previous three editions; Merckx's old adversary Roger De Vlaeminck, winner a record four times in the previous ten years; Marc De Meyer – winner in 1976 – and another rapid Belgian, Guido Van Calster, plus an opportunist Dutchman, Hennie Kuiper, who was to win Roubaix two years later.

On paper, in a straight sprint, all bar Kuiper were faster than the sixth man: Hinault.

However, the sprint at the end of Paris–Roubaix comes at the end of seven hours racing, including the cobbles, and the efforts needed to compensate for whatever tribulations have come along the way mean that sheer strength counts for more than top speed. Hinault could shine in such a sprint, and he read it right, positioning himself on the front of the string just before the bell rang for one lap to go. He was going to lead out the sprint. Most observers felt it was suicide, but had forgotten what happened at Amstel Gold ten days before. Hinault had looked at the flags in the velodrome, and noticed that the wind was going to be against them down the back straight, but on their backs for the finish. His tactic was to use his strength to gain a bike length's advantage coming into the home straight, hoping the wind would then impel him to the line.

His victory drew this tribute from De Vlaeminck: 'He was unbeatable. I was in my best form at the start and still fresh at the finish when we came into the velodrome. Hinault was leading out at 45kph, I looked around and thought, "This sprint is for me!" but he accelerated again and again without ever weakening. There was no way I could get past him. It sounds incredible but it's true. I've beaten Merckx plenty of times, but never Hinault. For me, he was the greatest ever. It's hard to say, because Eddy is a friend, but Hinault was even stronger than him.'

Afterwards, as Hinault was waiting for the anti-doping test, someone pointed out a small white mark on the tubular tyre of his front wheel. It was the inner tube poking through where the cover had worn away. He pinched it with his finger and thumb. Psssss, down it went. The making of a masterpiece can hang on the finest of margins.

CHAPTER 8

BADGER

The bulldog knows his match and waxes cold
The badger grins and never leaves his hold.
He drives the crowd and follows at their heels
And bites them through – the drunkard swears and reels.

– John Clare, 'The Badger'

I bought the little cuddly badger from a man in a van by the roadside on the Col des Saisies during the first mountain stage of the Tour de France in 1992. It was sold in aid of the Perce-Neige (snowdrop) handicap charity founded by the actor Lino Ventura but was one of those souvenirs that you acquire in a spirit of ironic disbelief, because of its total incongruousness. When I acquired it, I noticed that there wasn't exactly a rush among the roadside fans to part with their francs. 'Business isn't brisk for *blaireaux*,' I wrote at the time, but without dwelling on why. I now suspect the lack of interest was because the soft-furred, smiley-faced toy wearing a yellow T-shirt doesn't have any of the qualities the cycling fan of the time would associate with Bernard Hinault. The connection could not be more explicit: the badger bears a large label with a portrait of the cyclist. But it has no visible teeth; its winning smile makes Kenneth Grahame's Mr Badger from *The Wind in the Willows* look like a grumpy old curmudgeon. Its massive tail is more squirrel than badger. In its cuteness and fluffiness, it is the sort of badger you would give to a small child at bedtime.

The cuddly *blaireau* was a rare attempt to market one of the most distinctive nicknames in cycling. Bernard Hinault as *Le Blaireau* is one of the few occasions where identification of the nickname with the person it describes is instant and total. This is one of the last in a line of distinctive cycling nicknames, which were often anthropomorphic, and always seemed to capture the essence of their subject – the Leprechaun, the Eagle of Toledo, the Little Goat, the Angel of the Mountains, and of course, the Cannibal. Unlike Merckx with the Cannibal – which he seems never to have appreciated – Hinault bought into the Badger persona lock, stock and stripy nose.

Hinault's nickname has dual parentage. When Hinault's neighbours Maurice Le Guilloux and Bernard Talbourdet began training with the hot-headed young professional in the mid-1970s, they called him *blaireau*, probably in a vain attempt to put him in his place. There is a slightly derogatory undertone: given how he half-wheeled them on the road – once they had hauled him out of bed in the mornings – they probably needed some way to emphasise their superior age and experience. One day, Le

Guilloux used the term in front of the late Pierre Chany, one of the leading French cycling writers of the late twentieth century. Chany picked up on it, and the rest was history. The *L'Équipe* man knew that a good nickname is part of a great champion's register, in a tradition going back to Henri Desgrange, the founding father of cycle race organisation and journalism, which were synonymous in the Heroic Era.

Why did it capture the essence of Hinault so perfectly? There is a slight physical resemblance that has been noted by some, such as by the journalist François Thomazeau – 'Very little eyes, his nose, the shape of his face.' The nickname also reflects a key part of Hinault's identity: Hinault remains *un paysan*, in the literal sense of 'a man of the country'. When he told me that he could shoot, pluck and cook a pheasant, and choose the wine to go with it, that wasn't mere bravado. His teammate Jean-François Bernard recalled one occasion when they were setting off to go training from Hinault's home at Quessoy, when a pheasant walked down the drive. The pheasant was in the wrong place at the wrong time. Hinault returned to the house, Bernard said, without taking his cycling shoes off, and shot the pheasant, still in his training kit. Another time, Bernard recalled, they went out for a ride – this was just before Hinault won the 1984 Tour of Lombardy – and the Breton bumped into a farmer who wanted to show him his land. 'There he was on a tractor in the middle of these vast beetroot fields and there we were waiting by the road.'

There is a rural element to Hinault's adoption of *le blaireau* that in our urbanised times can be hard to appreciate. The way the badger is seen in the countryside is light years away from the idyllic vision created by Kenneth Grahame. This is not an animal which is loved by country-dwellers – it destroys crops and breaks into hen-coops and its vast burrows make a mess of hedges – but, in the days before bovine TB became an issue, it was respected, albeit grudgingly, for its immense strength and the tenacity that John Clare noted, and which badger-baiters were so ready to exploit. Hinault shows a countryman's lack of sentimentality towards the animal. When I visited him in 1993, he pointed out a wood behind his farmhouse and said, 'There are loads of them in there, thirty or forty. I don't have time to hunt them but I have colleagues who go and catch them.'

Most importantly, Hinault's persona as *Le Blaireau* reflected the way he raced, and the way he wanted to be perceived as racing. It's far from sentimental. 'A devil of an animal to deal with in a tight corner,' he told me with relish in 1993. Ten years later, he went into more detail for *L'Équipe*, 'A badger is a beautiful thing. When it's hunted it goes into its sett and waits. When it comes out again, it attacks. That's the reason for my nickname. When I'm annoyed I go home, you don't see me for a month. When I come out again, I win. You attack me; I get my claws out. I go home, get myself sorted out, then I win. I'm a badger. I'm not a nice animal.'

What can't be denied is that this was his way, as he told me in 1993. 'If you don't win, [people] say, "He's finished, tomorrow he won't be there any more." At times like that you turn in on yourself. You prepare quietly for your comeback, then when you are morally and physically ready, you attack for the win.' Those around him saw it: 'When he was needled, he would react. And usually, that meant pain,' wrote Laurent Fignon in his memoirs.

The maxim that a rider should attack the day after a defeat dated back at least to the legendary team manager Marcel Bidot, who ran the French team in the Tour from 1952 to 1961 and in 1967 and 1968; Guimard and Robert Le Roux had the same way of thinking. Hinault wasn't the first to adopt the philosophy, but it exemplified the way he raced, the way he saw racing as a constant challenge. The best example would be the stage win that so surprised Sean Kelly at Saint-Étienne in the 1978 Tour. This came the day after a major setback in the Puy de Dôme time trial and exemplified the fact that Hinault never, ever wanted to remain on the back foot.

It's impossible to tell which came first: Hinault's portrayal of himself as the vengeful badger waiting in his lair, or the events that it exemplifies in his career, most notably the comebacks after knee injuries in 1980 and 1983. But you have to look at it this way: Hinault didn't ask to be called *Le Blaireau* any more than he claimed leadership at Valence d'Agen. He was thrust into the front row at Valence; he was given the nickname. In both cases, he was bright enough to sense the moment and seize it.

That is borne out by both Guimard and the Swiss Paul Koechli, who coached Hinault at the end of his career.

They noted that their charge followed his Badger's nose most of the time, and the approach served him well. As Guimard put it, he had 'instinctive intelligence. He would put his foot over the abyss, then do a U-turn at the right moment. He didn't necessarily know why but instinct prevented him from doing the wrong thing. He "felt" things.' Early on, however, he sometimes went too far, and Guimard's view was that he became Hinault's 'safety net' – the one thing that stood between the cyclist and disaster.

Koechli identified in Hinault a thirst for knowledge and a high capacity to absorb it, prioritise it and put it into action. 'He wanted to know everything. He was very practical. He has what you might call practical intelligence. He has an innate ability to select rapidly what he judges to be important. He gets rid of the rest. What's always impressed me most is his speed of action, his ability to target something, his ability to close himself to the world. For example, at the Tour de France, where people constantly come at you wanting this or that, quite aggressively, he can completely distance himself from the stress of competing, simply by his thought processes. He does naturally and rapidly what others take years to learn through sophrology. He can let his feelings go slice by slice and he builds them up in the same way.'

For the *patron* of the peloton, a rider determined to have every advantage he could over the opposition, the Badger was a useful persona to project, dominant and aggressive, vengeful if injured morally or physically. It helped Hinault race the way he wanted, and to control the races in the way he wanted. As Hinault said, 'If you hit a badger in the face with a spade, it just chews it. It's the only animal that does that.' It tied in entirely with his vision of himself: 'My principal quality is that I fight, always.' Not all those who were close to Hinault agree about the extent to which the *Blaireau* persona was a bluff. 'Hinault the human being and Hinault the cyclist were the same person,' was Fignon's view.

Hinault's self-belief was, and remains, his key characteristic; in comparison to the more existentially challenged Merckx and Coppi, he wasn't – and isn't – a man who admits to having doubts. 'He didn't say much,' said Fignon of Hinault. 'He didn't show off in front of us. He just showed his internal power through the jut of his chin. Everything about him exuded confidence. His whole being expressed a single thought: "I know who I am."' Anquetil, who had a strong connection with Hinault due to their shared love of rural life, felt the same, and drew this comparison: 'I always had doubt in my mind, and that was perhaps what gave me my strength. Hinault, on the other hand, gets his strength from his total certainty.' Hinault's 'certainty' wasn't as total as it appeared. He admitted to moments of weakness; others observed them in him. But he was fundamentally different from other champions in that he didn't feed off uncertainty, or if he did, he wouldn't admit to it. Merckx and Coppi's greatest performances were inspired by a fear of failure, a perfectionistic need to go the extra mile – or fifty – to guarantee a victory. Hinault always seemed driven by forces that were far more visceral: a need to fight, be it for vengeance, because he felt threatened, or because he had to prove a point.

'Hinault's real driving force was his pride,' wrote Guimard. 'Often he reacted more like a boxer than a cyclist' – remember his early nickname, 'Cerdan'? – 'He was never stronger than when he was in a genuine fight: he would leave bodies on the floor. Managing him meant keeping to basic principles and leaving him some auton-omy. He had to believe that he was the master of events.' The manager recognised that Hinault's ego and machismo were the qualities that 'made him do seemingly impossible things, just to show that he was the strongest', and Guimard's great feat was that he managed to accommodate these character traits for several years. If something went wrong, Guimard said, 'He had to be put in a situation of conflict, so that he would recoup his losses. He felt obliged to demonstrate that he hadn't made a mistake. That meant in the end, he would be able to say, "You see, I was right."'

Guimard recalls occasions when he would deliberately annoy his protégé, knowing that the reaction would appear on the bike and the ones to suffer would be Hinault's fellow cyclists. One example he cited was the Grand Prix des Nations in 1976, when Hinault – who had a knee injury – and Raymond Poulidor were fighting for victory in the Prestige Pernod; Hinault was leading, and needed only to beat Poulidor to win the trophy. 'At the first time check Poulidor was third, the Badger was about tenth, so

I had a right go at him – "Jeepers, Poulidor, that far ahead of you, at his age"; just like that, he forgot his sore knee and was the fastest rider over the last twenty kilometres.'

This only worked with Hinault, Guimard said: 'If I had provoked Laurent Fignon, he'd have undone his toe straps and got off his bike. If I'd used the same words with Greg LeMond he'd probably have given me a straight right.' Hinault wasn't always patient and he wasn't always restrained, as we have seen. A teammate from his early days, Bernard Quilfen, recalled, 'It was at the start of his career, at the start of the season some time. I heard him bellow, "This year, I'm going to do them all in. I'm going to make them look small, I'm going to win everything, one thing after another: Classics, big Tours . . ." It was not appropriate, it was incongruous, but the most striking thing was that he believed in it as firmly as iron.'

Robert Millar considers that Hinault was essentially bipolar, but stresses that he needs to be placed within the context of a sport that appeals to extreme characters and forges them. 'Most bike riders at that level aren't normal human beings. What they are thinking and how they go about what they want to do are not what a normal person would call sane or nice. Of the people I've raced against at that level, Hinault was probably the most aggressive. You'd get the feeling that he hated you deep down and he would use that feeling to beat the crap out of you. His saving grace was that now and then he would switch off the aggression and turn into a normal human bike rider. I only saw that side of him when he was with teammates, or the stress was off. He'd be almost normal, you could talk with him about normal things – farming, cars and so on.'

If there was another Hinault maxim to go with 'racing for fun', it would be *ne pas se poser de questions*, as in, 'I was there to ride a race, not to ask questions.' But in Guimard's view, the doubts existed, and were behind his aggression at times. 'He needed a conflictual relationship to function,' argued Guimard. 'Unconsciously, he needed it to justify his aggression. He needed it to gain motiva-tion. Secondly, it allowed him to dispel his fears. The bigger his doubts, the more aggressive he became.' When you talk to Hinault now, it's clear that there is more to him than machismo and self-belief, although these qual-ities were so obviously thrust to centre stage when he raced. He is a subtler character than some of his utter-ances might imply, and than some of what is said of him might suggest. 'To understand Bernard, you have to look at his teeth: flat, worn down by anger,' said Jean-René Bernaudeau.

Guimard believed there was a downside to the brutal inner force that drove his protégé: 'The other side of the coin [was] a lack of discernment, a lack of diplomacy, and a certain arrogance that sometimes played against him.' According to Millar, Hinault showed a disdain for the normal courtesies that were the stuff of life in the peloton, largely because he did not need to observe them. 'When you work with people you try not to be disliked. You avoid rubbing people up the wrong way, but these were subtleties that never came across Hinault's mind, not until 1986 when he began letting go of the anger and hate that made him race the way he did. Most teams share out favours, but Hinault's teams never needed to because physically he was so dominant. He would give out favours, but only when you'd earned them. You had to do [him and his team] a favour first. His team rarely got people to ride for them, and you rarely saw them bailed out by another team. I would ride alongside him and he wouldn't say anything. It would be up to me to start a conversation. If it was Fignon, he'd start talking.'

Hinault was more than just an angry farmer. Millar's vision of him is of a supremely opportunistic athlete, along the lines of Eddy Merckx, who would choose bad weather, crashes, punctures, crosswinds in order to get the opposition on the wrong foot. 'There were no tactics to it. He'd just set about killing you. Say there were three mountains on a stage in the Tour, or a big day on a stage race, he'd set a pace that hurt on the first two, then he'd set about you properly on the third. It didn't have to be uphill. It could be anywhere, when you were getting a *bidon* from the car, on a descent, on a false flat, early in his career it might be a bunch sprint. I used to call it cruelty because he didn't need to do it. He seemed to take delight in choosing just when to do it because it would hurt us the most.' Millar also notes that Hinault had a unique ability to recognise his rivals' weaknesses – physical and mental – and store them up on a mental log for use in future, 'on another day when he thought it might work'.

The Scot admired Hinault's willingness to embrace any means available to make him more dominant, underlining that he was not merely a man who worked off brute force. 'Technically he was excellent. He took every new form of technology and tried it. Guimard was always trying to think about how to make his riders better, wondering whether having the bottom bracket two millimetres higher might make you corner quicker. Hinault would buy into that. He wouldn't say, "I'm not putting that silly aero helmet on"; he'd put on the helmet, go out and half kill himself then assess whether it had made him faster. He wasn't an old traditionalist who would say, "I'm winning the bike race, I don't need to go faster"; he'd ask, "Can I win by 0.5sec rather than 0.4sec?"'

The *L'Équipe* writer Philippe Brunel believes courage was Hinault's key quality: intellectual bravery as well as the obvious lack of physical fear. The flipside of Hinault's lack of diplomatic subtlety was that by and large, if he said he was going to do something, he stuck to his word. 'The most extraordinary thing in Hinault's career [was] the way that he kept every promise he made, in spite of seeming to be constantly picked up and thrown around by destiny.' Brunel points to Hinault's conduct in the Valence d'Agen strike – where he could have just faded back into the crowd when he was projected to the front row – and his eventual move away from Guimard as the obvious examples: '... he would take what he thought to its logical conclusion, and he would fight for what he felt was just'.

Brunel feels that Hinault didn't set out to get rich, and that celebrity 'weighed him down like a sack of bricks'. 'I don't think he imagined he would ever make so much money,' his teammate Alain Vigneron told the writer. 'Sometimes he would marvel at the fact that he was treated so lavishly for doing something that he liked to do. In his youth he had got used to doing without very much, and he kept the instincts of his milieu. As for glory, he really didn't care about it. You never felt he was flattered by anyone. He never seemed aware of being a star, so much so that he had to be reminded that that was what he was.' This explains, in Brunel's view, why Hinault never became a personality on the scale of national notoriety to compare with Yannick Noah or Alain Prost. 'Popularity was never a real part of the equation [for him].'

That might explain why Hinault's ways were not always to the liking of the French media. Many of them were based in Paris and had an instinctive distrust for anyone who hailed from *La France Profonde*, let alone one who dared to treat Parisians the same as he would anyone else. And Hinault clearly did not court popularity. 'Hinault has the most handsome face and the happiest smile, but elegance isn't his thing,' wrote Philippe Bordas. 'His pedal stroke is like a smith's hammer rebounding off an anvil. He has Jacques Anquetil's calculating nature and the worst of Merckx – his obsession with power, his lack of pity…He is not like Merckx, who was desperate for a *palmarès* that covered everything. He doesn't train very much. He doesn't cherish victory for its own sake but for what it signifies: submission. He's as happy as a tree-stump and his heart is tuned in to detect other people's weaknesses... Hinault is the first great [cycling] champion with a vindictive mentality.'

By 1982, there was debate over Hinault's character, with the *L'Équipe* journalist – and future editor-in-chief – Jérôme Bureau addressing an open letter to him, requesting that he closely examined the way he interacted with the public. It was a stinging indictment of the sport's leading champion. 'What use is class and talent if you only use them when you are on your bike, and then only in small doses?' asked Bureau. 'I have observed you refusing to sign autographs because there were dozens of them pressing you and you needed to be alone to get ready, to concentrate, like a champion. You were right. To leave, but not to grumble. I've seen you turn up at the anti-doping caravan and rattle the door so they hurry to open up for you. Threatening with a smile on your lips to piss up against the door. Was it funny? Pretty much, but you didn't have to keep on with the act and boil up a whole potion of anger within your head. And use that to send on his way a radio reporter who was only trying to do his job. As you were doing yours.

'When you climbed on to the podium to receive your yellow jersey, part of the crowd whistled, and part of the crowd were chanting your name. Like the little lad who was hanging on to a tree branch and almost breaking his neck with the pleasure of seeing you and applauding you. Be it only for that child, you do not have the right to whistle the crowd in your turn. To insult them. To say you would like to put on a jersey with tintacks on it because you are fed up of being tapped on the back... I wonder if you would rather have the back of one of the fourteen riders who didn't get through the stage? Or the fitter you could have become? You are Bernard Hinault. Day and night. And you are incredibly lucky to have that gift.'

Bureau probably wouldn't have approved of Hinault's reply to an autograph hunter who had turned up without a pen: 'You wouldn't go out on the pull and leave your cock at home, would you?' The story was told by Jean-François Bernard, who added, 'He wasn't super-easy around people, but that's more a matter of shyness. He was on the back foot.' Christian Prudhomme's first journalistic contact with him was in 1985 when he had to write a piece entitled 'Has Hinault changed?' He asked Hinault and received the answer, 'I'm fed up of answering this kind of question, go and ask the public what they think.'

'I was afraid of Hinault,' recalls Philippe Bouvet, who covered the Hinault Tours for the newspaper *L'Équipe*. On the other hand, Bouvet felt that he was easier to work with than Laurent Fignon, who would simply rip you to bits with a glare. Hinault may have been grumpy, but it was nothing personal. 'Hinault might curse at you, but you'd always end up with something interesting. Fignon was devastating – Hinault would tell you where to go, then call you back.' 'I never let anyone walk all over me, and when I had something to say, I said it,' was Hinault's view. 'There were some who got fed up with that.'

Macho he certainly was, but Hinault wasn't a machine, as the occasions on which he wanted to return to his wife and child indicate. Maurice Le Guilloux shared a room with him in many campaigns and remembers him as a character who never slept. 'Bernard always watched rubbish on the television – [in Belgium] films in Flemish subtitled in English. I'd tell him to turn the sound down because he didn't understand any of it. He'd answer, "OK, but it brightens things up."' Hinault would read magazines on hunting, *Lui*, *Reader's Digest*, and according to Le Guilloux, he made a point of washing his own kit, which was rare for a team leader. 'Traditionally, the *domestique* did the washing for the leader, but Bernard did his own, he was proud of doing it. He was the first rider in the peloton to bring along liquid soap – before that we all carried a sliver of a soap bar in the bag. He would wash his shorts with the yellow jersey still on his back, then hang them up on a cord. He would black his shoes as well, with the blackest wax he could find. He loved it.'

Unlike the obsessive Mercxk and paranoid Coppi, Hinault didn't particularly like training, or, to be accurate, he didn't like training if there was no immediate objective, and he didn't like getting out of bed on certain days. He wanted to compete, not train. There were apparently times when his regular training partner Le Guilloux would turn up on time at the Hinault house and find him still in his dressing gown. But they would then spend fifty kilometres 'at war' – because Hinault always wanted to have his front wheel one metre ahead of his partner's. Jean-François Bernard recalled covering twenty kilometres in ninety minutes, including a stop at a bakery to buy cakes. 'Training with him was always special. When he had his mind on it you would come back dead, so dead that you wouldn't even want to eat, but when he wasn't in the mood, you would just go out and waltz about without doing anything.'

This was a pattern that Laurent Fignon observed as well, at the start of both the two seasons he spent with Hinault. In his memoirs, *We Were Young and Carefree*, he wrote, 'In winter, he would train so little that at early training camps he looked like he had been on holiday for a year. He looked as if he had been inflated. If you didn't know the Badger you would wonder how long it would take for him to get back to what he had been. You would be making a huge mistake.

'The man who turned up at training camp was a distant relation of the champion who had snaffled every trophy going the previous season and had then hung his bike up for three months. As soon as we began to train as a group he adopted the facial expression he wore on his bad days. He sweated all over and swore at us. Sometimes he yelled that we were going too fast. When he saw that one or two of us looked a bit surprised, he would shout, "Go on you clever dicks. You'll see how good you are in a few months' time." He could do whatever he wanted.

Less than a month later he would win the first race he rode.'

There were other occasions when Hinault's carapace of certainty would crack. Fignon recalled Hinault on home soil in 1982 at the Tour de l'Armor, a four-day race held in Brittany, when he was 'so stressed out, so obsessed with winning that he was rarely his usual self. We wondered if he could sleep at night.' Hinault won the prologue at Châteaulin, and one night he turned up at the team hotel laden with cases of red wine, so that they could 'toast Brittany'. The team staff had disappeared, to Hinault's disgust, 'Bloody Guimard, he's never around when he's meant to be. In a state like this, Hinault was terrifying: he exuded primeval anger', wrote Fignon. They drank a good deal, broke into Marc Madiot's room to upend his bed, roamed up and down the corridors singing. 'It was a riot.' Hinault was told to quieten down by the hotel manager: '"This is my turf," the Badger replied, and told him where to go.'

The next day's turn of events was intriguing in what it shows of the sporting mindset, and of Cyrille Guimard's man-management. Most of the Renault team had hang-overs; the teams who were staying in the hotel were aware of this, and decided to pay them back. 'It was a rough old day,' recalled Fignon. 'We had to keep Hinault in the race, although he was as hung-over as we all were. Guimard hadn't said a word. We had to prove to him that the night's activities hadn't affected our willpower or our ability to control the race. Guess what: Bernard Hinault ended up winning that Tour de l'Armor.' Fignon's argument was that the episode pulled the team together and cemented relations between Hinault and his *domestiques*. 'Hinault never forgot anything. We had had a big evening and together we had helped him win. He had been put in a situation where he could judge our friendship and our willingness to hurt on his behalf. He was a man of honour and five days later he helped me win the Critérium International.'

Later in his career, Hinault could bluff, but he doesn't seem to have been the best actor on his bike. When he was suffering, according to Millar, 'Hinault would start moving about more on his bike, as if he was chewing something. His facial expression would change and his pedal stroke would be more laboured. I was used to the sight of his back going away from me, so you'd see his pedal stroke change. He would use a bigger gear than usual when he was feeling bad.' For Zoetemelk, it was about his teeth. 'It was easy to guess what Hinault was planning. You just had to watch him grit his teeth. From that moment on, it was going to hurt.'

Like the cuddly toy, the Badger caricature does the complex man that is Bernard Hinault a considerable disservice. Hinault comes across as honest, in the sense that he is a straightforward person, perhaps too straightforward for some tastes, and also – old-fashioned though this may sound – a man of his word. Nowadays, Hinault is gentler than might be expected, in many respects. He hasn't turned into a recluse, along the lines of Rik Van Looy, who barely talks to the media, but he takes some pains to keep his life in Brittany separate now; mostly, if you want to talk to him, you do so at a race where he is contracted to work for ASO. He's direct, which makes him impressively easy to deal with. He is impressively, sometimes remorselessly, professional. He rarely uses four words where two will do. Sometimes his briefness can seem borderline brusque, but it never strays over the boundary into rudeness. He seems at his happiest and most relaxed when discussing the countryside, and bike racing in the abstract, and watching him interacting with press and cycling fans, he seems to enjoy the contact. And he seems to enjoy it for what it offers in the present; he has never dwelt on the past when it comes to his racing. I noticed at our first long interview in 1993 that he seemed far less interested in discussing his own racing than in talking about the sport of the day. It might sound rose-tinted, but you have to conclude that he actually enjoys bike racing for what it is, with all that comes with it.

'Depending on when you see him, the *Blaireau* can seem like an extraordinary person or a dimwit,' said Alain Vigneron in an interview in November 2014 to mark Hinault's sixtieth birthday. 'He was extraordinary on his bike, in an unimaginable way, but not off it. Anquetil was a gentleman everywhere.[15] I would have liked Hinault to be like that, he wasn't, but I can accept it. It's not necessary; it's just something we expect. Hinault is an

---

[15] Except perhaps in his tumultuous, convoluted private life.

average Frenchman, but that's not a criticism. He's a Poulidor who won races. He's a Poulidor not an Anquetil. That might not seem like praise, but it is. Poulidor was a gutsy racer, not as calculating [on his bike] as when he was playing cards. Hinault's extraordinary, but I don't worship him. I want to say, you're sixty, drop the mask, you are the good bloke, the countryman, not a special personality, but that doesn't mean you are a bad guy.'

Millar won't profess to liking Hinault as a person but respected him as the ultimate example of what he tried to be. 'I admired him because the way he rode a bike is how you ride in your dreams, when there is nothing nature can throw at you that can stop you. Other aspects of him – the domination, the hatred, the need to hurt people – are almost insignificant alongside the sheer ability he had. He was so good at the bike-racing bit.'

CHAPTER 9

RUPTURE

'You either love Guimard or you hate him.'

– Bernard Hinault

On the afternoon of 8 July 1981, the British photographer John Pierce was trying to shoot the finish of stage 12 of the Tour de France at the Zolder motor-racing circuit in the far east of Belgium, when the Belgian police got in his way. The *politie* prevented him from poking his camera over the high wooden fence that cordoned off the finish area so Pierce went as far down the fence as he could, to a point about a hundred metres from the finish line, where the fence turned a corner. He stood in the angle, hoping to take a side-on shot of Sean Kelly, knowing that for British media, the Irishman was a sure-fire sell.

Pierce didn't catch Kelly. Instead, thanks to the obstructiveness of the *politie*, what he captured was one of the most celebrated cycling images of the 1980s: three riders simultaneously launching their final effort for the finish line side by side. Eddy Planckaert, the eventual stage winner and Guido Van Calster, who came fourth, are in the same jersey, the blue of Wickes-Splendor; Hinault – sixth across the line – is resplendent in yellow. The image is extraordinary. It gives the impression of perfect composition while in fact it arose from sheer fluke: not only does Pierce capture the moment when the three men are all out of the saddle at maximum effort, but Planckaert – to the left – and Hinault – to the right – are equidistant from Van Calster, while the eyes of the two nearest the camera – Hinault and Van Calster – are both fixed on the finish line. Their mouths are open, white teeth bared and necks humped due to the cold sponges they stuffed down their collars to stave off the thirty-seven-degree heat.

The picture is panned, the blurring background reinforcing the image of speed. The blinding sunlight hits the spokes of the front wheels identically, 'stopped' by the shutter. Look closely at the image, and you can spot the logo on the shorts of that year's top sprinter, Freddy Maertens, between Hinault's two braced arms. Few images better capture the essence of precision, power and nerve that is bunch sprinting. Incredibly, the image only emerged to become one of Pierce's calling cards when an industry contact finally spied it and bought it for a backdrop in a trade-show stand.

The image is one of the standouts from two Tours de France that are widely denigrated as 'boring'. 'Hinault's Tours from 1978 to 1982 followed one another in identical fashion, and are among the most boring and nerve-aching of the post-war years,' wrote Olivier Dazat in *Seigneurs et*

Forçats du Vélo, conveniently forgetting the strike of 1978, the dramatic fightback of 1979 and the succession of freak events in the first half of the 1980 race. 'The route was made to measure like a chartered accountant's three-piece suit by organisers who ardently wished for a win for the little lad from down home, upping the number of time-trial stages so that by the end of the first week the Tour would be over with the climbers in the depths of the standings.' Dazat made the accusation that the opposition Hinault faced was not of a high calibre. On the one hand there were survivors from the Merckx era such as Van Impe, Zoetemelk and Joaquim Agostinho. On the other, there were fine climbers such as Mariano Martinez, Robert Alban, Bernard Vallet – beaten by Hinault in the French national junior championship in 1972 – and Beat Breu; none of them was a good enough all-rounder to threaten the Badger.

In the 1981 and 1982 Tours it was obvious from day one that Hinault was going to win, making for a palpable lack of suspense. But Dazat's criticism also reflects a dislike among the French media for champions who win consistently and straightforwardly. This may partly derive from the fact that for forty years the most prominent journalist at *L'Équipe*, Jacques Goddet, was also the organiser of the Tour and his colleague Félix Lévitan was highly placed at *Le Parisien Libéré*. They both needed an exciting Tour de France to sell newspapers and draw in sponsors for the race. On various occasions, Jacques Anquetil, Eddy Merckx and Hinault all failed to provide the epic victories that were required by the circulation department of *L'Équipe*, and thus were denigrated as champions lacking in panache. It's not a phenomenon limited to the period when *L'Équipe* ran the Tour; more recently, Bradley Wiggins faced the accusation after dominating the 2012 race, and Miguel Indurain's five Tours of 1991–95 were lambasted as the most soporific ever.

The criticisms of Hinault resemble those levelled at Anquetil, who noted bitterly that during his rivalry with Poulidor, his younger opponent was consistently more popular. The distinctions between the two were exaggerated and sentimentalised to create the picture the media and fans wanted. If Anquetil was given less than his due, Poulidor was no 'eternal second'. In fact, he was capable of major victories such as Milan–San Remo or the Tour of Spain. He was also far removed from the image of the bumbling countryman that he and his manager Antonin Magne cultivated. He was a cunning character who would earn all the money he needed to pay for an early season training camp by beating his teammates at poker, which is hardly the behaviour of an ingénue. The truth is that, since the 1960s, the French media and public have tended to prefer a noble loser to a dominant winner.

Hinault had never been quite what the French media wanted. He was just too prickly, too unwilling to compromise. 'You tread on his toe and he reacts,' said his former teammate Alain Vigneron. 'When competing, given his incredible physical strength, it was a very effective formula. Elsewhere, obviously, he'd leave a bit of fallout along the way. But what astonishes me is that he has never lowered his guard over the years. He has never smoothed off the corners, as if his reputation hung on his initial way of functioning, as if he was locked into a personage that was bounded by orders and certainty.'

Hinault's 'boring' tag takes on a new dimension when you look at that photograph from Zolder. Getting involved this closely in a bunch sprint is not the act of a conservative rider, the more so when you consider that Hinault was actually leading out a teammate, the sprinter Yvon Bertin, who was wearing the green jersey of points leader at the time and would finish third on the stage. Hinault was not racing entirely in the way that Merckx did – as Zoetemelk told me, he wasn't as voracious as the Cannibal – but he and his teammates were going for everything on offer, and the notion that he was riding through the Tour counting every pedal revolution is wrong. Dominant as he was, that hid an underlying fragility. Severe strain was being placed on two elements that had underpinned his rise to the top – his physical robustness and his close relationship with Cyrille Guimard.

In one sense, Dazat's criticism of the 1981 and 1982 Tours is merited: there was none of the high drama, on and off the bike, that marked the 1978, 1979 and 1980 races. They were Tours typical of a mature rider at the height of his powers – think Anquetil, Merckx, Indurain or Lance Armstrong, Bradley Wiggins even – where the opposition flounders and the champion has a psychological stranglehold. Plus, Hinault had seen the risks he ran

Bernard Hinault, Brittany, 1977

Hinault's early mentor
Robert Le Roux (*top*) believed
his protégé should be proficient
on a velodrome, and Hinault's
track career took him as far
as the world championships
in Montreal in 1974 (*bottom*);
under his second coach Cyrille
Guimard (*centre*), his track
racing days came to an end.

Pull and push: after being dragged out of a ravine following a crash in the 1977 Dauphiné Libéré, Hinault came to a brief standstill on the climb to the finish at Grenoble's Bastille.

The young Badger chez lui: a 1977 photoshoot for *Paris Match*
at Hinault's Yffiniac home shows him with his wife Martine
and their son Mickael.

Centre stage: Hinault stands firm at the riders' strike at
Valence d'Agen, 1978, and is greeted warmly by the crowds after
winning the yellow jersey later in his first Tour de France.

Leading the frontrunners through the Pyrenees in the 1979 Tour (*above*), en route to victory from Joop Zoetemelk on the Champs-Élysées (*below*).

Man for all seasons: cyclo-cross was a handy discipline for even the best of road racers; competing in winter helped Hinault cope with freezing temperatures at spring Classics such as Liège–Bastogne–Liège in 1980.

Big gun: in 1981 Hinault and Guimard visited their new signing Greg LeMond at his Nevada home, and produced some novel images for what was then a parochial sport.

Guimard, (*left*), Hinault, LeMond, (*right*) and Fignon, (*below right*), would be variously friends, teammates and rivals as the 1980s progressed.

In tandem: getting in the saddle with controversial magnate
Bernard Tapie in 1984, (*above*), enabled Hinault to fill the
last remaining gap in his collection of yellow jerseys,
with a record-equalling fifth Tour the following year.

Eddy Planckaert, (*left*), Guido Van Calster, (*centre*), and 'the Badger' sprint for the finish at Zolder in 1981. The eventual stage winner, Freddy Maertens, can be glimpsed behind Planckaert; his left thigh is visible under Hinault's armpit.

In the wars: 16 months after an altercation with strikers on Paris–Nice, (left), resulted in a broken rib, Hinault crossed the finish in Saint-Étienne with his nose fractured and his fifth Tour win in question. A brace of black eyes and a bloodied face weren't going to stop him.

Celebration time: the stage victory hand-in-hand with LeMond
at l'Alpe d'Huez in the 1986 Tour, (*above*); (*below*), time for a quick pint
in Cragg Vale as the Tour prepares to visit Yorkshire in 2014.

physically if he gave too much of himself too often, as he had done in 1980. He came to the 1981 Tour as the world champion, with enormous momentum behind him: the clean sweep in Critérium International, the sprint in Amstel Gold, his dominant Paris–Roubaix, plus another crushing win in the Dauphiné, twelve minutes ahead of Agostinho, with the points and mountains prizes along the way and the nineteen-year-old prodigy Greg LeMond finishing third for Renault.

The 1981 Tour was won in the time-trial stages, where he took a clean sweep of all four to give him the overall title from his one-time team leader Lucien Van Impe; the margin was a Merckx-esque 14min 34sec, and Hinault was never shaken. It was also won, however, by taking the fight to the climbers early on the key mountain stages, leaving them little chance to spring a surprise. On the flat, hunting time bonuses at intermediate sprints kept up the pressure. There was one minor shock: the young Australian Phil Anderson took the yellow jersey at the early mountaintop finish at Pla d'Adet in the Pyrenees, but in the following day's time trial, Anderson was history. By a happy symmetry, the time trial finished in Pau; Hinault regained the lead where he had left the race in such secrecy twelve months earlier. He clinched the Tour at l'Alpe d'Huez, where he finished second to Peter Winnen, and the next day he added the road race stage which convention demanded, at Le Pleynet-Les Sept Laux in the Alps.

It was a classic of the genre – he sat tight on the first mountain, the Col du Luitel, and launched himself in pursuit of his former teammate Jean-René Bernaudeau, on the second, the Col des Mouilles. There was a point to prove here: Bernaudeau had left Guimard for Renault's big French rivals, Peugeot, and the 1981 race had been billed as a match between the master and his former servitor. It took a one-hour pursuit to close the two-minute gap to Bernaudeau and Juan Fernandez, which he did at the foot of the climb to the finish. At 4.5km to go, on a tight left-hand hairpin, Hinault had a good long look at his companions, and accelerated, leaving them behind. Bernaudeau was thirty-two seconds back at the finish and was no longer cited as a potential Tour winner.

A few weeks later at the world championship in Prague in 1981, Hinault came surprisingly close to defending his title on a course that manifestly didn't suit him – it was too flat – and even though he rode in a way his old master Robert Le Roux criticised as tactically naïve. His mistake was to allow a group of thirty-five riders to get away – he complained afterwards that he was too closely marked – although he then closed the two-and-a-half-minute gap on his own. Even after that he had kept enough strength to come a close third in the bunch sprint, half a wheel behind Freddy Maertens. The French had planned the finish well, appointing Gilbert Duclos-Lassalle to lead out from five hundred metres, setting up the kind of extended sprint in which Hinault would have his best chance. Unfortunately the Italians had the same tactic in mind, and Baronchelli did precisely the same job for Saronni; Baronchelli sat up too early, and Saronni was easily outsprinted by Maertens, who had briefly reversed his decline to dominate the sprints in the Tour before taking this, his second world title. After the World's, he went back to the obscurity he had left.

The year 1982 saw another piece of unfinished business completed – the Giro–Tour double which had proved elusive two years earlier. Until the final week, the Giro had looked as straightforward as a major Tour can be, a prologue team time trial win for Renault, a brief spell in the pink jersey after the first solo time trial at Assisi, where he beat Moser by thirty-nine seconds. Moser was permitted a five-stage spell in the *maglia rosa*, until the mountaintop finish at Campitello Matese, where Hinault seemed to be set fair after regaining the lead. The race came off the rails at the end of the second Alpine stage, where Guimard thought the key climb was relatively easy, and they would be able to give a little leeway to climbers such as Silvano Contini, Tommy Prim and Gianbattista Baronchelli because when the climb toughened, Hinault could make his move.

'At the team briefing, Guimard told us to ride flat out as far as ten kilometres to go, at the foot of the final climb,' recalled Marc Madiot. 'We would pull over, the *Blaireau* will come past and the race will be over. We got moving, flat out, pulled over but the *Blaireau* didn't come past, he blew up, Contini took the pink jersey. That evening, [Hinault] was shouting, "Bloody hell, tomorrow [Montecampione] we'll start again."' The Montecampione stage was short – three laps of a fifteen-kilometre circuit, followed by a fifteen-kilometre climb to the finish. 'We did the same thing [as the day before], with him yelling, "Faster, flat out,"' recalled Madiot. 'We parked up at the foot of the climb, and off he went. In five hundred metres he broke Contini, who realised he would never be a great champion. He got the pink jersey. The Giro was won.' It was, Hinault said thirty years later, one of the most violent attacks of his entire career.

The 1982 Tour was more straightforward, thanks partly to the organisers' decision to again include four time-trial stages, with two in four days midway through. Hinault won the prologue, ceded the yellow jersey to the Belgian Ludo Peeters and then to Anderson, regaining the lead nine days later in a time trial at Valence d'Agen – the location where he had led the strike in 1978. A second time trial at Martigues three days later enabled him to extend his lead on Anderson to over five minutes with a week of racing left; all that remained was a holding oper-ation in the Alps and victory in the final *contre la montre* at Saint-Priest. That looked all very much along the line previously traced by Anquetil, particularly when Hinault stated openly that he was saving his strength to try and win other Tours in future. However, winning on the Champs-Elysées, as Hinault did for the second time, was something Anquetil would not have attempted.

This time on the Champs, Hinault followed convention, to begin with at least: he refused to take any risks and was actually in the middle of the bunch at the *flamme rouge*, marking one kilometre to go. But then a teammate, Charly

Bérard, came alongside, and the red mist came down: 'I forgot the *maillot jaune* and everything else. I could only think of the finish.' It was Bérard who moved Hinault from the back to the front of the string, while Hinault's strength – as in the 1978 finish at Saint-Étienne – did the rest. An elbow in the ribs from Sean Kelly – the classic sign from a sprinter to make an interloper aware he is in hostile territory – did nothing to stop him, and Hinault maintained his record of winning at least one road-race stage in all his Tours. He is the only Tour winner to win the road stage up the Champs – and he has done so twice.

Renault's star was winning as much as ever, but the team around him was mutating. The arrival of Laurent Fignon and Pascal Jules in 1982 was partly responsible: the Parisian duo were the spearhead of a new generation, ironically enough inspired by none other than Hinault himself. They had precisely the attitude that he had shown in his early days, fearing nothing, respecting nobody unless they were stronger on the road. 'When Fignon, Jules and the others arrived, they wanted to wind me up,' Hinault told me. 'But it was good as well. I didn't feel like an old man among youngsters.' An older pro, Alain Vigneron recalled Fignon and Jules sitting at one end of the table at training camp in 1982 with Hinault at the other. 'It was two worlds – Hinault came out of deepest Brittany, they were two young Parisians. Fignon began shouting at Hinault, "You over there, I give you a year at most." What he meant was that he would take his place in twelve

months. It was to wind him up – Fignon admired Hinault
and deep down he knew that Hinault was the better rider.
But Bernard had no answer – there was a generation gap,
a gap in background, culture. As far as Bernard went, he
would sort it out on the bike.'

The best account of the change of generations comes
in Fignon's memoirs. 'In the evening at the dinner table,
the Badger liked to behave like our big brother. He would
recount his exploits, tell us of the things he liked to do
in the bunch when he was going well.' Hinault was quick
to put the irrepressible, irreverent Fignon and his close
friend Pascal Jules in their places. 'We would make a daft
comment or two, one day, Hinault said something, in his
usual way, calm yet firm, with the implication that if we
didn't agree we'd sort it out on the bike tomorrow. "Well
guys, just remind me how many races you've won?"'

Fignon adds, 'We stuck to the basic rules of the team.
But only the basics. You should have seen the faces of
older riders like Hubert Arbes and Maurice Le Guilloux
when we teased Hinault at the dinner table. They put their
faces down in their soup bowls. The shame they felt on
our behalf.' Fignon and Jules were the standard bearers for
a new generation, with less respect, less sense of hierarchy,
less willingness to wipe out their personality in order to be
a good *domestique*. It could be seen as the more individu-
alistic 1980s taking over from the more structured 1970s.

Guimard felt the same, noting that, 'The generations
had less and less in common. On the one side there was
Hinault's generation with a basic structure inherited from

the 1970s, and on the other the generation of Fignon, Jules, Madiot and the others who devoured everything the early eighties had to offer, not just on the sporting side but culturally, socially and emotionally. The two groups didn't watch the same television programmes, didn't read the same magazines and still less the same books. They didn't listen to the same music and mostly didn't look at the same girls. They didn't see the world in the same way and didn't talk the same language. On the bike they worked together, off the bike they were separate – it was a gradual process, slow, insidious and progressive but inexorable.'

One day, Hinault said to Guimard, 'I don't feel as if I know my own team any more.' Fignon too could sense his leader's unease, although having finished fifteenth in the Giro at his first attempt at only twenty-one, he knew his time would not be long in coming. He felt it more strongly after an episode in 1983 when he said to Hinault – who had been off the pace at an early season race in Italy – 'All you have to do is train, mate, it'll make life a lot easier.' A young teammate of Merckx, Rik Van Looy or Anquetil would never have dared make a comment of this kind to his leader. It marked a turning point, so Fignon felt, a moment that symbolised the tension that would split the team apart: 'Hinault was no longer the untouchable godlike figure within the team.'

Hinault had always seemed untouchable physically as well, but that changed in 1983. That year's Vuelta a

España is described on the race's website as 'one of the most spectacular editions in history'. It was a legendary face-off with Hinault's Renault – where he had the support of Fignon and LeMond – pitted against the world champion Giuseppe Saronni, and a golden generation of Spaniards. Together, the likes of Marino Lejarreta, Julián Gorospe, Pedro Delgado, Álvaro Pino, Eduardo Chozas, Alberto Fernandez, Vicente Belda formed what is now referred to as 'the Spanish armada' – an unofficial coalition of senior home professionals who were determined that victory should go to one of their own. It was this group who saw off Robert Millar's challenge on those roads a couple of years later.

Hinault had started the season slowly, as usual, not helped by a trip to the US to help promote the Tour of America, and a return by Concorde for Paris–Roubaix. Even so, he arrived in Spain fresh from a win in Flèche Wallonne six days earlier, taken in foul weather from his compatriot René Bittinger, and a crushing victory in the Grand Prix Pino Cerami, where he escaped forty kilometres from the finish to win by five minutes. The Vuelta didn't go to plan, however. Four days in, Renault got their tactics wrong when Fignon made a late attack and was joined by Lejarreta, a pencil-thin, lugubrious-looking character known as 'the Reed of Berriz'. The 'Reed' was actually the defending Vuelta champion, having been awarded the win after Angel Arroyo had tested positive the previous year.

The move meant Lejarreta gained valuable time on a disgruntled Hinault on the day before the first major

mountain stage. However, the Frenchman took the race
lead the next day on a tough Pyrenean finish at Castellar
de Nuch; on the stage after that, amid heavy snowfalls,
Lejarreta, Gorospe, Delgado and Alberto Fernandez
escaped on the descent from the Puerto de Bonaigua,
with Lejarreta taking the lead as ten Spaniards filled the
first ten places on the stage. Hinault's deficit was only
twenty-two seconds, so the script suggested he would
take the leader's jersey back in the stage 8 uphill time
trial at Panticosa, and his cause was helped a little when
Saronni and the Belgian teams – Aernoudt and Boule
d'Or – staged a protest about the condition of the roads
as the snow fell again, and seventy-three kilometres were
cut off the route of the third Pyrenean stage.

Panticosa was where Hinault's lack of form became
apparent. This was the sort of stage he had dominated in
the Tour de France, but in the snowfield at the top of
the climb he managed only ninth, 2min 13sec behind
Lejarreta. Knowing that the Spaniard's team, Alfa Lum,
were relatively weak, he joined forces with his fellow
'foreigners' Hennie Kuiper and Saronni in an attack in a
crosswind en route to Soria two days later. The race lead
switched to young Julián Gorospe, whose team manager
Jose-Miguel Echavarri had been warned that something
was about to happen; Lejarreta missed the split in the
bunch and slipped to fourth. As he had done with
Zoetemelk in the 1979 Tour, Hinault kept the pressure
on constantly, and the very next day Gorospe was out of
the lead, with Alberto Fernandez taking over.

Gorospe now feels that he and his fellow Spaniards got the race wrong. 'Hinault was Hinault, he'd won three Tours, the Giro and a Vuelta, so that was intimidating at first. But we quickly realised that he wasn't in good shape, and there was one stage when he was really up against it, when he could have lost the race or even abandoned. The thing was [either] the director [of the Reynolds team] didn't want to eliminate Hinault completely, or as a result of the way the race was panning out, we didn't wipe him out. And at the end, he got stronger and stronger and then he finished us off instead.'

Asked if he feels they could have turned things around and perhaps won the Vuelta if they had raced to eliminate Hinault early on, Gorospe says, 'For sure. Had we played things differently in a stage to León going over the Pajares climb [stage 14], he wouldn't have won it. We had a teammate in a break ahead; Hinault was dropped behind, and he was in real trouble, more than five minutes down. The director didn't let us work, because we knew that could screw up the teammate's chances, and Hinault caught our group with ten kilometres to go. We had him totally sunk, he could have been forced to abandon the Vuelta there. Then again, nobody knew that he was going to get so good.'

Fignon could sense that his leader was not his usual self. 'The overall win seemed to be slipping away but our Hinault was clinging on through the pain, scraping down his last bits of strength down to the very bone. He seemed oblivious to the [sore knee] that was affecting him a little more every day, and to any doubts. He was such a proud devil.' To add to the pressure, the home crowd took against the 'foreigners' – they threw stones, spat at them, leading to a threat from the non-Spanish stars to quit the race. The atmosphere settled only when the president of the UCI, the Spaniard Luis Puig, went on television and made a public appeal for calm.

There was one more time trial, a relatively brief twenty-two kilometres at Valladolid, four days from the finish; Hinault won as expected but Gorospe took the lead, by a mere ten seconds. The entire Renault team were given the job of setting up Hinault's attack on the one mountain stage remaining, stage 17 from Salamanca to Avila, over four mountain passes in the Sierra de Gredos east of Madrid. Hinault and his teammate Pascal Poisson caused the initial damage on the climb of Pena Negra – thirteen kilometres culminating at 1,925m high – early in the stage, but Fignon had been told to go flat out on the climb of Serranillos, twenty-two kilometres long, the penultimate ascent. 'I hit the climb as if there was no tomorrow, on the big ring for five or six kilometres, with Hinault on my wheel.' Hinault recalled later that he 'believed he was going to blow up', but they burned off the big threat Gorospe first, with Lejarreta hanging on for dear life.

'I was a very young rider, twenty-three years old and this was just the second Vuelta I rode,' explained Gorospe. 'That stage was one of the hardest and they [Renault] planned that stage really well; Hinault was strong, but I think Fignon was going equally well. Fignon went all out in the first part, and I tried as hard as I could to hold on to him. But then Hinault took over, and the only rider who could hold his back wheel on the Serranillos [climb] was Lejarreta.

'I wanted to hold on, wanted to hold on, and I managed to do that for the first few kilometres, but it was simply that I wasn't strong enough. That completely did my head in, and it took me quite a while to come round to the idea that I had lost the race and I couldn't do anything against Hinault, given who he was. Then I tried going at my own pace, and I cracked again, and I just crawled home about twenty minutes down. It was really hot, and that didn't help me either.'

Hinault and Lejarreta bridged to Vicente Belda and two other riders who had escaped earlier; by the time the trees cleared near the summit, they were two minutes clear of Gorospe, who had just one teammate to assist him. What followed was an epic eighty-kilometre escape in which only Lejarreta and Belda were able to cling on to Hinault. 'Whenever the Spanish TV cameras returned to the trio, the images were always the same: Hinault driving at top speed, his two fellow breakaways a few metres behind, visibly struggling,' says one version of events. His victory on the velodrome at Avila was inevitable, the time gaps massive: three minutes on the next group led in by Fignon, Gorospe at over twenty minutes. Two days later, Hinault took his second Vuelta win with 1min 12sec in hand on Lejarreta and 3min 58sec on Fernandez.

Of Hinault's nine Grand Tour successes, this was probably the hardest fought. Ironically, the main beneficiaries were his defeated opponents. For the 'armada' this defeat was actually the start of a golden period in Spanish cycling, which coincided with Spain's emergence from the Franco years; that 1983 was the first Vuelta to enjoy live television coverage marks it out as an obvious turning point. The years of plenty would culminate in Pedro Delgado and Miguel Indurain's Tour de France successes and the brief emergence of Spain as cycling's economic powerhouse in the 1990s. For Hinault himself it was a Pyrrhic victory, one that came at a massive cost.

Whatever errors he made on his bike, until then, Hinault had always had the physical power to compensate for them. Guimard is biased, but is still well placed to claim that Hinault was the strongest cyclist ever, ahead of Merckx and Coppi and Anquetil. Sean Yates, a student of pedalling muscle power, concurs. 'From a brute strength point of view he was probably the best there was. A flipping beast. There is a picture of him in *L'Équipe* from 1986, when he won the prologue in the Tour d'Armorique; he's pushing so hard he has lifted his front wheel off the ground on the hill to the finish line. They talk now about marginal gains, about the need for riders to duck and dive to save a few watts, but Hinault just used to sit on the front all day in 53x13. He was a hard-core bike rider and he's a hard-core character.'

With the exception of the 1980 Tour de France, Hinault had always seemed physically unstoppable. The flight from Pau seemed cataclysmic at the time, but in the context of his rise and his dominance, it was a mere blip, given the speed with which he returned to win the world title. That robustness had gone, however, and the Vuelta left him with a knee injury. Gorospe doesn't recall seeing any visible sign of Hinault's knee issue and he felt Hinault was bluffing. 'He was constantly banging on about his knee problems, about poor form and physical problems. You couldn't actually see anything was wrong with his knee. It was purely internal. In any case, in the end it didn't matter.'

In his memoirs, Fignon states that his leader was carrying the injury before the race's finale; Hinault himself put the issue down to two changes in his saddle height made without his knowledge during the Avila stage. He recalled feeling his saddle was initially too low; he switched to his spare bike, which felt perfect, then changed back to his original machine, where the saddle had been adjusted and was now too high.

'It had been lowered by half a centimetre,' he told Pascal Sergeant, hinting it might have been sabotage. 'I felt a problem in the tendon, as if there were grains of sand in there [at] every turn of the pedals. The sheath of one of the tendons burst and bled internally – I had a huge blood mark behind my knee, and that intrigued everyone.' In *Le Peloton des Souvenirs*, Hinault explained that the issue was in the right knee, on the interior of the joint. The tendon became as thick as his finger and nodules formed. He fought the pain en route to the DYC whisky distillery near Segovia – a finish that became something of a Vuelta tradition. Sickeningly, he recalled, 'Once the [tendon] sheath had split, it was less painful.' On the final stage into Madrid, on the Col de Navacerrada, he had no option but to attack, to give the impression he was not vulnerable, although after the finish he had trouble walking. In spite of all this, it's easy to imagine why he hung on, given the stress and opprobrium that had accompanied his departure from the Tour three years earlier. He wasn't going to quit a major Tour while wearing a leader's jersey for a second time.

This has to be seen in context: it was the last in a series of knee issues, most of them relatively minor, which affected Hinault throughout his career. In his first autobiography he wrote that 'riding Madisons on the track I was short of a bit of skill, so what I lacked in finesse, I made up for with force. The upshot was that I had regular bouts of inflammation in the knees. That was why I didn't like to do Six Day races; at the point where I had to push my teammate I should have just been letting my legs turn with the pedals. Instead, to put more force into the change, I was pushing more on the pedals; I was completely askew at that moment and my knees were taking all the strain.'

He also recalled falling in the time-trial stage of the Étoile des Espoirs at the end of 1975 and dislocating his kneecap so severely that he was unable to climb the stairs.

'A *soigneur* put the knee back; I felt a violent pain. It was the very morning of the race, Gerard Porte, the Tour de France doctor, gave me an anaesthetic injection…the first injection I'd ever had.' At the start of 1980 he injured his right knee when his gears slipped and it smashed into his gear lever. He had also complained of knee pain early in 1983 as well.

Three days after the Vuelta finished, on 12 May, Hinault was down to ride the criterium at Pogny in north-eastern France, but he pulled out during the race and let it be known that he had tendinitis – it was the first official acknowledgement that there was a problem. Initially, he attempted to cure the knee injury with rest, as he had done in 1980; he competed next in the Tour of Luxembourg on 8 June, but again abandoned after a day and a half due to the pain. Ten days later, on 18 June, came the announcement that he would not start the Tour. A wisdom tooth operation did not help matters. 'It was over,' was Fignon's view, but no one knew quite what was over – Hinault's season? His career? 'For weeks there was a ridiculous game of cat and mouse with the journalists,' the same as there had been in 1980 at the Tour de France. 'Guimard put his head in the sand; Hinault played the fool. Neither was speaking to the other.'

During the Tour, while Fignon rode to an unexpected win, his nominal leader regained form and fitness with a training camp in the Alps, before making a third abortive comeback at the Callac criterium on 26 July, two days after the Tour finished, to test the state of the joint. After fifty kilometres, the pain returned whenever he rode out of the saddle; he abandoned and opted immediately for an operation, carried out on 2 August at the Saint Thérèse polyclinic in Lannion under general anaesthetic. The surgery was a synovectomy – opening part of the synovial membrane, which effectively seals the side of the knee retaining the synovial fluid within the knee joint, to remove the nodules which were preventing the tendon from moving in its sheath. With a Frankensteinian scar twenty-one centimetres long on the inside of the knee, he was back on his bike seventeen days later, for a ride of fifteen kilometres, but his season was over.

His days at Renault were also numbered. After the 1983 Tour, Hinault turned up at the team's after-party to celebrate Fignon's unexpected victory; Fignon admitted he was a little nervous, but was soon reassured. 'His body language was warm. He came over to congratulate me as if he was my elder brother.' He also noticed that Hinault seemed unhappy, ill at ease, as if he was no longer part of the team. 'The Badger looked as if his suit was too big for him. He seemed distracted, his mind elsewhere, as if he was barely involved. He was following Guimard's every move, as if he was wary of him and wanted to keep out of his reach . . . There was no prospect of what everyone feared, which was a fight for leadership. Everything about him led me to believe that the impending divorce between him and Guimard was set in stone. When Guimard was in the room . . . he reverted to being a tight-lipped, suspicious Breton. The pair of them could clearly no longer abide each other.'

The issues with Guimard dated back a couple of years. There were reports of arguments at training camps, one tale that Guimard and Hinault had a major dispute at the Vuelta when the manager spotted his leader drinking wine at dinner. Hinault's version is that the relationship began to deteriorate after 1980, when he showed the first signs of fragility with his knee injury. 'Cyrille wanted to do everything his way; the rider had only to pedal and keep his mouth shut,' he said.

Hinault was looking for more involvement in the team's workings, especially recruitment, and a say in what the various sponsors supplied; there was a disagreement over the generation issue with Hinault wanting to hang on to the team's older riders, Guimard keen to renew the squad constantly with enthusiastic youngsters. Guimard wouldn't have it, prefiguring the disagreement that would part him from Fignon a few years down the line. With the scale of the team's affairs growing, Guimard too had changed, and had moved gradually from being another rider who happened to be in the team car to being the head of a medium-sized enterprise. 'Guimard had always bossed him about, but Hinault always bounced back,' wrote Fignon. 'He gained strength when Guimard provoked him. His pride made him react and someone else would bear the brunt. But times were changing: perhaps Hinault was getting fed up with Guimard's ways, and was pondering a change of scene; Guimard might well have decided Hinault wasn't going to regain the hunger he had when he was twenty and it was time to think of the future.'

Another issue was the way that René Hinault had been removed from the team in 1979; there was also a disagreement when Hinault worked with the president of Gitane on some contracts and the *directeur sportif* disapproved and tried to intervene. There were spats over what now seem like trivia – a falling out when Hinault bought the mechanics a bottle of wine after a cold wet evening at Tirreno–Adriatico; an altercation when he changed the riders' jerseys at Milan–San Remo, at their request. Laurent Fignon had felt the tension between Hinault and Guimard in 1982, the year he entered Renault. 'We were kept well clear when they had any disagreements but we could feel it, like gangrene, slowly letting its toxins into the team day by day,' he wrote. The dispute took a back seat as Hinault and Guimard focused jointly on winning the Vuelta in spring 1983, but it burst into the open after Hinault's knee became increasingly precarious.

Hinault now sees his split from Guimard as a part of the growing-up process. 'With Cyrille it was "do this, do that"; you know it will work, but something is lacking – the passion. With Cyrille there was no discussion – you couldn't say you didn't understand or you didn't agree. Where the clash came was that I had signed a personal contract with La Régie Renault without going through him, and that was the beginning of the catastrophe. He wanted to be in control of that. We didn't fall out. I had a tax check a little bit later, and each time the inspector visited him, he would call me up and keep me posted. We never fell out. It was just that it didn't work any more.

Something was broken. We still get on really well today. It was like a marriage – it was better to separate, there were some disagreements. I wished him good luck and moved on, he said well done, off you go. We both succeeded on our own.'

Hinault had the end of his career in sight; he had set the date for his retirement at the end of 1986. He felt there was no point wasting time and energy on disagreements. At a meeting at the end of August 1983, he told Renault's marketing director Michel Rolland – who also ran AS53,[16] the team's holding company – that they needed to choose between him or Guimard. Renault went for the manager, as Hinault apparently suspected they would. Guimard had just won the Tour with Fignon while his other emerging star, Greg LeMond, had just taken the world road race title. 'We've been put in a position where we have to choose between the star and the team,' said the head of Renault. 'We've chosen the team.' Punt on the new Tour de France winner who had just turned twenty-three, plus a world champion of twenty-two, or stick with an ageing star with a dodgy knee and uncertain future who had given himself only three more years? The choice must have seemed obvious.

---

[16] So named because it was based at 53 Champs-Elysées.

CHAPTER 10

NO FAVOURS

'The Blaireau was a weird fellow: he frightened me. Sometimes he would attack and the peloton would string out into a long line. Then he would sit up and start laughing, mocking us. He had a godlike aura . . . [he was] a great champion but I didn't like him.'

– Paul Kimmage, *Rough Ride*

The descent from the Col de l'Espigoulier towards Marseille and Toulon is a sinuous one, eleven kilometres where one 180-degree hairpin comes on top of another with barely any respite. The lead group in Paris–Nice descended at the limit of their tyres' adhesion on 12 March 1984 as the end of the stage to La Seyne-sur-Mer approached. The descent had offered the perfect opportunity to dislodge the race leader, Scotland's Robert Millar, before the flat run-out to the stage finish on the eastern side of Toulon, and Sean Kelly, Stephen Roche and Bernard Hinault were among those who had taken full advantage. 'Hinault was in one of those moods, having one of his days,' recalled Kelly. 'There was a climb [l'Es-pigoulier] where he set a crazy tempo, there were ten or fifteen of us on his wheel, all just hanging on. Every now and then he'd look round and then give it full gas again.'

'Millar wasn't the greatest descender, so Hinault decided to give it a lash down the Espigoulier,' recalled Stephen Roche. 'We nearly broke our necks on that descent.' 'Hinault made the descent full on, right on the limit,' continues Kelly, 'and then on the flat section after the descent, one of the organisers' cars said there was a problem.' The road ahead of the race had been blocked by a group of strikers from the massive dockyard at La Ciotat, where restructuring had begun in 1982; the yard would be closed in 1987.[17] 'At a certain point we could see the road was blocked, it was a straight road and you could see it coming closer – six hundred metres, five hundred, four hundred ...'

The entire group slammed on the brakes, apart from one man. 'I was in front with Hinault because he'd got me to ride with him, and he started sprinting,' says Kelly. 'I followed him for a while, but then I backed off, and he just kept sprinting full gas into the strikers. One guy caught his bars, and down Hinault went, and started

---

[17] The La Ciotat dockyard had produced oil and methane tankers since the 1950s, including the Esso Westernport, the biggest ship in the world when it was completed in 1976. The yard hit economic problems in the 1970s; in 1982 it was merged with others in Dunkirk and La Seyne-sur-Mer; in 1986 the French state cut off subsidy, prompting closure; protests continued at the yard until 1989.

punching and kicking. He was throwing punches, one guy caught him by the hair...I said to Phil Anderson, "This is dangerous, let's get out," so we went round the side of them.' The brief bust-up – to a soundtrack of shouts from the strikers – lasted less than thirty seconds, Roche believes, 'although it seemed a lot longer', but 'Hinault would have broken a world record for the number of punches you can throw in that time'. He adds: 'He went into them like a sprinter going for the line. His arms were everywhere. We thought, "Shit, he's going to kill someone." But he calmed down pretty quickly.' According to one report, Hinault was stopped when a protester said to him, 'You know, Bernard, we are going hungry here.' By then, Hinault had received a cracked rib.

'Eventually they said they would neutralise the race,' says Kelly, 'they would stop it to get all the vehicles past the demonstration then restart it with the break at the same time gap.' As the entire race concertinaed into a small space behind the demonstration, the group containing Kelly and Hinault was caught up by the group chasing behind, including Millar and his teammate Sean Yates. Most of the riders tried to prevent their legs from stiffening up by riding up and down the small stretch of road, but not Hinault. 'He went to the team car and sat in there,' says Kelly. 'Then when the race started again he went off like a bullet, as soon as he got out of the car. Everyone was hanging on for dear life.' 'When they restarted the race, we were one minute behind, several of us from Peugeot who were with Robert,' says Sean

Yates. 'We pulled for twenty kilometres behind Hinault's group, all of us together with Robert on our wheels, but we made no impression.'

Roche explains the altercation as a combination of adrenalin – it happened as the race was absolutely at its height – and Hinault's natural territorial instincts. 'We'd been risking our lives coming down that descent and there are these people who come along and obstruct us. Hinault is a guy who stands his ground. There is no question – [he thinks] "You shouldn't be here, off you go." He stands his ground. He doesn't think about the best procedure, who's watching. The animal in him came out.' Both Kelly and Roche draw parallels with the episodes in 2008 and 2012 when Hinault removed interlopers who had intruded on the podium at the Tour de France, where he now runs the protocol ceremony. They also make the point that on both occasions, once his territorial instincts had taken over, safety concerns were not uppermost in his mind. 'You can see whenever you are in a room with him that he is a dominating personality,' says Kelly.

Hinault's explanation of the Espigoulier fracas is that he was brought down first: 'Only a madman would throw a cyclist to the ground, as happened to me. That was the background that made me react as I did. I didn't enjoy it,' he told Pascal Sergeant, 'but you have to be clear about these things. If there are problems in certain French industries, it's nothing to do with the bike riders. I felt it was completely out of order for us to be held hostage.'

It's a measure of how extraordinary that brief flurry was that those who were there have almost total recall of the altercation. 'I can still picture myself standing there,' says Roche. Thirty years on, he can still hear the sound of the aluminium cleats on Hinault's shoes clicking on the tarmac as he flailed at the protesters, and for Kelly the episode is crystal clear as well. If the strike at Valence d'Agen marked the start of Hinault's 'first career', the barney at the foot of the Espigoulier was where the second phase began. The boss was back in the bunch.

'There is a special delight in knowing that you are the boss, the *patron*,' said Hinault in an interview given to *L'Équipe* magazine in 2003 to celebrate the hundredth anniversary of the Tour de France. 'You are like a soldier, a general who dominates, who imposes his will on the others. I believe that you are born like that. Some are born to be workers, others to be in charge. I could have been a warlord. I would have waged war to win castles and land if I'd been born in the Middle Ages. Or I could have been an admiral.'

From his first Tour, Hinault took the reins. There was a good reason for this: he was the strongest, and he was the strongest-minded. Hence his definition: 'If you're the boss, you need to be capable of doing things. To be a *patron*, you have to be capable of winning the race overall, not just the points or the mountains. You hold the key to winning stages and can decide if someone can win. You need the strength to get off the front and catch an attacker, and there may be days you decide to do that, even if they haven't wound you up.'

There have been few true *patrons* in cycling and the few there have been have varied widely in their personalities, in the measure of influence they have asserted and in the areas they have tried to control. The role and powers of the *patrons* have mutated constantly over the years as the sport has changed, but what they have always had in common is that they were not men who should be crossed. In Rik Van Looy's case, he and his team were so strong that they could have a huge influence on who won in almost any Classic. With Eddy Merckx and Jacques Anquetil, it was more insidious: a rider who annoyed them and who refused to race the way they wanted might well find wins hard to come by. In general, before cycling expanded in the 1980s, the elite wanted to keep the circle of big-money earners as small as possible. Similarly, until Guimard broke the agents, the big stars had influence with the handful of brokers who doled out appearance contracts, so a word or two from a senior rider could affect a lesser man's earning power. This all meant that the 'heads' of the peloton could wield considerable influence.

As cycling evolved, so did the nature of the *patron*. By the 1980s, teams weren't always as rigidly structured as in the past; they increasingly followed the hydra-headed model created by Peter Post, where there was no single leader, but a plethora of talented individuals who worked together to ensure that the team won rather than one star. That made it harder for one rider to dominate. Hinault's manager Cyrille Guimard played his part in killing off the agents, meaning that senior riders lost leverage among the lesser lights. By the 2000s, the role of those with power and influence was circumscribed: settling personal scores – Lance Armstrong's assault on Filippo Simeoni in the 2004 Tour being the best example – or highlighting safety issues (Armstrong in the Giro in 2009, Fabian Cancellara in the Tour in 2010, or Bradley Wiggins in the 2012 Tour). There was no longer space for a *patron* who could boss a sport in the style of Van Looy, Merckx or Anquetil.

Stories of the Badger playing the role are legion, but follow a common theme. There were occasions – Valence d'Agen being the most notable – when he stood up and represented his fellows along the lines of a union leader. There were times when he and other senior riders would unite and protest against excessive amounts of cobbles or racing in the mountains in the snow. In 1982, he led a protest at the Callac criterium against the sudden imposition of doping controls at the race, earning a one-month suspended ban and a fine of 1,100 Swiss francs, which was never applied. But most famously, Hinault seems to have acted as the *patron* in order to ensure that the riders raced in the way that he wanted to, and – it can be conjectured – to cement the psychological stranglehold he enjoyed over his fellows.

His intimidating personality made an impression on new pros immediately. Stephen Roche remembers bridging to Hinault when he attacked in one of his first races. 'It was a big effort to get to his wheel, and when I did I started swinging a bit, wanting to get my breath back. He turned round, looked at me and growled, "*Passez*" – "Do your turn." I had no option.' Later, Roche recalled a 'small race, something like the Tour du Tarn', where Hinault decided to make a point and set a searing pace down the left-hand gutter, with the peloton strung out behind him. Roche set up another line in the right-hand gutter, directly opposite the Badger and the pair rode along, 'him looking at me, me looking at him, looking, looking, looking'. This episode could be compared to the occasion when Hinault and Moser 'half-wheeled' each other up the first climb in the Tour of Lombardy in 1979, but it had a different ending; the eyeballing ended when Hinault swore and pulled over.

What sets Hinault apart from Merckx, Anquetil or Van Looy, Paul Sherwen believes, is 'that Hinault came in as a *patron*, with a big ticket on his back. There were some good teams and riders around back then, but he always acted like a leader. His actions said "this man is the boss".' 'He controlled the Tour completely,' says Kelly, who recalls that usually, when the Tour had a flat stage after the mountains, Hinault would want a steady start to the day. 'We'd roll out and do the first sixty or seventy kilometres at a very easy pace. Hinault would ride at the front making sure no one attacked. If somebody did attack they would get a fucking bollocking,' says Kelly. 'I've seen it myself: Hinault go after somebody and say,

"If you do that again, you won't ever win another race."' Kelly grimaces and mutters, 'Fout pas le bordel'. 'Don't mess with me.'

Mainly, recalled Graham Jones in conversation with the writer Richard Moore, Hinault asserted himself 'physically on the bike rather than verbally. He would occasionally shout a bit but usually it was because he was on a bad day. I remember once at the Tour of Romandie he went to the front for twenty kilometres and strung it all out, and then he sat up and said, "Have you had enough?"' Another tale comes from a small French race, the Tour de l'Aude, in 1980, when the Spanish rider Alberto Fernandez attacked. Hinault went after him, tapped him on the shoulder and said, 'Are you going to attack like that often? Nope, because I'm going to do it.' Off he went, and was not seen again until the finish.

Inevitably given their combative characters, Robert Millar was among those who fell foul of the Badger. 'At the Tour of Romandie in my early years, the directeur sportif told me to attack. I didn't have the legs; Hinault got really annoyed and came past about three times faster than me. It happened again at the Tour de France in 1985. I attacked in the Pyrenees at the start on one of the mountains when there was no racing going on. Hinault got his team to work to catch me, but they ran out of legs, so he had to finish the job himself – he came past with a glare on his face, and said, "What did you do that for? No one's racing." I said, "I'll decide when I race," and the glare got really horrible. By that point, I'd got tired of his persona. So at certain times when he was struggling a bit, I'd go to the front and ride hard so it would hurt him. Pedro Delgado would do it, Stephen Roche would do it, and eventually even Greg LeMond cottoned on, but he would do it subtly.

'If you were going to race with Hinault, you would wonder how much he was going to hurt you,' continues Millar. 'I wasn't afraid of him, but he gave me worries. You had to adopt the attitude that you were going racing, he was going to hurt you, but you weren't bothered. You couldn't disrespect him because he had built up this persona for himself, and it wasn't bullshit. If he said he was going to beat the crap out of you, he'd take you on physically and mentally even if he wasn't in good condition. Sometimes when he wasn't good or going for the win, if he was irked enough he would attack at just the right moment, everyone would be in the red for a long, long time, then he'd swing over. If you were a bit weak or not as good physically, your day would be over.'

Roche recalls just such an episode, from the Dauphiné Libéré in 1981. 'We started a stage with five or six cols in it, ending up at Alpe d'Huez or somewhere. Hinault was riding on the front and turned round, and said to us, "We've got six cols today, how do you want it? We can all go for it now and half of us go home tonight, or we can take it easy now and hit it from three cols out." Mariano Martinez attacked, and Hinault said, "What did I say?" He rode and rode over the six cols, and I finished something like forty-five minutes down. It was a statement:

"Listen guys, I gave you the option but if you play with my balls then you pay the price."'

'There has never been a boss like him,' recalled Sean Yates, who inevitably encountered Hinault after he turned professional in 1982. The former Peugeot pro says now that he had no objection to the fact that Hinault ruled cycling, because like the Badger he felt that riders should respect each other, and personally he didn't want to race hard over multiple Alpine passes on certain days. However, Yates, renowned as one of the hard men of cycling, feels that Hinault's intimidation tactics would not be tolerated in cycling today. 'It was not a time when it was considered to be bullying, but Hinault was bullying and intimidating people. He was definitely pushing the envelope.'

Hinault would argue that young riders such as – most famously – Joël Pelier but also Jean-Claude Bagot should conserve their energies and attack at the appropriate moment. An episode from the 1985 Tour, where Hinault and Pelier had a legendary altercation,[18] makes the point. It occurred on the stage to Limoges, late in the race. 'Like I did with Pelier, I had to have a fight with [Jean Claude] Bagot' – a new pro, riding for the Fagor team. 'He wanted to give it a lash forty kilometres from the start. These young riders need to be better advised. When I was their age people always told me not to attack too far from the finish, so I didn't use up all my bullets. I told Bagot in the same terms I gave it to Pelier and I hope it bears some fruit.'

---

[18] See chapter 12.

Hinault's notion that young riders should conserve their resources was more than ironic given the way he had stirred the pot when he was an impetuous young professional, until Guimard got hold of him. His long-standing friend Maurice Le Guilloux recalled the young Hinault at the Étoile des Espoirs in 1974, an amateur racing with the pros. 'We pros couldn't wait for the race to end; we were low on motivation because it was the end of the season, and my form had completely gone,' he told the historian Pascal Sergeant. 'In the rain, Hinault was attacking every day, going for all the *primes*, all the intermediate sprints. He could have won the race if he'd actually used some tactics and ridden differently.' Then again, Le Guilloux also recalled that Hinault was not exactly welcomed with open arms. 'We didn't roll out the red carpet because he just attacked non-stop.'

There were practical reasons why Hinault didn't like to be disturbed by riders like Pelier and Martinez. He wanted a given race to be structured in the way that suited him. As Guimard saw it, Hinault was like a boxer: he loved a fight, or he would be bored – and he wanted to be the one who decided when he was bored. 'When he had something on his mind, you didn't want to wind him up because he would just turn up the throttle and you would pay in full,' said Jean-François Pescheux. It was Old Testament stuff, inspiring 'fearful expectation of judgement and fiery indignation, which shall devour the adversaries'.

As Millar underlines, Hinault did not merely want to win bike races, he needed to dominate his fellows. There is a clear difference here with Eddy Merckx, who wanted to win everything he rode, who was addicted to winning, and found that domination was a way of achieving that end. With Hinault, controlling the world around him came first. 'His way of racing was to dominate you, break you. It was the way he would go about his day. As I came up through the ranks he stopped being able to break me physically all the time, some days I could race with him. When he discovered he couldn't hurt you, he worked on you mentally, he'd say he didn't like foreigners, ask what you were doing there in front. His teammates would come and lean on you, annoy you in the wind.'

In the years after Hinault's retirement, cycling changed and so did the nature of its bosses. The *patron* emerged in a close-knit, almost closed society whose members rubbed shoulders from February to October; when the big names only troubled to race seriously a few times a year, the cycling peloton became less structured, less parochial and infinitely more diffuse. This is why Hinault can fairly be described as the last man to dominate cycling. The figures who followed him were different and they operated in a different world. 'I always say things changed in cycling in the Indurain era,' says Julián Gorospe, who raced with both the Badger and Big Mig. 'Miguel was a good guy under any circumstances and as a racer he wanted to be even nicer, if possible, than he was off the bike – to the point where when he was top dog he'd give races away.

'Cycling before Miguel was different; back then you wanted to win as many race as possible and you won them – and Hinault was part and parcel of that era. He was a rider who you felt intimidated by as a matter of course.' The same could be said of Lance Armstrong, who dominated cycling in the early 2000s, even if his seven Tour de France wins are now null and void. At times, Hinault seemed to appreciate the Texan's utter ruthlessness. 'It was telling that when Lance Armstrong didn't let Jan Ullrich win at Grand-Bornand in 2004, he told us that Bernard Hinault said "no favours" to him on the podium,' believes Sam Abt, who does, however, point out an important difference between the two. 'Lance did some extraordinarily cruel things and I don't remember Hinault doing anything I would characterise as cruel. I don't remember hearing Hinault demean any of his rivals – he never said, "Joop Zoetemelk, six times second," never did that.'

For Abt, Hinault belongs to a more innocent era. 'There wasn't much difference in racing from Hinault's days to the 1920s, not compared with the difference between Hinault and Lance Armstrong. I remember Lance boasting to me once that their new team bus had windows we couldn't see through from outside, but they could look out and see who was there. I said, "Why do you even care who's there?" He answered, "There might be someone we don't want to see and anyway we can sit and make fun of them." With Hinault's team no one would have even thought of that.'

'I think with Armstrong it was more calculated aggression,' is Robert Millar's verdict. 'With Hinault it was more natural. [With] Lance you felt that he was thinking, "Wait ten minutes, then do it," while with Hinault it was, "Kill, kill, kill, they're hurting, I'm liking this." In their heads it was the same desire to dominate the people they were racing with, but Lance wasn't as opportunistic as Hinault. One moment of weakness and Hinault would jump on you. One of the mechanisms he used to push himself was to act like he hated you.'

In his series of portraits of the Tour's champions, *Forcenés*, Philippe Bordas wrote that Hinault represented the angry, upwardly mobile lowerclass, with an element of anarchism that Johnny Rotten might have recognised. 'When he arrived in the peloton, he did not recognise any superiors. He defied Merckx and the established hierarchy. He planted his molars in old legs stiffened by structured events.' In Bordas's view, however, Hinault had a cold-blooded focus on the present at the expense of anything broader. 'Hinault dreams of life where everything is sub-jugated to the present – no legends, no dreams, but perpetually renewed exploits with a simple immanence: I am what I am, I do what I do.' Hinault, he concludes, 'drags each exploit out of his guts in the same way you pull a blackjack from the glovebox'.

When Hinault took his enforced break through the second half of 1983, the cycling world moved rapidly on. Laurent Fignon won a Tour de France in which the nation dis-covered a new tragic hero in Pascal Simon, whose *calvaire* captured headlines for a week in which he tried to retain the yellow jersey despite a broken shoulder blade. Greg LeMond won the world road race championship while Kelly took the first of his run of Classic wins in the Tour of Lombardy. Fignon, Kelly, LeMond: three of the biggest cycling stars of the late 1980s all made immense strides in Hinault's absence. That was no coincidence.

Roche also progressed in Hinault's absence even if, in common with Millar, his Tour debut in 1983 was stymied by the need to assist their Peugeot teammate Simon. The Irishman noticed a massive difference when Hinault was absent from the peloton. 'When he was around there was a certain pattern to the races. The races that really suited him – the stage races – you would base your tactics on him. If there was a time trial, you would have to get rid of him somewhere, catch him napping or blow him out. He knew what needed to be done in a race so, for example, he'd want to make sure the dangermen weren't near him before a time trial. You knew he would chase if anyone dangerous got away – it would be his team on the front, and you might put yours up as well.'

At the start of 1984 no one knew how the racing was going to unfold, says Roche. 'The question everyone was asking was whether [Hinault] would get his form back, will he be as strong in the time trials, in the mountains? Who can beat him now if they try? Everyone was afraid of him but actually his form took a long time to come back. His margins of victory after his injury were smaller and he didn't get the margins he had when he won before the operation. There was a definite question of whether he would come back to what he was and there was a definite element of everyone trying to test him in the races. Before, you knew that getting rid of him in the mountains would be complicated, but it wasn't the same when he came back. He calculated far more. And in 1984 he definitely wasn't at the level he had been.'

When Hinault set such a searing pace up the Espigoulier in Paris–Nice and tried the nerves of the survivors down the descent before laying into the strikers waiting on the flatlands, the Badger was not quite the man he had been twelve months earlier. When he had his operation the previous August, he had no idea what the outcome would be: 'I didn't know where I was going, if I was going to come back to 30, 40, 50 or 100 per cent of my old strength, or if I was going to come back at all.' The alter-cation at the foot of the Espigoulier was not staged to impress on his companions that the Badger was back and that he could be as bad as before – it was too sudden and adrenalin-fuelled an episode for that – but it reflected a new insecurity, which would last all through 1984. 'All that spring we were going up the wall, the conservative elements within cycling were rubbishing everything we did,' recalls one team insider. 'And on the road it was painful. We weren't a strong Classics team and there were expectations of Bernard and the team in every area.'

Hinault had got back on his bike in late August 1983; he began walking again a week after the operation, to get the joint moving. His first bike ride was a short outing with Mickael; by 6 November he had built up enough strength by riding on the road that he was able to race cyclo-cross, a key test of explosive power which puts immense pressure on the knees compared to the more supple action of riding on the road. On one weekend, 11 November, he raced three 'crosses in succession.

He raced those events in a Renault jersey, marking the end of an era as his next team, La Vie Claire, took shape. A defining shift in cycling was under way as Hinault switched sponsors. The contrast was immense: the world's leading cyclist had swapped the lumbering state-owned giant Renault for a freewheeling capitalist buccaneer who courted controversy at every turn. Cycling was about to be dragged kicking and screaming into the 1980s. Enter (drum roll) Bernard Tapie.

UN BERNARD PEUT EN CACHER UN AUTRE – BEHIND ONE BERNARD THERE MAY BE ANOTHER

'Setbacks are a thing that Bernard simply cannot take.'
— Martine Hinault

'Lorsque ce soir je suis rentré, toute ma vie s'est écroulé et j'ai vu la vérité, avant d'entrer j'aurais dû frapper ...' The tale of heartbreak and descent into alcoholic stupor, 'Vite un Verre' (Get me a drink, quick), is delivered in a style where Sacha Distel meets Tom Jones, with a hint of Scott Walker along the way. The lyrics are gloriously banal, the tune backed by a full orchestra and female backing singers easy on the ear as only French *chansons* can be.

The singer is fresh-faced, kiss-curl falling down his forehead, hair artfully cut over his ears, a little pudgy perhaps, à la Brian Wilson. The name on the sleeve is Bernard Tapy – an Americanisation apparently pronounced *Tapay* that looks like a vain attempt to garner a little Anglo-Saxon lustre – but nearly forty years after Bernard Tapie's brief career as a crooner he is still recognisable as the man who relaunched Bernard Hinault's career in 1984.

Tapie is said to have written his own sleeve notes on his first single, describing himself as 'a unique character. A child of common stock, his origins have left him with a ready wit, and the charming smile of a Parisian urchin...Young, handsome, sporty, he appeals to fans of all kinds. His inspiration lies in the tradition of French *chanson*...a distinctive personality with punch and expressive power which are all his own ...' Like many would-be imitators of the king of *chanson* Charles Trenet, Tapy did not appeal to enough fans of any kind to have a career of any note. His contract with RCA in 1966 was not renewed, although he released two more singles nineteen years later, by which time he had achieved notoriety for reasons that had nothing to do with his voice box and everything to do with his capacity to reinvent himself.

Had his career as a singer blossomed, Bernard Tapy would probably have ended up on a rostrum animating the post-Tour *spectacle* that rocked stage towns until the 1970s. As it turned out, Bernard Tapie ran a team that won the Tour, twice. To say that the *chanteur* turned tycoon is a unique character in Tour history is an understatement.

Tapie is unique in France, one of the most multifaceted and larger than life figures to emerge in the last half-century, a chameleon who has constantly reinvented himself, forging myriad identities in a world where business, sport, showbiz, politics and controversy all rub shoulders.

Tapie's résumé – not to mention the various unauthorised biographies and the twenty-one-page Wikipedia entry – confirms the old saying that the truth is stranger than fiction, although in his case the two are hard to distinguish at times. Tapie began his working life as a car salesman, then switched to selling televisions after a hilarious episode in which an unsuccessful salesman knocked on his door; Tapie decided to join him and hit upon a way of getting the boxes into the houses of unwilling customers: persuade them it was a market research exercise and they were on loan before coming back to clinch the deal. He was persuasive, quick to learn, determined, but with a short attention span, flitting from one enterprise to the next.

The key move came in 1977, when he formed a company to buy up and re-establish bankrupt businesses; his first move on to the French national stage was in 1980 when he bought a set of *châteaux* at a knockdown price from the Central African dictator Jean-Bedél Bokassa, only for the dictator to take legal action to reverse the deal – upheld by a French court – on the grounds that Tapie had incorrectly informed him that the French authorities were on the point of seizing the buildings. Three methods were used to reboot the businesses:

renegotiating their debts, cutting costs, and – critically for Bernard Hinault – diversification into other areas.

The two Bernards met in Tapie's Paris office in September 1983. The initial contact came through Jean de Gribaldy, an *éminence grise* of French cycling through the seventies and eighties, the Besançon viscount who had discovered Sean Kelly and ran his Sem-France-Loire-Skil team. De Gribaldy had contacted Tapie earlier in the 1980s to see if his La Vie Claire chain of health food shops would be interested in supplying his team. Tapie had bigger ideas, as might be expected: 'Can you get me Hinault?' De Gri couldn't – for a while. When Hinault came on the market in mid-1983, there was interest from the Italian team Malvor, and a long-standing French cycling sponsor, Guy Merlin – although the latter was ruled out as he was already sponsoring the Tour itself – but De Gri remembered Tapie's words, and advised the Badger to meet the businessman.

Hinault pulled no punches, pointing out to Tapie that he was uncertain whether he would return to racing at his previous level; it was a 50–50 chance, he said. He had no idea what standard he would reach. But Tapie had no hesitation in putting his money behind a sportsman with a dodgy knee. The four-times Tour winner was an uncertain proposition, but he was as viable as any of Tapie's knockdown acquisitions. The tycoon's best-known companies had all been bought at one franc apiece from liquidators. Health food chain La Vie Claire, Terraillon (scales), Wonder (batteries), Testut (more scales, along with meat-cutting machines) and Look (bike and ski components) would be sold between 1988 and 1995 for sums varying from 125 million francs (Terraillon) to 470 million (Wonder).

Tapie's thrust was that Hinault's sporting success was a marginal factor for him: he had just acquired Look, and wanted the Badger to publicise a radical new venture, a system of pedals with clipless bindings based on the 'step-in, step-out' system used in skiing. It was a classic piece of Tapie diversification: the idea was that on top of the seasonal ski business, producing pedals would enable the factory to remain active all year round.[19] There were other Tapie companies that could be involved: Mic-Mac, an iconic couture company with shops in Saint-Tropez, founded by Brigitte Bardot's husband Gunther Sachs; gym equipment makers Adams. And as well as publicising his companies in the biggest sports arena that France had to offer, a tie-in with a figure such as Hinault would help turn Tapie into a figure on the national stage in his own right. That could only help his ambitions in business, in other sports such as football, and in politics.

The deal was confirmed live on French television on the evening of 25 September as part of its coverage of the Grand Prix des Nations. A press conference two days later in the Hilton hotel near the Eiffel Tower drew

---

[19] Apparently he also had his eyes on an equestrian project for the company.

between 100 and 150 journalists from all milieux, way beyond the couple of dozen cycling specialists who would usually attend. Key personnel were recruited, among them Philippe Crepel, briefly a professional in the 1960s, who had managed the La Redoute team. Crepel sees that press conference as a defining moment in Tapie's career. 'He's a phenomenon in French society now but he was barely known then, and that was the rocket that put him into orbit. He is an exceptional communicator, with an astonishing ability to manage a situation at speed. He's permanently on the rebound.' The key line from the press conference was this one: 'Whether Hinault races or not is irrelevant, it doesn't matter if he wins or not…I'm counting on him to make as much money as possible. As far as success goes, that's the only measure.'

A central figure in the negotiations was Philippe Riquois, a businessman responsible for handling the Tour's television rights outside France, who had been tasked with finding a sponsor for Hinault. Riquois did the financial planning, Crepel the logistics and practical side – bikes, vehicles and so on. The budget would be 10 million francs, roughly £1 million, or double what Crepel had had at La Redoute. Initially the goal was to bring in sponsors from outside as well as Tapie's own companies, in the end the only one to buy in was Citroën, whose interest in setting themselves up against Renault is easy to imagine.

A year or so earlier, Hinault had explained to his former junior rival Bernard Vallet – when they were sharing a room at the world road race championships – that he intended to set up a team where the roles of general manager, *directeur sportif*, and trainer would be separated, rather than being the duty of one man as was the case with Guimard and others. To that end, a call was put in to Guimard's former tutor in Switzerland, the bespectacled, slight, boffin-esque Paul Koechli. He would be the trainer, and would direct the team on the road. Maurice Le Guilloux, Hinault's old training partner, would move from Renault to become a *directeur sportif*; a couple of the Renault old guard – Charly Bérard, Alain Vigneron – joined along with a Swiss contingent who came with Koechli.

The now-iconic jersey inspired by abstract paintings by the Dutch artist Piet Mondrian was born at a meeting in a bistro in Paris's Place de la Bourse involving Crepel, Koechli and a stylist from Mic-Mac, who initially suggested a black design, which was turned down on the grounds that the riders would overheat in the sun. 'I wondered about something to do with patchwork, so the stylist went to the Louvre and bought a Mondrian book,' recalls Crepel, 'and then we worked out the design on the table in the bistro.' Designs inspired by Mondrian could already be seen elsewhere – in television backdrops, in a collection by Yves Saint Laurent in 1965 and in the logo used by cosmetics company l'Oréal. Between the three of them, they came up with a design using blocks of red, white, blue and yellow – one for each of the sponsors: Look, Terraillon, Citroën and La Vie Claire

– separated by thick black lines. The La Vie Claire jersey design owes something to the celebrated cocktail dress by Yves Saint Laurent, but can be clearly traced to Mondrian's works of the 1930s such as *Composition II in Red, Blue and Yellow*, and *Composition No. 10*.

The jersey design also included a key, novel feature: whereas in the woollen jerseys used in cycling hitherto, the logos and names had to be woven into the wool or stuck on with flocking, La Vie Claire's *maillots*, made by Santini, would be polyester-based, with the designs printed on the material. 'It was a huge turning point – the first printed jersey,' says Crepel. 'There were no limits to what we could do.'

Philippe Bouvet wrote that relaunching himself with La Vie Claire was 'the biggest challenge of [Hinault's] career, the most emotional because it was done for its own sake. It was personal. It's a victory that doesn't figure on his *palmarès* because it was a victory over his own body. He said he wanted to live a sort of ideal life, live purely and simply because he reproached Guimard for suffocating his personality.' Crepel recalls that getting the team on the road in three months was 'complicated, because the people around me didn't understand the urgency of getting bikes, cars, training plans'. He notes, however, that it was a far smaller enterprise than putting together a squad in the twenty-first century.

Key to relaunching Hinault would be the partnership with Koechli, Swiss amateur champion in 1966, and a professional until 1970, including a ride in the Tour de France in 1968 for a combined Swiss-Luxembourg team.[20] He was not among the sixty-three who finished. After retirement due to a femoral artery problem, Koechli studied coaching in Macolin, the headquarters of the Swiss Federal Office of Sport and home of its education centre, the Haute École Fédérale de Sport. Guimard was among the alumni who had studied the coaching programme devised by Koechli. By 1984, when Tapie's lawyer called him, he was flirting with the notion of forming an American-backed cycling team and he had trained the double Grand Prix des Nations winner Daniel Gisiger, an early devotee of aerodynamics.

Gisiger's time-trial success proved Koechli's sporting credentials. The Swiss – who later became the country's national trainer – had begun working with Koechli in 1978, having seen his success with Joseph Fuchs, the climber who by then had twice won the Swiss national road championship, and who would go on to win Liège–Bastogne–Liège in 1981. 'Before Paul, training was empirical,' says Gisiger. 'You went riding on your bike but no one said what you should do. You played with your friends, sprinted for milestones and hills. Koechli devised zones of training to develop this or that physical aspect. I began working at different intensities. It wasn't defined by the volume of training but the volume at certain

---

[20] Trivia lovers should note that one of Koechli's teammates was Johny Schleck, father of the 2010 Tour winner Andy.

intensities.' Gisiger says that Koechli's methods were greeted sceptically by professional team managers who were set in the idea that hours on the bike were all that mattered; then again, he heard later that the East Germans had studied Koechli and his methods.

Gisiger says that he discussed Koechli with Hinault – 'the peloton was a small world in those days' – and the trainer's methods were written about in *L'Équipe*; it was he who gave Hinault or a representative the coach's number. Hinault says that his new mentor's *modus operandi* marked a radical change. 'The Guimard way can take you a long way, but the thing about Koechli was he wanted to give the information out – he didn't want to keep it for himself,' he told me. 'I'm still convinced that Guimard was a very good trainer, but the small thing that Paul taught me was lacking. Paul's way of doing things was different again. Cyrille would say, "Do this," but he wouldn't say why. Paul Koechli would say, "This is the thing to do, and you will develop in this way, what particular aspect." For me, Paul Koechli was the best trainer there has ever been.'

He continues, 'I didn't learn to train until I was twenty-eight. Before, I trained but not as specifically as I did later on. Above all with Koechli, when I began a training session on a given day, I knew what I was setting out to do and what it would achieve. His role was to tell you, "I will teach you now to train, how to put together a training plan, but then you will be independent." You would send in your files, of course' – Koechli still has the ring binders of Hinault's training diaries – 'but he wasn't the one telling you what to do. At the start he would tell you, then it was up to you to tell him what you did, how you felt during the day.

'Initially he drew up the training plans, but later on it was up to you to do them depending on your racing pro-gramme. I didn't have a pulse monitor, but [how I trained] was based on the intensity over a given time. For a very high intensity, the time [of the interval] was very short. When the intensity was lower, the time was longer. I used a pulse monitor once. Paul wanted me to use one at all costs at the start and I said it was pointless. But I rode up a *col* wearing one, recording my heart rate, that was all. I didn't look at the watch – it's your body that you listen to when you make an effort, not a machine. Over a fifteen-kilometre climb with a gradient of 7 per cent, there was a three beats difference between the bottom and the top: 168–171.'

Koechli, a trainer rather than a *directeur sportif*, was a rarity in cycling at the time and he was far removed from the traditional figure of the old pro who hands down the ideas given to him by other old pros. He lacked Guimard's bombast, Robert Le Roux's evangelism, or the Godfather-like geniality of Jean Stablinski. Radically, he was openly against the use of banned drugs; he would stay that way until he left cycling in 1992. In the pre-Internet dark ages, he was occasionally lampooned for his reliance on his computer, in which he kept a database of riders around the world and their results. One of his experiments was a four-day track-training camp in spring 1984; another was to make Hinault change the side on which he dismounted when doing cyclo-cross, purely in order to show that he could change anything if he really wanted to. More importantly, he persuaded Hinault to train more regularly in the winter and made his future leader visit him so that he could get to know him; there were several such stays, Hinault recalled.

In *Le Peloton des Souvenirs*, Hinault wrote that under Koechli he regained his love of cycling as a pastime. 'You had to enjoy being on the bike. It was almost a philosophy. A cyclist shouldn't hold the handlebars, but caress them as if he was playing the piano. He insisted on us being relaxed so we could use our energy more fully.' Now, he says, 'I learned to train again. Before, I trained according to instruction – do this, do that. You do it because you are a competitor and it will help you win. But you're not interested or involved, there is no research, no reflection. With Paul, once you have gone through all the process, you've got a bit of physical data, you say, "In order to do this, I have to do that, and that's the way I will do it." You are far more involved.' That said, it was not always sweetness and light, notably in the Grand Prix des Nations in 1985, when Hinault quit in a fury after the Swiss didn't give him the time checks he wanted.

Interviewed later, Koechli said he felt that Hinault 'wanted something different to what he had experienced before. He wanted to be in charge. And above all he wanted to understand the mechanics of his career, his preparation and the things that made him react more or less. He is an impulsive person, a complete person, and often it wasn't desirable to discuss things further. In a team, it's fatal to have conflict. The important thing is to seek out the reasons and confront them intelligently. In the three years since we met he has matured massively, because he's in charge.'

'[With Paul] you had a plan for seven days in your head,' says Hinault. 'You don't need seventy bits of paper to do it. You go out in the morning and say, "Today it's high intensity, short duration, but it will be very hard." You have a basis that you work from. When you begin it's high intensity, then at the end of the week it's longer and lower, perhaps seven hours at 130 bpm. You might go fifteen days without seeing Paul – and when you see him you give him what you've written down on your fifteen files. He would analyse it and see roughly what it meant. He could see if it made sense or not. The first three months together we talked an immense amount – because I wanted to learn from him. It wasn't a daily process of him following you, of being on your back – you were given ownership. That's what was interesting. You have an objective and you figure out your training. Otherwise you are a child.'

La Vie Claire was launched in the Crazy Horse cabaret club, whose blend of slightly sleazy glamour, front and *animation* fitted the Tapie persona to a T. For cycling, it was radical then; even now it would raise eyebrows. Cycling was a tough world to enter, 'fundamentalist, sectarian,' says

Crepel, 'but Tapie had no inhibitions. He wasn't there to be liked, but to make things happen.' The team broke with tradition by training in Spain and won their first race there, the Tour of Valencia, where Hinault won the final stage, a sixty-kilometre criterium. On 13 May 1984, a year to the day after winning the Vuelta a España with a very sore knee, he took the Four Days of Dunkirk.

The Four Days has a respectable history but is not one of cycling's flagship events. By that point in the season, however, Hinault simply needed a win of note. He had finished third in Paris–Nice, abandoned Milan–San Remo, had not ridden strongly in the Ardennes Classics – where he had won so often in the Renault days – and as the Tour de France hove into view, something was required. Tapie and the other key figures in the team had already decided that a stronger team was called for in 1985.

Guimard, for one, believes that Hinault never returned to his previous standard, but said it wasn't entirely a physical matter relating to his recovery from the knee operation. 'He lacked the necessary motivation to impose on himself the extra work that his increasing years required. He would have had to work harder to remain the rider he was before 1983. And there was another psychological factor: he had won everything.' What was certain was that his old protégé wasn't the same. The carapace of invulnerability had been shattered. He wasn't quite his old self in the mountains.

Among the riders who sensed this were a bunch of Colombians who raced that year's Dauphiné Libéré wearing plain jerseys because they were officially a national team, but had no proper kit. Most of them came from a semi-professional team, Leche Gran Via, including Pacho Rodriguez, who dominated stages five, six and seven – winning two and finishing second in the other – to take a commanding lead before cracking on the penultimate day. On that snow-hit mountain stage to the Col du Rousset, Hinault lost six minutes on the winner on the final climb, while another Colombian, Martin Ramirez, took over the leader's jersey. Ramirez went into the final Sunday with a 27sec lead on Hinault, and – interviewed years later – claimed that the Frenchman spent much of the morning's road-race stage trying to intimidate him and shouting at him. The little amateur wasn't unnerved and clung on to finish the afternoon's final time trial ahead of Hinault. But this was a far cry from the Badger who had dominated the Dauphiné so outrageously in 1979 and 1981.

Meanwhile, Fignon had gone on to run Francesco Moser close at the Giro and as the Tour de France approached, the Parisian's dominant win in the French national championship – on Hinault's home turf at Plouay – made it clear that he was the favourite for the Tour, although, as Guimard recalled, many of the home media wanted the returning Hinault to win. He took the prologue in Paris but after that it was an uphill struggle. Guimard and Fignon knew their man well, and played him like an angler with an energetic salmon on the hook. 'I was convinced that he would make mistakes. Calculating, waiting, playing with other people's strategies was not his strong point,' said Guimard. He also felt – rightly – that Koechli didn't have the strength of character to tell Hinault what to do – or more crucially, when to hold back.

Renault dominated the team time trial, with La Vie Claire losing 55sec; in the first solo *contre la montre* from Alençon to Le Mans, over 67km, Fignon clearly had the upper hand, winning by 49sec; the 1min 29sec cushion created meant Fignon and Guimard could relax a little. Hinault then attempted a classic war of attrition, chasing bonus sprints, trying to get breakaways established at unlikely moments, but to no avail. 'It might have worked on a rider who was mentally weaker than me, but I never lost my head,' said Fignon. For example, on the marathon stage from Nantes to Bordeaux, 338km, Hinault pulled back a total of 28sec in bonuses, and he pressed on after the third sprint of the day, pulling a group of twenty-one riders clear, including several La Vie Claire teammates. Fignon was unruffled.

Fignon said later that he and Guimard 'knew that Hinault was an impulsive, angry rider who didn't have the best tactical awareness. He would return blow for blow or simply knock everyone senseless, but when he needed to race with his head, he needed Guimard.' And the Renault boss knew how his former protégé functioned, as Robert Millar observed: 'Guimard was smart. During that Tour, he continually poked Hinault's inner monkey so that he got angry and [would do] something rash like attacking too far from the finish. As soon as Hinault heard the *deedle-dee-deedle-dee* of the Renault team car horn he would start to tense up, Guimard would appear at the back of the bunch smiling and giving out orders to his riders. The smiling part probably annoyed Hinault the most.' In the first Pyrenean stage to Guzet Neige, Hinault dropped another 52sec after a sharp attack from Fignon; as had been the pattern at the Dauphiné, he spent the whole day riding hard, but unlike of old, the climbers – new faces such as Luis 'Lucho' Herrera of Colombia and Pedro Delgado of Spain – didn't melt away.

Fignon wrote in his memoirs: 'The very next morning, in a move which was unexpected and almost pathetic, the Badger showed he was racing on pride alone. He attacked *en route* to Blagnac, on his own, sixty kilometres into the stage. It was total folly but he had to keep going for twenty kilometres as he left himself no way out.' Renault could not take it seriously: 'He's gone mad, *Le Blaireau*. He didn't really believe that he could make us blow all by himself,' said Madiot. 'We should have let him wear himself out for a bit longer,' reflected Fignon. There was a method, of a kind, to Hinault's apparent madness: he recalled that there had been days when he led the Tour when he had been vulnerable, and the only way to expose Fignon, he felt, was to test him, as often as possible. In the next key stage, however, a mountain time trial from Grenoble to La Ruchère-en-Chartreuse, Fignon won again; again the gap on Hinault wasn't massive – a mere 33sec – but it underlined his physical superiority. 'I felt completely unbeatable,' he recalled. The next day, crossing the Vercors, it was the turn of Renault to put Hinault under pressure, sending Greg LeMond up the road in an escape with another possible podium contender, Pascal Simon; Fignon and his team had no need to chase, instead Hinault had to rally La Vie Claire in pursuit.

The moment that epitomised Hinault's eclipse in that Tour came on the stage to l'Alpe d'Huez, where the Badger's aggression finally backfired on him. The stage crossed the Col du Coq and the super-steep Côte de Laffrey before finishing on the Alpe; there were multiple attacks from Hinault, followed by one incisive move from Fignon, all observed by Robert Millar, who had a ringside seat en route to fourth place overall. 'Hinault couldn't drop Fignon on the Côte de Laffrey, so at the top of the hill Guimard came up and spoke to Fignon, just before the descent, which is pretty dodgy. Fignon and Herrera pissed off a kilometre before the top, and we were all dropped – that was obviously a plan, so that Hinault wouldn't do the descent flat out and kill us all.

'As soon as we [i.e., Millar, Hinault and company] made the junction to Fignon and Herrera in the valley, Guimard appeared and started saying stuff to Fignon like, "You hurt them there, they're hanging on," stuff that was calculated to annoy Hinault. Hinault's face just went even redder, and he attacked again, and the same thing happened – as soon as Fignon caught him, the car would come up, Guimard would have a chat, Hinault would go again, then Fignon put us all in the gutter, made a tempo behind him, so the gap wasn't growing – Hinault was just left there to fry.' For Félix Lévitan, Hinault's vain attacks were an effort 'to show that whatever happened he was not and he never would be a rider like any other. There was something derisory in the attempt, but even more panache.'

As they climbed l'Alpe d'Huez – on roads that look disconcertingly bereft of crowds when the images are seen now – Guimard realised that this was their chance to hammer the final nails into Hinault's coffin. After a few seconds, Fignon put in the *coup de grâce*. 'Hinault's defeat was complete,' wrote Philippe Bouvet in *L'Équipe*. 'When Fignon flew past under his nose, it was as if his youth was flying away with him.' The *directeur sportif* asked Fignon to take up station thirty metres ahead of Hinault. The effort he made trying to pull back his former teammate broke him; he eventually lost three minutes. There was something of the King Kong about the moment; a majestic beast brought low by his own strength.

Millar was riding just a few yards behind, and recalls, 'By the time I caught Hinault, he looked as if he had hunger knock; maybe he hadn't eaten enough because he was so worked up.' Overtaking Hinault was a process in itself, because Millar knew that if he humiliated the Badger, one day he would pay for it. 'I had to calculate the speed I went past him to make sure that I didn't upset him. I made sure that I went past fast enough that he couldn't get on my wheel, and fast enough that it looked like I was at cruising speed. Normally, you jump the guy, but I didn't want to jump him, as that would be humiliating.'

In the La Vie Claire team car behind Hinault, Paul

Koechli, Philippe Crepel and Bernard Tapie all looked on as Hinault was put to the sword. 'It was like a silent film,' recalled Crepel. 'Hinault was chivalrous, but that was the physical reality. Fignon just went straight past. I can imagine Tapie thinking that Hinault was finished.' That evening, the La Vie Claire boss said publicly that he might be interested in signing Fignon; as it was, he was already tapping up LeMond.

Fignon's comment that he had laughed when he saw Hinault attack time after time in vain inevitably caused controversy: this didn't seem respectful to a four-times winner of the Tour de France and former team leader from a youngster, who, at times that July, admitted he had become an unpleasant character. 'Everyone thought I was laughing at Hinault. That simply wasn't it. Not in the slightest. He understood.' Fignon explained that his laughter was not contempt for the old champion, it was more an expression of delight at his own physical superiority, and an acknowledgement of the absurdity of the situation. If Hinault understood, it was because he and Fignon shared that sense of joy, of 'play', when they were racing. 'It's easy to say I made him laugh,' said Hinault later. 'But he didn't know why I was doing what I did. There were days when I knew if he'd attacked me, I'd have been in trouble, so I applied that principle to him. I tried to make him crack. It came back and bit me but I had no other answer. I didn't get angry when Fignon said what he did. I just thought, one day perhaps I would be the one who would be laughing.'

Ten minutes after the finish, Hinault's verdict was, 'It didn't work out, but I won't stop attacking until we get to Paris.' That was front worthy of his team owner. Alain Vigneron, who was sharing a room with Hinault on that Tour, recalled that his leader hit crisis point that evening. 'He was saying that he couldn't ever get back, it was doing his head in. He was close to tears.' There was a surreal side, as so often on the Tour; the pair were rooming on the ground floor of a holiday chalet, and Hinault's near-breakdown was witnessed by cows chewing the cud while they peered at the windows.

The next morning, Millar recalls, Hinault seemed back to his old self. 'We were going up a hill, it was roasting hot, I was hiding halfway down the bunch, someone attacked and he went past them, dropped them, then turned round and asked the guy what he thought he was doing. He had already recovered. He had to maintain his indestructible persona.' But at La Plagne the next day, any slender chance that Fignon might be defeated finally evaporated as the young Parisian achieved the most dominant victory of his career, simply riding away up the slopes to win by a minute from Jean-Marie Grezet and LeMond, with Hinault struggling in at 2min 58sec – a margin which would have seemed unthinkable a couple of years earlier. 'It was easy,' said Fignon. 'I took time out to admire the scenery and even look at Hinault a couple of hairpins below me.'

'Fignon just played with Hinault,' concludes Millar. 'For the rest of us, it was a case of picking up what was left behind. Obviously Guimard had worked out how to get the best out of Hinault by controlling his anger, so he knew how to annoy him, what would grate on him and make him react at the wrong time so he would waste energy. I don't think Fignon would have beaten him in that Tour without Guimard pressing Hinault's buttons and making him do the wrong thing at the wrong time. Physically, Hinault wasn't far behind Fignon in that Tour. That day on l'Alpe d'Huez for example, without the histrionics beforehand there was no reason he couldn't have ridden up with Fignon.'

L'Alpe d'Huez and La Plagne looked like the classic phase when the old champion finally has to give best to a younger man who goes on to succeed him. It was not that simple. 'Even in 1984, I was not Bernard Hinault,' stated Fignon later. 'Hinault was a better all-rounder, a better time triallist' – borne out by the fact that even when Hinault was under par and Fignon at his best, the newcomer did not open vast margins in the time trials in that Tour. Fignon added that Hinault was better at hurting himself and less susceptible to getting ill at the start of the season – in fact, all round, Hinault was more robust. Fignon won only three major Tours in his career, and a handful of Classics; that was down to his health failing him. 'I did not have the class that Hinault had. To me that was obvious.' Compared to Fignon's five-year fight to return after his knee gave out, Hinault's six months in the doldrums seem small beer.

The paradox was that, in finishing ten and a half

minutes behind Fignon overall – among the mere mortals with LeMond and Millar not far behind him – Hinault finally won the hearts of France's public and press. 'Hinault's youth appeared to fly away each time Fignon disappeared around a hairpin bend,' wrote Philippe Bouvet. 'But he lost in such a way that people came to love him, taking on the character of a magnificent underdog. Fignon dominated, so much, so much more than before. But Hinault won the heart of the crowds, much more than in his greatest days. The bravura of the one – Hinault – raised the triumph of the other – Fignon – to a new level.'

It was an intriguing turnaround from the Jérôme Bureau editorial of two years earlier. 'I'm popular and that makes me feel really good,' said Hinault afterwards. 'But the people who come and tap me on the back or come and try to touch me [as I ride] scare me. I have the impression that they sometimes consider me to be an animal and that they don't respect me sufficiently.' But he was gracious in defeat – 'We have all taken every risk in the book, and I've lost, but that's the game.' Philippe Brunel concluded, 'among the journalists who went slowly back to the press room, some were reproaching themselves for having waited so long to like Bernard Hinault. It's certainly not too late to write it.' The morning after l'Alpe d'Huez, the headline in *L'Équipe* said it all: 'Now, let's love him.'

It is hard to find the panel that commemorates Laurent Fignon among the hundreds in the crematorium wall at the Père Lachaise cemetery, but it's not hard to distinguish when you finally spot it. The marble plate forty centimetres square bears three pictures of the 'professor': racing in the Tour de France's yellow jersey in his pomp, with his earphones on as he commentates for French television and – largest of the three – stubble-headed and pasty-faced during his attempt to fight off the cancer that took his life in 2010.

It's not a dramatic memorial in comparison with Tom Simpson's stone on the blasted Ventoux or a place of worship like the shrine in Fausto Coppi's native Castellania, but in its understatement it is what the sober, philosophical man Fignon became in his later years would probably have wanted. Fignon didn't like a fuss being made of his attempt to get rid of the cancer, just as he didn't like going over the most dramatic moments of his cycling career; he simply wanted to be appreciated for what he was rather than for the headlines he created.

What do I have left of Fignon? The small panel on a breezy autumn day, the translation I wrote of his memoirs *We Were Young and Carefree*, the sound of his voice harsh with the cancer as he commentated for television at the 2010 Tour, his last, a few flashbacks to interviews here and there, and the memory of one golden summer spent glued to a television screen in a Normandy village watching him rip the Tour de France to shreds with Bernard Hinault put to the sword. During that sweltering July, thirty years before that chill autumn, he became the first cyclist to get the better of *Le Blaireau* in ten Grand Tours. Then, it had seemed that the years of the Badger were over and a new star was set to rule France and the Tour for years to come. Fignon himself joked that he would win seven Tours and then stop.

That 1984 Tour now has an elegiac feel to it, the epitome of a summer where there was barely a cloud in the sky and Fignon could claim that 'we were young and carefree'. This was the last Tour *franco–français*, the terminus of a line stretching back through the duels of Jacques Anquetil and Raymond Poulidor to the very first Tour in 1903. It was the last Tour when French cyclists won the bulk of the stages, a high water mark for French cycling, which could boast seven out of seventeen teams and fifty-four of the one hundred and seventy starters. It was the zenith of Fignon's career; he would spend the next six years trying to get somewhere near the form that led him to be dubbed 'the ogre'. This was one of the most dominant team performances the Tour has ever witnessed, with first and third overall for Renault, plus ten stage wins including the team time trial, and those stages shared among five riders within the team. Guimard's personal series of management successes had stretched to seven of the last nine Tours but it was the end of his run: the gradual decline of the stable that bred Hinault, Fignon and LeMond would run in parallel with French cycling's gentle slide into the doldrums.

In the thirty years after his entry to the world of the Tour, Tapie travelled far from cycling as his career entered its roller-coaster phase: he moved into soccer with Olympique Marseille – bought in 1986 for a symbolic one

franc and subsequently four times French champions and
Champions' League champions – and briefly into yachting
for a transatlantic record; by 1990 he was among the
twenty richest men in France. Adidas was the 'deal of his
life', bought in 1990, sold in 1993 after François Mitterrand
made him a minister. Olympique Marseille descended
into chaos and bankruptcy – and a six-month jail term for
Tapie – amid allegations of match-rigging which saw the
Champions' League title removed. The Adidas deal
morphed into an epic court case against the bank charged
with the sale, Crédit Lyonnais, which eventually embroiled
the head of the IMF, Christine Lagarde. With business
and politics off limits to him, Tapie then reinvented himself
as a singer, writer, television presenter and actor before
launching a discount website, *bernardtapie.com* and
acquiring the media group that includes the newspaper
La Provence. The group's ventures include health cruises
around the Mediterranean, 'with evenings animated by
Bernard Tapie'. Nearly thirty years after RCA said *non*,
he is still onstage. You can't help thinking it: aboard the
Costa Clasica, somewhere on the crest of a wave between
Marseille and Malta, with his kiss-curl and his winning
smile: Bernard Tapy still wants to be Sacha Distel.

CHAPTER 12

THE KILLER AND THE KINDLY LAD

'You haven't seen the end of me yet.'

– Bernard Hinault, 14 July 1985

It's hard not to like Greg LeMond, most probably because Greg LeMond seems to want people to like him. LeMond is always described as naïve, but it's the wide-eyed naïveté of a Labrador puppy. Over the years, the issue most journalists have had with LeMond is not that he won't answer a question or that he is impolite. It's precisely the opposite: he can give up so much of himself, and so freely, that the journalist ends up feeling a little disquieted. In his racing days LeMond was that rare thing for a sportsman: he was lovable, a man who would make you wait an hour in a corridor then bumble his way out of his hotel room and win your undying affection by baring his soul as if you were the only journalist he had ever bared it to.

Few people in sport seem so trusting; few can have carried such hurt.

Visiting LeMond in Minnesota on his retirement in 1994, I was surprised at how much pain a man could express at the end of a career that had included two world championships, three Tours de France and one of sport's most dramatic comebacks. But this was before the revelation that he had been abused by a relative as a child, and before the lengthy, stressful years he and his wife Kathy spent fighting their way through the legal, financial and business maze that Lance Armstrong had constructed to conceal his doping. LeMond was hiding the early hurt within him; the later pain was yet to come.

Even after a career that spanned fifteen years at the highest level in European cycling – including a lost year, 1987, spent recovering from the shooting accident that nearly cost him his life – LeMond still sounded like an outsider, more so than the other English-speaking riders I'd come to know. He had travelled further than the likes of Sean Kelly, Stephen Roche or Robert Millar, and never seemed as integrated as riders like Phil Anderson or Allan Peiper, Australians who had embraced Flanders. LeMond's unbuckling refusal to change was part of the quirkiness that made him such an attractive character: here was a man who defied the deep-rooted precepts of European cycling, who ate ice cream, who brought his wife to races, who liked air conditioning and Mexican food.

The spectacular success of 1989, when he returned from his injuries to win the Tour and World championship – a rare double that eluded Hinault and Anquetil – had failed to mellow the memories of 1985 and 1986. These two Tours de France were dominated by a diverse trinity: LeMond, Hinault and their patron, Tapie; three characters so big that they made the Tour rather crowded. LeMond has been convinced for thirty years that he could have won the 1985 Tour ahead of Hinault had team orders not restrained him; he was equally convinced that the following year the Frenchman had moved heaven and earth to defeat him, going back on an agreement reached after the 1985 race.

The focus on these two Tours in recent years has been intense following the publication in 2011 of Richard Moore's account, *Slaying the Badger*, the release of the film of the same name by John Dower in 2014 and a French film, made almost simultaneously for *L'Équipe 21* by Patrick Chène, *Parole de Blaireau [A Badger's Word]: Hinault vs LeMond*. The films come to a similar conclusion: Hinault – and his supporters – have one version of events, LeMond and those around him recount another; both are radically different and never the twain shall meet.

The two-year-long LeMond–Hinault imbroglio can only be viewed through the prism of their respective characters. 'A killer, in the best sense of the term,' is Guimard's view of Hinault. No one has ever said that of LeMond. '[Greg] doesn't have Hinault's destructive rage but he doesn't have his single-mindedness either,' was the verdict of Bernard Vallet. 'He's a lovely boy, but certainly too kind.' No one, to the best of my knowledge, has used either of those epithets for the Badger.

*

By 1985, the 'Killer' and the 'Lovely Boy' had several years of shared history. Before Cyrille Guimard even clapped eyes on Laurent Fignon, he had LeMond lined up as the Badger's replacement at Renault. Guimard signed the American when he was only twenty; LeMond had yet to reach twenty-one when he took his first professional win at the Tour de l'Oise. The clincher for Guimard, or so he said, was watching his potential signing in the Ruban Granitier Breton at the end of 1980. LeMond was already legendary as one of the most precocious junior racers that cycling had ever produced, having won three world championship medals in 1979, one of each colour. Guimard was driving behind the winning break in a stage of the Breton race, when the young American had his chances wrecked by a puncture. LeMond's team car took an age to give him a spare wheel, and the rider threw a mighty strop, punching his *directeur sportif*.

For Guimard, this was clear evidence of 'character' as demonstrated so often by his current leader. But LeMond did not have Hinault's ability to turn events to his advantage or his willingness to pursue a lost cause: six kilometres after the wheel change, with the race clearly out of reach, he abandoned. Famously, Guimard and Hinault visited the LeMond home in Reno, Nevada, to clinch the signing; according to LeMond, a priority for the French pair was to visit a Wild West store and acquire Stetsons, boots and jackets. The picture of the trio sitting on a fence in complete *A Few Dollars More* rig is now an iconic image of cycling moving into the new world of the 1980s.

For LeMond, the money being offered by Renault wasn't the real draw; more important was the fact that Guimard had restrained Hinault until he was physically mature. He was a coach who would manage a young rider's career. LeMond's early years had the same template as the Badger's: three formative seasons in which he targeted smaller stage races, most notably taking a dominant win in the 1982 Tour de l'Avenir. He did not show Hinault's talent for one-day Classics, but a silver medal in the 1982 world championships was followed by gold the next year. His debut in a major Tour was, like Hinault's, in the Vuelta, which he rode in 1983. He has been described as a thoroughbred, supreme in talent, fragile in nature, mentally and physically. He certainly did not enjoy Hinault's rude health; that Vuelta was wrecked by illness, while in his first Tour, 1984, he struggled early on with a throat infection before coming good late on – as he tended to do when at his best in a Grand Tour – to take third behind Fignon and Hinault.

By the end of the Tour, LeMond's former leader and his new boss Tapie were making overtures. Hinault's indifferent form early in 1984 had led to a crisis meeting a couple of months into the season, at which it was decided to strengthen La Vie Claire for 1985. Steve Bauer of Canada, the Dane Kim Andersen and Hinault's sparring partner in his junior days, Bernard Vallet, were the main reinforcements, plus – eventually – a co-leader: LeMond.

According to one account, Hinault first mentioned the possibility of joining La Vie Claire to LeMond as they sheltered from a snowstorm at the end of the penultimate stage of the Dauphiné Libéré that June. Hinault had just had a brutal reminder of his need for a strong co-leader as he finished second to the Colombian Martin Ramirez.

In keeping with Tapie's image as French sport's playboy king is the tale LeMond tells in both films, of being whisked away from his hotel by a beautiful brown-haired woman on a motorbike during the evening after the finish of the 1984 Tour stage to l'Alpe d'Huez. With LeMond clinging to her waist on the pillion she piloted him to the top of the resort, then took him to a twelfth-floor hotel room where the two Bernards – Hinault still getting over the kicking he had received from Fignon, and the crisis he had had in front of Alain Vigneron – were waiting. Just as when he won over Hinault, Tapie's mind was on his Look pedals: he held one out and asked LeMond if he would like to make more money than he thought possible. As LeMond recalled, it was all terribly James Bond, but with a twist: years later he found the contract promising him a dollar for every Look pedal sold in the US and realised that he had not received a dime.

Being tapped up by Tapie was light years from the olde-worlde way Guimard functioned; the price Tapie offered LeMond was worthy of a new world. For cycling at the time, it was astronomical: a million dollars over three years. It is understood to be at least twice what Hinault was making, although, as Tapie pointed out at the time, it was less than 5 per cent of Look's publicity budget in the US. It more than tripled LeMond's wage at Renault, although he made more than his basic $100,000 at the French team thanks to appearances and endorsements. Guimard tried to retain LeMond, telling him he would win another three Tours at least with him, but with Fignon at his physical peak, both men could see the obvious disadvantage of LeMond remaining at the French team. The La Vie Claire move was an obvious one, given that Hinault was an ageing leader yet to return to his best, and Guimard made no attempt to match the offer.

The cycling historian Benjo Maso highlights the arrival of Tapie in cycling as the start of an era he terms *The Big Money*: the time when cycling made the transition from a small-time sport to a cash-rich business. 'A ten million franc (£1,000,000) budget was pretty over the top back then,' recalls Philippe Crepel. 'This was a time when there were teams of riders who were unemployed and were riding in blank jerseys. You could say you had a ten million franc budget and Bernard Hinault; after that there wasn't much talk of cyclists being *smicards*, low-wage employees.' It marked a massive expansion in budgets: a few years earlier, the French magazine *Miroir du Cyclisme* detailed running costs for one of the country's smaller teams, which had a budget totalling 1,510,000 francs (£151,000).

Bernard Tapie's willingness to buy his way to success was not the driving force behind cycling's economic revolution of the 1980s, but what can be said is that the magnate, Hinault and LeMond joined forces at a key moment in cycling history. From 1982 France's national-ised television stations had had to compete commercially, and from 1984 the Tour could be transmitted worldwide due to the development of communications satellites. That drove the race's viewing audience from 50 million in 1980 to a billion in 1986, making it a marketable commodity for the company who produced the images. Hence French national television's willingness to stump up epic sums for the rights; by the 1990s the rights fees underwrote the entire event, as they still do today.

Worldwide exposure and the TV rights explosion is what has led to the Tour de France being the centre of the professional racing calendar in the twenty-first century, to the unhappy exclusion of events with notable traditions but less lustre. It had other knock-on effects, particularly an influx of multinational sponsors – Panasonic, Hitachi, Coca-Cola and so on – and their need for worldwide publicity led them to hire riders from outside the European heartland. That in turn drove income for the biggest stars, and gave greater market value to cyclists from 'emerging markets' such as the US, Colombia, New Zealand and Scandinavia. Wage inflation drove up team budgets, and here Tapie's willingness to buy success – and critically, to make LeMond's status as cycling's million-dollar-man public – had an effect across the board. In 1980 Renault's budget was £450,000, which was substantial for the time; three years later, La Vie Claire started on more than double that, and that million-pound budget was upped for 1985 to meet LeMond's salary. 'Tapie took LeMond to conquer the US, to give the team a global look,' believes Crepel. Plus, he adds, by July 1984, Tapie was not convinced Hinault would return to his best.

The other Bernard felt differently. Towards the end of the 1984 Tour, during the marathon 320-kilometre stage from Crans-Montana to Villefranche en Beaujolais, Hinault fell into conversation with a young French professional, Guy Gallopin. The Badger was heading for the biggest defeat of his career, but he was bullish: 'You wait until you see the end of season I'm going to have: I will win the Grand Prix des Nations, Tour of Lombardy, then next year I'll win the Giro and Tour.'

The Grand Prix des Nations on 23 September 1984 was a classic turning point, a key test as Hinault had been beaten in all the long time trials in the 1984 Tour. He came in well ahead of some of the pretenders who had progressed in his absence: Kelly, Roche, and most importantly, Fignon. He registered the fastest average to date on the Cannes course in spite of a strong, swirling wind: 44.193km for the 90km. On his low-profile bike with a small front wheel and various aerodynamic bits, he laid the spectre of Fignon to rest – the double Tour winner could manage only fourth, 2min 4sec behind. *Le Grand Retour* was the verdict of *Miroir du Cyclisme*; for the magazine, this was Hinault's return to his old dominance, also the first time that 'he has proved that he is not only a talented athlete but a champion revered by the public'. It was the Poulidor paradox: he had become popular because he had been defeated, and shown human frailty. 'Talent, success, reverence: Bernard Hinault had never managed to unite the three qualities at the same time. But in Cannes, the transformation took place.' He was cheered from start to finish and he compared the reception to when he won the world championship at Sallanches – and the background was the same: a return from injury.

Hinault's view was that he had not won a race since the Four Days of Dunkirk. He clearly didn't include the prologue time trial at the Tour, which is a sign of the prologue's comparative stature back then. Nowadays it would be worth an entire season's racing. The Nations was followed by victory in the Baracchi Trophy. This was a throwback to the glory days of Anquetil, Coppi and Merckx, a two-man team time trial in northern Italy, far more than an exhibition event.[21] He was teamed up with Francesco Moser, who had gained new stature in the winter and spring of 1984, having taken the world hour record, then followed up with Milan–San Remo and the Giro. It was an intriguing match where the two long-term rivals were temporarily teammates but were still determined to look better than the other – so Hinault forced

---

[21] The Baracchi ran from 1949 to 1990 in its two-rider format, reverted to a solo time trial in 1991 – when it was merged abortively with the Grand Prix des Nations – and was then abandoned.

the pace up every hill, and made a point of crossing the finish line ahead of 'Cecco', who had the benefit of using more aerodynamic equipment.

The win that sealed the comeback was the Giro di Lombardia: a classic solo effort, after an attack on the climb of San Fermo della Battaglia, ten kilometres from the finish. 'He was sharing the room with me, he got up and said, "Today I'll win."' recalls Jean-François Bernard. 'He'd abandoned in the Giro del Piemonte three days before, he was completely at a standstill. I was with him there and said to myself, "If he wins today, I don't understand anything any more." That afternoon I was dropped twenty-five kilometres from the finish from the front group, an Italian picked me up in his car and took me to the finish with my bike in the boot – it was always the way in Italy, you didn't have to wait for the broom wagon – we took a short cut and I remember seeing Hinault coming into the finish on his own, putting his arms in the air.' With exquisite irony given Fignon and Renault's utter domination of the Tour, that was enough to give Hinault the Prestige Pernod prize as best French professional of the year. The autumn run of form also made the point that the La Vie Claire project had come of age against the odds, given its leader's form that spring.

The Lombardy win led neatly into the big challenge of 1985: a third Giro victory to set up a Giro–Tour double. The home fans' passionate hostility at the Giro harked back to the past (and ahead to the scenes that formed the backdrop to Stephen Roche's win of 1987). A year earlier an unholy alliance between the organiser, the late Vincenzo Torriani, and the *tifosi*, helped to set up a win for Moser ahead of Laurent Fignon. The 1985 route was relatively flat, with two long time trials designed to favour Moser; the atmosphere was no more favourable to Hinault, who took a decisive advantage on Moser in the stage 12 time trial through Campania from Capua to Maddaloni. So high were feelings running towards the French, that one writer at the race, Robert Guennegan, said he didn't dare go and buy cigarettes on the day of the time trial. As the small French press corps watched Hinault's victory on the television screens in the press room, they could see him wiping the spittle from the *tifosi* off his face, and at one point, a vast poster of Moser wielded by a fan nearly knocked him off his bike.

What they couldn't work out, however, was why the La Vie Claire team car had one back door held wide open, all through the stage. It seemed as if the mechanic was permanently ready to leap out with a spare wheel – but in fact, it was to ensure that the Italian fans kept back off the tarmac, as the *carabinieri* were struggling to create enough space in front of Hinault. They had collided with at least one *tifoso*, confided Tapie afterwards. At the finish, the fans had to be forced back off the finish line to let Hinault come through; as he did, he was narrowly missed by a flying Coke can. 'Next time we will do a Ben Hur,' was Hinault's response. 'We'll put blades on the wheels and cut them up if they don't get out the way. The more they shouted, the more they threw at me, the more they spat at me, the more it stimulated me. I said to myself, "I'll show them what a great champion really is: now, their Giro is over."' The Giro ended with another time trial, from Camaiore to Lucca; Moser won the stage but by only seven seconds, although Hinault's eventual winning margin of just over a minute was well short of what he would have expected in his halcyon days.

LeMond had finished well adrift of Hinault and Moser in the Giro, and the Breton had good reason to be confident when he turned up in Plumelec for the start of the 1985 Tour. The irony was that had the American stayed at Renault he would have ridden that Tour as their leader; that spring, Fignon had suffered the knee injury which was to wreck his career. It was the end of an era for him and Guimard. At the end of 1985, Renault pulled out of both Formula One and cycling, partly due to pressure from the unions, who objected to the money Renault paid out on sport. 'A catastrophic industrial decision and a national trauma,' was Guimard's view.

'Without Fignon I don't see who can beat us,' was Hinault's verdict. 'Millar, Roche, Anderson? They always have an off day.' The prologue was made for the local boy, drawing a crowd of 50,000 to the circuit at Plumelec. It included the celebrated Cadoudal hill, which is still used for the Grand Prix de Plumelec Morbihan, including, the day before the main event, an open time trial on the course so that amateurs can match themselves against Hinault's winning time from 1985. A total of four days were spent in Brittany, with the third stage a team time trial into Fougères dominated by La Vie Claire, not surprisingly given that four of the team had finished in the first nine in the prologue. Koechli adopted a radical strategy, making the riders who were slightly lower on form use slightly faster wheels than their stronger teammates, so that everyone raced on an equal footing. Afterwards, eight out of the nine figured in the first nine overall, with only the Belgian Eric Vanderaerden in yellow, thanks to generous time bonuses. In a classic show of strength, the next day La Vie Claire sent their Dane Kim Andersen up the road en route to Pont-Audemer and put him in the yellow jersey.

Another twenty-four hours later, the stage into Roubaix over the cobbles put paid to most of the Colombian climbers, who lost time apart from Fabio Parra, but LeMond began to move up the standings as he picked up one time bonus after another. Following stage 7 into Nancy he was two seconds ahead of Hinault, meaning that he would start the time trial between Sarrebourg and Strasbourg ahead of his nominal leader. At seventy-five kilometres, this was an extraordinarily long *contre la montre*, designed to play to Hinault's strengths as the ones at the Giro had been for Moser. The moment that summed up his dominance came after fifty-three kilometres when he overtook Kelly, who had started two minutes earlier – it was also an image of cycling's transition from ancient to modern, with the Irishman time trialling on a standard road bike with toe clips and straps, floppy brake cables and making no concessions to aerodynamics other than a skinsuit. Hinault, on the other hand, was sporting a teardrop-shaped helmet, and riding a low-profile bike influenced by the aerodynamic aids popularised by Moser after his hour record the previous year: it had a small front wheel and rear disc, not to mention his clipless pedals.

The time trial left LeMond the nearest challenger at 2min 32sec but both Anderson and Roche were nigh on four minutes adrift; the Tour was not over, but it was La Vie Claire's to lose. The next morning, to make the point, Hinault put his team on the front for the first hour through the Vosges, covered at 45kph, so that the climbers were worn out by the time they reached the opening first-category climb of the Tour, the Champ du Feu. What followed three days later on the first major mountain stage was classic Hinault: amid expectations that he would ride defensively as in the past, he made a pre-emptive attack on the Pas de Morgins with the strongest climber in the race, the Colombian Luis Herrera. 'I had warned my teammates I would attack at the foot of the climb – I attacked on a level crossing, and it was so unlikely that no one expected it.'

The unspoken agreement en route to Morzine between Hinault and Herrera was standard; the mountains jersey for the Colombian, a big boost overall for the Frenchman, who pushed his lead to exactly four minutes on LeMond, with Roche the only other rider within six minutes. According to Pedro Delgado, it went further: 'As he was intelligent, [Hinault] reached a tacit agreement with the Colombians. He would help Herrera to win the King of the Mountains and to win stages [Herrera won two]. In exchange, the Cafe de Colombia team would control the stages on the crucial climbs, and his riders would not carry out those mad attacks that blew the race apart.' The time trial at Villard de Lans enabled him to push his lead to 5min 23sec. This was positively Merckx-esque.

Hinault's immense lead after Villard de Lans prompts the question: what would have happened had the Badger stayed upright on Cours Fauriel at Saint-Étienne the following day? Had Hinault ridden untroubled right through to Paris with such a huge advantage, might he have been tempted to state loud and clear that he wanted to go for a sixth Tour in 1986? Quite who or what caused the crash at Saint-Étienne remains open to debate. Hinault was in a group sprinting for tenth place behind a small group including LeMond, Delgado and Millar; the race leader blamed Phil Anderson, the Australian is adamant he was not responsible. What mattered was the outcome of the touch of wheels: Hinault landed on his face, breaking his nose in two places after his Ray-Ban aviator sunglasses slammed into the bridge. The images of him picking himself up and crossing the line covered in blood were impressive: one, from *Miroir du Cyclisme*, shows his face close up in a double-page spread, blood dripping off his temple and down his nose. A few seconds after the crash, however, he had the clarity of mind to ask the race organiser Jacques Goddet if the group had been in the final kilometre, which meant he would be given the same time as the first rider in his group; they had, so there was no need to hurry across the line.

The double fracture of the nose left him looking like a boxer who has had a bad day in the ring, with two black eyes. 'When I look in the mirror, I'm scared of myself,' he says. The next morning, the major issue – on top of the debilitating effect on his system as his body coped with the toxins released by the contusions – was that he had slept in a T-shirt and the wounds had wept into it. His priority was to show that he was anything but a broken man. 'He rode in the front line all day to show how hard he was; he insisted on riding at the front so no one would attack,' recalled Robert Millar. 'Everyone thought that with the injuries he had received, he would never finish the next day and sure enough the Colombians all attacked on the climb out of Saint-Étienne,' recalled Paul Sherwen. 'He got to the front with his team, and rode tempo for ninety minutes, then turned round and said, "OK, what do you think guys?"' This was not the only show of strength from the peloton's *patron* in that Tour: one subplot of the race was a battle with a new professional, Joël Pelier. Hinault called him to order when he attempted to break away early in the mountain stage from Morzine to Lans-en-Vercors, and chased him down again later in the race. 'I'm not riding the race to sit on his wheel,' was Pelier's summary, which was worthy of the Badger in his youth.

Two stages across central France took the Tour to the final major challenge: the stage through the Pyrenees to Luz Ardiden, via two major *cols*, the Aspin and Tourmalet.

Hinault was suffering, mainly due to bronchitis brought on by the congestion in his broken nose; at the stage finishes he could be seen wrapped up like a child going to school in winter. In chilly, misty conditions which did nothing for his inflamed lungs, it was Renault who set the pace on the Aspin – quite possibly Guimard's way of getting revenge on his former protégé – with the upshot that the lead group split apart on the Tourmalet. 'I [could] see Hinault yelling at Herrera,' recalled Delgado. 'And that was the moment I attacked.' With the Spaniard went LeMond and Roche, and a few other opportunists. After the lead built up, what happened remains a matter of controversy; LeMond was told to remain in Roche's slipstream unless he could dislodge the Irishman and escape solo.

'He didn't know what to do,' said Roche of LeMond's dilemma. 'He wasn't fully committed really…He kept jumping away, but he wasn't going full on. He would attack, get a gap, then let me get back up to him and ride, then he'd attack again.' Roche confesses that he didn't commit fully either. 'He was peed off with that, I was peed off with him because he wouldn't ride. It was a stalemate. I didn't want to ride 100 per cent because Hinault was two minutes back, and I calculated that if I let Greg get the overall lead I might beat him in the time trial. I was just controlling Greg – the only way I could ensure he didn't get away was not to give it 100 per cent.'

The arguments between LeMond and Maurice Le Guilloux in the team car – Koechli was behind Hinault, further down the mountain – were played out on live television, with LeMond's frustration all too apparent. Koechli, on the other hand, remains adamant that there is no way the American would have been permitted to collaborate with Roche. His specific orders were to get rid of the Irishman, as Roche well knew, but the Dubliner's recollections of the time gaps the lead group were given is at variance with that of LeMond, who believes Hinault was several minutes behind. 'They misled me,' says Roche. 'Hinault was only a minute behind us, they told us it was two minutes because they knew I would figure Greg was the threat. If I thought it was a minute I was going to ride hard, but I thought it was two minutes, so I thought Hinault had blown. In fact he was at forty-five seconds, he was closing. Koechli was trying to save the Tour, because he wasn't sure whether Greg would beat me in the final time trial, so he wanted to keep his options open. Greg was frustrated because he wanted to get away from me, but I wasn't going to let him go.'

Supported mainly by the Swiss Niki Rüttiman, Hinault lost just over a minute to LeMond and Roche at the finish, where the American was clearly outraged that he had not been given the go-ahead to collaborate with Roche. 'If Hinault was in my place he wouldn't have waited,' he angrily told the television cameras. His immediate reaction was that he wanted to quit the Tour. The next day, the race climbed the Col d'Aubisque via the Col du Soulor for what was essentially a fifty-three-kilometre hill-climb stage where Roche scored a solo victory. Behind, Hinault suffered when LeMond set a hot pace in the chase group, from which he was dropped before he managed to grapple his way back on. It was dramatic stuff, the more so because it was simply impossible to tell whether LeMond was chasing Roche, or trying to dislodge his nominal leader. But as at Luz Ardiden, Hinault's Tour was saved, just.

'Without my crash, it would have been an easy win,' Hinault told Jean-Marie Leblanc of *L'Équipe* at Bordeaux, as the race headed for Paris, with his fifth win beckoning. 'The opposition was trapped between me and Greg. We blocked them easily. It's true that Greg's support has really helped. I've played straight with him: he had his chance at Saint-Étienne and he repaid the favour at Luz Ardiden. There was no clash. He had the normal reaction of an ambitious young rider. He was wound up by the people from CBS who led him to believe he'd been deprived of the yellow jersey.'

'I could have easily taken the Tour in 1985 – I would have won by three minutes that year,' was LeMond's view when I interviewed him in 1994. Perhaps, but had the break ridden flat-out en route to Luz Ardiden, Roche would have had a say in the matter too. In Richard Moore's *Slaying the Badger*, LeMond went further: 'It's not just the stage to Luz Ardiden that made the difference: it was the next day. If you watch the stage on the Col d'Aubisque, Hinault was dropped four or five times. I basically pushed him up the climb to keep his lead. He had his peak at the first time trial and then he was going slowly downhill.'

*

Hinault doesn't buy the LeMond version of events, obviously, but he remains convinced that of his five Tour de France wins, 1985 was probably the toughest, due to his broken nose. 'But even when I was lying on the ground I never thought I might have lost. As long as my legs were going round well, in my head I knew I could win, no problem. I never asked myself if I might be going to lose a Tour, even in 1979 when Joop Zoetemelk took a lot of time out of me on the stage to Roubaix.'

But that Tour comes down to one question: could LeMond have won it, and should he have been given his head? For Roche, La Vie Claire's management of the Luz Ardiden stage made sense – as it did to most European observers – although Roche believes that had LeMond been given the all clear, he could probably have won. Robert Millar feels that 'Greg was probably better than Hinault in that Tour, but Hinault was smarter than Greg. Greg was probably slightly intimidated, even though they were on the same team.' Bernard Vallet had a subtly different view at the time: 'Bernard is more sure of himself and his strength than he's ever been. He may not be as good as he used to be in the high mountains, but he knows how to be at his best precisely when he needs to be. Greg has the class to win the Tour, but I don't know if he's hungry enough.'

When on song, LeMond always finished a Tour strongly, and 1985 was no exception; his extraordinary final week enabled him to close to 1min 42sec behind Hinault in the overall standings. However, his victory in the Lac de

Vassivière time trial, his first stage victory in the Tour, could not make up for the fact that he had not performed at the two key moments when Hinault built his Tour-winning lead: the Strasbourg time trial, and the stage to Morzine. There was even speculation in the French press that Hinault had slowed down deliberately at Vassivière, to give his teammate the win; LeMond asked Hinault the question as well.

Hinault was not having any of that, but 1986 would be different, he said: at the start of the Tour, he had told a packed press conference in Brittany that he would return the following year as *capitaine de route* to ensure a win for LeMond, and he repeated that after Vassivière. 'The *caravane* have seen a passing of the baton. I will repeat it again, loud and clear. Next year in the Tour, I will be just the road captain. I will raise hell in the race to make Greg win and make sure I have some fun. That's a promise.' *L'Équipe* didn't view it quite so solemnly: their cartoonist drew Hinault on a bicycle and LeMond on a child's scooter. 'Because you've been so well behaved, I'll put you on my handlebars next year,' says the Badger. LeMond's reply is: 'Thanks, Uncle Bernard.'

CHAPTER 13

HEADS I WIN, TAILS YOU LOSE

'If Hinault wins [the Tour] a sixth time he'll be a hero. But if he makes LeMond win, he'll also be one.'

– Jacques Anquetil, *L'Équipe*, 1986

The mind loves the unknown, said René Magritte. Indeed, much of road cycling's allure lies in what it leaves unsaid. Mystery has lent an aura of myth to the Tour de France since its creation in 1903, and it remains one of the things that sets cycling apart even in the days of live television, live blogging and real-time power outputs. It is no longer quite the case that, as Geoffrey Nicholson wrote, riders spend much of a Tour de France stage in slightly worried ignorance of what is happening around them, but there are plenty of times when the totality of events in a given race cannot be grasped, because there can be a plethora of actors – many of whom don't know precisely what is going on at a given moment, even though they are major players in the drama – and an endlessly changing tactical dynamic. The result is clear; the intricacies of what happened usually far less so.

The bare facts of the 1986 Tour de France are well known: Bernard Hinault versus Greg LeMond in the ultimate fratricidal/parricidal battle between two teammates. Hinault has agreed to help LeMond win but he takes an early and emphatic lead overall in the Pyrenees. He makes a second, fruitless attack and crumbles, enabling LeMond to recoup most of his deficit but by now LeMond is convinced his teammate is out to entrap him. Hinault suffers a calf injury, enabling LeMond to take the yellow jersey in the Alps; the next day the pair attack together and cross the line hand in hand at l'Alpe d'Huez only for Hinault to declare immediately that the Tour is not over, not just yet. Treason, cries LeMond, and the atmosphere remains poisonous all the way to Paris. In fact, it remains pretty tense to this day. In 2013, to celebrate the race's centenary, Philippe Bouvet of *L'Équipe* got the two men together on the Alpe to pick over the moment. It was perfectly amicable, he told me, but LeMond's conclusion didn't exactly spell truce: 'I was fucked over a bit, but I'm not angry about it.'

Pressing the button marked '1986 Tour de France' was an entertaining part of interviews with Hinault and LeMond in 1993 and 1994, when memories of the race were still relatively fresh, and feelings still raw. Hinault was defensive, bordering on the grumpy. 'For me, there was nothing to discuss. As far as I was concerned, he was the one who was going to win the Tour and that was all, right?' He was adamant that if he had wanted to win the Tour, 'OK, there would have been no problem. Of course I could have won. When you've got five minutes on the first day in the mountains, what do you do? I didn't win five Tours by being on holiday. I could have just sat on Greg's wheel and from then on the race would have been over. With five minutes' lead, I could have been under-hand. Who pays the team, who gives them their salary? I could have just said, "OK Greg, now you're working for Bernard Hinault."'

A year later, I was able to put Hinault's view to LeMond, something that had not been done since 1986. LeMond, predictably, was outraged. 'That's total bullshit. It was a nightmare on that team. It was pure war. We didn't even talk at dinner. He can look at it and say there's no doubt that the pushing and fighting made the race so aggressive that we destroyed everybody. But I remember that l'Alpe d'Huez stage. If he could have taken two or three minutes out of me with my teammates, that is what he would have tried to do. That is what would have happened if I had not gone for it on the [Col du] Télégraphe. Everything Hinault did was in some way to screw me.'

On 21 January 1986, Hinault was awarded the Légion d'honneur by president François Mitterrand, the ultimate proof of his acceptance into the establishment. The photo-graph shows Hinault – bow tie around his neck – looking the president firmly in the eye – the two men were pretty much the same height. Mitterrand's speech eulogised Hinault's tenacity and courage, the latter quality being, the president said, 'the raising agent of a nation. It is an exemplary value, and examples are what a nation seeks above all else.' To win a bike race, Mitterrand said, required 'bravery, steadfastness, intelligence. You gauge your effort as you conduct your life. When a race is being led by Bernard Hinault, you know what's going on in his head and that's very important.' Fine words from an Elysées speechwriter, but it didn't look that way in July that year to LeMond and the rest of the cycling world – perhaps even to Hinault himself.

The key decision that informed the background to that Tour had been taken several years earlier, in 1982, when Hinault announced that he would retire on his thirty-second birth-day. The knowledge he was leaving cycling on 14 November 1986 impacted on every race he rode after his fifth Tour had been won in July 1985. The next fifteen months would be an extended *Tournée d'Adieu*, or farewell tour, in which Hinault would race in unaccustomed places – the Coors Classic in the US, in which he won a brace of stages in August 1985 and which he would win overall the following year, the Clásico RCN in spring 1986. The 1986 Tour would be the highlight but he was under no pressure other than the need to end his career respectably.

LeMond's position was the complete opposite. At the start of the 1986 season, the La Vie Claire coach Paul

Koechli said publicly that it was time for the American to lose his timidity and 'take the reins'. But a major win kept eluding him: he had taken the silver medal at the 1985 world championship in Italy, and finished second in Milan–San Remo in March 1986. In the run-in to the 1986 Tour he would finish fourth in the Giro – a target where he was foiled partly by a route that was light on mountains to favour Moser and company – and third in the Tour of Switzerland behind his and Hinault's teammate Andy Hampsten. LeMond was at precisely that tough stage in his career when an electric prospect has to become more than a promise; a single stage win in the Giro was not the level of success required of a leader who needed to assert his authority.

The Tour was presented as a rerun of the Hinault–Fignon match of 1984, as Guimard's leader – now sponsored by Système-U supermarkets – had regained something that looked, superficially at least, like form. The resonances of a rematch of 1984 were impossible for the French press to ignore in spite of the promises made to LeMond at the end of the 1985 Tour. And from the off, Hinault acted more like La Vie Claire's leader than LeMond; he finished two seconds ahead of the American in the Friday evening's prologue time trial won by Fignon's teammate Thierry Marie, the rider my club-mates and I had travelled to the Lisieux criterium to support the previous July. It was Hinault who decided that La Vie Claire should slow down in the team time trial the following afternoon, to wait for the Swiss riders,

Niki Rüttiman and Guido Winterberg, who were suffering the after-effects of crashes in the morning's stage. Hinault and LeMond's loss of almost two minutes to Système-U placed the ball firmly in Fignon's court.

Compared to their early dominance in 1985, La Vie Claire took a back seat for a few days, so much so that Tapie called Maurice Le Guilloux and asked him, 'What the hell are you all up to?' The paymaster flew in to Nantes airport the night before stage 9, the first long time trial; Le Guilloux expected the boss to gather the team together and deliver a hair-drying. Instead, Tapie told them wryly, 'Well done, you've been invisible for a week, you must be as fresh as daisies.' That ignored a classic Hinault move on stage 6 to Cherbourg, when he pressed on after taking second in an intermediate sprint, taking eleven others with him to gain ninety seconds with the stage barely begun. The chase lasted seventy kilometres, earning him plaudits from the home press. 'We love our Bernard Hinault, a champion pure and simple,' wrote Jacques Goddet, 'capable of turning any situation upside down, seizing the initiative in the most unlikely manner.' The time gain was minimal, the tone for the Hinault PR offensive was set.

The time trial, over 61.5km, went Hinault's way, with LeMond 44sec slower after a wheel change. Although Fignon crumbled here, other favourites were taking position thanks to strong earlier rides in the team time trial: Stephen Roche was now 5sec ahead of Hinault with Robert Millar just 1min 24sec back after riding one of the best time trials of his career. Afterwards, Millar was hotly favoured to win one of the most mountainous Tours of the 1980s; Hinault's goal was to eliminate climbers such as the Scot and Colombians Luis Herrera and Fabio Parra: 'They aren't well built, they have no reserves. So you have to attack them until they have nothing left, until they don't manage to recuperate enough. It's easy.'

Another tactic Hinault frequently adopted was a pre-emptive strike on the first mountain stage as the specialist climbers struggled with the transition from churning massive gears on the flat stages to spinning tiny ratios in the mountains. They would improve as the mountain stages piled up; all-rounders like Hinault would hold their form at best. The stratagem had worked in 1985 en route to Morzine with LeMond marking the chasers; in 1986, the scenario between Bayonne and Pau on stage 12 was exactly the same, but rather than Lucho Herrera, Hinault had Pedro Delgado for company. 'Hinault always had a concept of cycling as something epic,' says the Spaniard. 'It must have been a good hundred kilometres from the finish when he said to his teammate Jean-François Bernard that he should go for it, just after a hot spot sprint.'

'[Hinault] said to me, "Accelerate,"' recalled Bernard, 'so I went for it, the gap opened and he said, "À *fond*, flat out, we'll ride as far as the intermediate sprint." Delgado and Erik Breukink came across to us, but the peloton didn't budge. He said, "Go flat out." I didn't think about waiting for LeMond.' Delgado takes up the story: 'Bernard took us to the foot of the Col de Marie-Blanque; on the climb, Hinault said I shouldn't attack and it would be better if we both went for it all the way to the finish. I had a lot of respect for him and I knew it was a long way from the top to the finish in Pau and there wouldn't be any way I'd stay away even if I dropped him. So we tackled the stage as a unit and without having spoken about who would win the stage, he was good enough not to fight for the sprint.'

Asked if it was clear that Hinault was going for the yellow jersey on the stage to Pau despite nothing being said, Delgado agrees. 'It was clear. What he wanted was that sixth Tour de France. We didn't talk in the break. We didn't even bother to negotiate. That's why I went behind him in the last kilometre, and he just went flat out, the whole way to the finish. What he wanted was the general classification. He didn't care about the stage win.' Luckily for LeMond, the American was able to elude the remnants of the chasing group late in the stage, with only Herrera for company, but he still rode into Pau 4min 37sec behind Hinault and Delgado, and his nominal *capitaine de route* pulled on the yellow jersey with 5min 25sec in hand.

'After that stage, LeMond said to us, "I don't know why Hinault is doing this to me,"' recalled the television commentator Phil Liggett. LeMond had been taken by surprise – 'It looks like I'm going to finish second again,' was his view after the stage – but he was not the only one. 'No one told Hinault to attack on the first Pyrenean stage, especially not with a *client* like Delgado,' said Le Guilloux. 'We weren't happy, neither me nor Paul Koechli. He did not behave like someone who was trying to set up the win for his teammate. It provoked a total schism in the team.' But in reality, who was going to gainsay the Badger? At the finish, Hinault was in high spirits: 'Now we are sure of winning the Tour.' His aggression had eliminated Roche, who lost twenty minutes, and Fignon, who was twelve minutes back and would abandon the next day.

The following day, Hinault was at it again. This attack was completely unexpected, on the descent from the Col du Tourmalet, just after the village of La Mongie, where there are few tight hairpins, making for a super fast run to the bottom. It was early in the stage; there were three major climbs to come. It was completely against tactical convention, and against team orders. 'We had all met together [before the stage], the only thing that was said was, "Above all, Bernard, you don't attack. That is the key thing. You remain in the peloton. You have only to follow,"' recalled Jean-François Bernard. 'Suddenly, bam! Off he went. We thought it was a joke. He wanted to kill off the Tour.' 'I didn't brake until the bottom,' recalled Hinault. '[There] I had a forty-five-second lead. I wasn't going to sit up. I wanted to force riders like Delgado, Roche and Anderson to chase, which they did.'

As Hinault has stated repeatedly, if he had been determined to win the Tour after Pau, he had only to follow

LeMond. In spite of his reputation for attacking at every turn, this second attack was very much out of character. In the ten Grand Tours he won, Hinault never made a superfluous attack in the mountains once he had a comfortable time cushion. On the other hand, in nine of those races he had Guimard to guide him, and in the tenth, the 1985 Tour, he was handicapped by illness. What's certain is that this was not a move that Guimard would have tolerated; his former *directeur sportif* said, 'The Tour was over, then he made the mistake he should not have made.' In his memoirs, Guimard described the attack as 'foolish...to no purpose'.

Hinault's contention has always been that 'LeMond had only to come with me. I was in front, he had only to follow.' 'I'd have waited,' he told Chène; on the other hand, Le Guilloux recalls driving alongside him and telling him to steady up, only to be told, 'I'll put fifteen minutes into them.' This was mere bravado: hunger knock ensured that LeMond caught up with him on the descent from the penultimate climb, the Col de Peyresourde, along with a little chase group that included Millar, Herrera, Hampsten and Urs Zimmermann of Switzerland; LeMond went on to win the stage, winning back almost all the time he had lost en route to Pau.

As is well known, LeMond does not accept his teammate's explanation that all this attacking was a plan to tire out the opposition: 'Hinault has to justify that attitude,' he told me in 1994. 'But I don't know how people could interpret his breaking away with Delgado [to Pau] and again the next day [on the Tourmalet descent]. He knew he had to do a knockout punch on me to be assured of victory.' By now, La Vie Claire was an unhappy team, with the atmosphere in the hotel variously described as 'wretched' and 'highly tense'. LeMond, says Abt, was 'almost hysterical'.

Two days of uneasy truce followed – including a stage win for La Vie Claire's Niki Rüttiman at Blagnac – then as the race reached the Alpine foothills, Hinault went on the attack again, en route to Gap, where Jean-François Bernard took the stage; LeMond was incandescent after a forty-five-minute chase. 'What's his problem?' was Hinault's riposte. 'Are his legs hurting? It might be just as well if he quits if he doesn't want to win the race any more.' Realising that there might be occasions when he would not have teammates around to help him chase – on the Gap stage, Bernard and Niki Rüttiman were ahead with Hinault – LeMond resorted to asking Millar if his team, Panasonic, would assist him. In exchange, he said he would not impede the Scot if he looked likely to win a stage.

Millar says, 'I seem to remember some kind of deal was done [but] it would have been a decision above my pay grade and made about a kilometre behind in the melee of team cars by those better placed to judge the merits of such an offer.' According to the Scot, as well as having to worry about LeMond, Hinault faced opponents who were only too happy to make him suffer when he was on the back foot. 'There were also times when Hinault was suffering and there were plenty of volunteers to keep him that way. I don't think the Badger would have liked it any other way as he raced to dominate and therefore must have expected retribution from the weaklings when he fell to their level.'

'LeMond was green with rage,' wrote Hinault in his memoirs. 'I explained that it was me who was the boss in the race and I knew what I was doing. The proof was that Bernard won the stage.' In Gap, when he spoke to the press after finishing the stage, LeMond threatened to quit the Tour, and he repeated this to Tapie's face later in the hotel. Interviewed that evening, the La Vie Claire boss was adamant that LeMond was the team's chosen leader: he would love Hinault to win, he said, with an eye to French hearts, but adding, 'We made an agreement last year, the best man will win and we know who that is.'

On the first day in the Alps, LeMond was the best man, taking a conclusive lead when Hinault was overcome by pain at the back of his left knee, at the top of the calf muscle – which he later put down to an unexpected change in saddle height, as at the 1983 Vuelta. At the stage finish on the Col du Granon – the highest summit finish in the Tour to that date – he dropped back to third overall behind LeMond and Zimmermann, 2min 47 back from the American.

The La Vie Claire hotel in Gap that evening was a busy place. Hinault called a meeting and told the team he was disappointed at losing second place to Zimmermann;

attacking the Swiss would now be their priority. Later that night, Tapie flew in, and tried to restore order between his two leaders. That set the scene for what those present felt was a moment of sporting beauty – a celebrated stage finish with Hinault and LeMond, the old champion and the young pretender, the two rivals, crossing the line hand in hand atop l'Alpe d'Huez, their faces wreathed in smiles. But it followed a tense little spell after more Hinault attacks, initially on the climb of the Galibier and – successfully – at the top of the descent from the Galibier towards the village of Valloire.

LeMond's response, after the drop into Valloire, was to ask Koechli – alongside in the team car – what he should do. 'You want to win the Tour – drop Zimmermann and catch Hinault,' was the answer. The coach added: 'It was probably the only time I saw Greg attack, as hard as he could, not a counter-attack.' A few metres from the top of the Col de Télégraphe – the five kilometre ascent that follows the drop to Valloire – LeMond finally dislodged Zimmermann. Later, he told me that had he not done so, he could have ended up in precisely the same situation as on the drop off the Tourmalet – but with the difference that Hinault had two teammates with him, Bauer and – at that point – Guido Winterberg. 'If he could have taken two or three minutes out of me with my teammates, that is what he would have tried to do. That is what would have happened if I had not gone for it on the Télégraphe.'

On the plunge from the Télégraphe to the Maurienne valley, LeMond saved his race. Up ahead, Hinault overhauled two earlier escapees, his and LeMond's team-mate Steve Bauer and the Spaniard Pello Ruiz Cabestany; by Saint Jean de Maurienne, the three had been joined by LeMond, with Zimmermann chasing behind. The race then headed south again over the Col du Croix de Fer, where Hinault and LeMond forged ahead, with Zimmermann cracking behind. 'On the Croix de Fer we let him get close; Greg wanted to react. I said, "Let him come, let him come." When we got a time check that [Zimmermann] was at thirty seconds, whee…Bye-bye. You kill the guy; that's the game, it's pure pleasure when you do that.' A breakneck descent to the Romanche valley took the pair to l'Alpe d'Huez; Hinault led them up the climb, although it was impossible to tell whether it was to protect his teammate from the crowds, or to ensure that LeMond didn't set too severe a pace.

The finale was, said LeMond, orchestrated by Tapie, who told him that he had won the Tour, and Hinault should be given the stage in recognition of his career achievements. The shared moment at the top looked like reconciliation, shared recognition of their joint dom-inance. It was the latter rather than the former: Hinault wasn't prepared to give LeMond peace of mind, yet. As he and LeMond faced that evening's post-stage television interview with Jacques Chancel, the crowd could be heard shouting his name; Hinault had the look of a man who has broken the teacher's ruler as he answered the question, 'Will you continue to attack each other?' '*Si nous faisons la guerre, ce sera une guerre loyale,*' he answered – 'If we fight, it will be an honourable battle.' He added: it will not be over until the time trial at Saint-Étienne.

The following day Hinault sowed more seeds of doubt, at the press conference during the rest day at the Alpe, in the ski resort's chapel. 'I'm very proud, but let me say one more time: the Tour isn't over. Who was the stronger on the climb? Go on, ask Greg.' The response from the French press was all there in *L'Équipe*'s headline: 'Hinault: It's Not Over'. A sceptic would note that this is a headline which would sell far more papers than one that read: 'Hinault: I Give Up'.

'I couldn't believe what I was hearing,' recalls Sam Abt. 'Hinault was saying it wasn't over after this glorious moment in sport. I'd have thought he went through that night thinking, "Jeez, I did a beautiful thing," but from his reaction he went to bed thinking, "I didn't shake Greg but I can still win the Tour." The finish hand in hand was overwhelming, beautiful, one of the great moments in sport – everyone thought it was perfect, Greg letting Hinault win the stage, the way they had wiped out the opposition, the setting – those twenty-one hairpins, hundreds of thousands of people. It was monumental. Monumental. It was obvious the race was over; it would have been a big part of Hinault's legacy if the morning after l'Alpe d'Huez he had said, "I did my best, I've tried to make Greg tougher, it's not going to happen for me, so for the next week I'll work for Greg." Instead ... the basic treachery – "it's not over". It wasn't

Hinault's fault that he was so ignoble because he's a pretty base guy. He's from a background that doesn't expect nobility.'

'Ignoble', 'base', 'treachery': that is one way of looking at it. An alternative view would be that Hinault was stating the obvious and that the old champion had the right to decide when he would abdicate. But this in turn set the scene for what has been described as a cycling thriller – two days where every word and act could be interpreted, reinterpreted, and overinterpreted. LeMond was warned by the organiser Jacques Goddet to be 'careful' – his wife Kathy and his father Bob bought all the food he ate, to ensure no one tampered with it. When LeMond fell off on a right-hand corner in the Saint-Étienne time trial, Kathy immediately thought, 'Sabotage.' There was a rumour that Hinault's old junior rival and former teammate Bernard Vallet had offered to nobble LeMond by falling off in front of him.

Going into Saint-Étienne, Hinault was again on the attack – with Bauer and Hampsten leading a feverish chase behind their own teammate – and in the time trial, the Badger did finish ahead of LeMond, but only by twenty-five seconds in spite of the American's crash and subsequent bike change. The pair's dominance was easily read: at the finish, Hinault caught Zimmermann, who had started three minutes ahead of him, and the Swiss ended up almost eleven minutes behind LeMond in the overall standings. By the final mountaintop finish at the Puy de Dome, Hinault had at last given up the fight, and he then made a point of assisting LeMond when he crashed on the final stage into Paris.

Hinault made his case for the way he had ridden at the end of the race. 'I've thrown everything at Greg. I've pushed him as hard as I can and spared him nothing and have put him under maximum pressure. If he doesn't buckle that means he's a champion and deserves to win the race. I did it for his own good. Next year maybe he'll have to fight off another opponent who will make life miserable for him. Now he'll know how to fight back.'

LeMond's interpretation of events has changed little over the years. '[Hinault] made promises to me that he never intended to keep,' he told Abt. 'He made them just to relieve the pressure on himself. I wish he had said at the start of the Tour that it was every man for himself. But he didn't.' Eight years later, he told me, 'He can look at it and say there's no doubt the pushing and fighting made the race so aggressive we destroyed everybody. Everything he did was to try and screw me. At l'Alpe d'Huez he asked to lead the race up because I'd won overall...then he said it's not over.'

The notion that the Badger was racing purely to help LeMond seems absurd; as the American said the next morning to Sam Abt: 'He wanted to win the Tour, and so did I.' If Hinault had been racing purely to win the Tour, however, with the intention of stabbing his teammate in the back, he would have wielded the dagger far more efficiently. Jacques Anquetil's view was that

Hinault had acknowledged there was a chance he might win the Tour – apparently he had a clause in his criterium contracts that stated that if he won the Tour, he would have the right to pull out. As Anquetil saw it, that meant he had the notion that if he were to win the Tour, he would simply announce his retirement on the Champs-Elysées. But accepting the possibility he might win does not mean he set out with the intention of breaking LeMond.

Abt's conclusion at the time was this: 'Once it started, [Hinault] went for victory – not to set a record of six triumphs, for Hinault is sincerely uninterested in records, but because he was unable not to try to win. Even LeMond, who felt betrayed, could acknowledge that Hinault had not acted out of malice, but simply had been unable to restrain himself from seeking victory.' Now, the writer says the same thing: 'Hinault was unable to hold himself back. I don't think he went to the Tour determined to try and win it. I think he was honest enough to keep his word and help Greg to try and win it. Things got out of hand, suddenly he's five minutes ahead and it just ran away with him.'

Robert Millar believes that in 1986 Hinault was trying to beat LeMond, in the only way he knew – by psychological warfare. 'He was trying to crack Greg. He saw that Greg was better in the places that mattered [so] he rode to his strengths, used Greg when he could, and intimidated everyone to keep things under control. Tapie didn't care who won – it was fantastic publicity either way, it was back to the days of Anquetil and Poulidor, two rivals who didn't like each other.'

It may be merely being wise after the event, but Koechli maintains that at La Vie Claire that year he was trying to implement a new kind of cycling, an unstructured model, 'a concept where there was no leader. Anyone could do anything at any time. We didn't have a leader.' In this reading of the race, Koechli supports Hinault's view that by racing so anarchically he was favouring LeMond's ultimate victory. 'Hinault didn't attack LeMond, he attacked. Period. LeMond thought Hinault was only riding against him. That's not true. To use Hinault against our opponents, by definition he has momentarily to ride against LeMond.'

Millar agrees that Hinault achieved his aim of destroying the riders who might give him trouble in the mountains – Millar and the Colombian climbers. 'He would attack on the downhills, he would attack on the false flats. If he saw you down the back of the bunch, he'd put his team on the front and make them ride.' He says this was the hardest of the four Tours he had ridden to that date; after riding strongly as far as the Alps, he finally quit when his health gave out. 'It didn't suit us climbers at all. By the bottom of a descent I'd be suffering because I'd been doing so many sprints to keep up coming down the mountain; I'd be in trouble in the valley and he'd ride there too, and on the next hill I'd be dropped. It was because I started in good condition, and he saw me as a threat. He saw I had that weakness and seized on it. I wasn't alone either.'

Hinault has frequently asserted that the notion of winning a sixth Tour to take the absolute record was not important to him, and he repeated it in 2014: 'I don't care about records. Records are there to be broken but I never wondered whether I was going to win five or six Tours. What was important for me was the pleasure of riding. When I was racing the question never entered my head. I could have won in 1986 but I wasn't bothered about winning six Tours.' Hinault was consistent in this: when he won his fifth Tour, he expressed no interest in it as a milestone.

In 1986, Hinault fell into two pitfalls he had set himself. Think Pooh Bear falling into the Heffalump trap – twice. Pitfall one: the Badger is not a man who goes back on his word; this means that having said he will ensure a LeMond victory he has no option but to go through with that. Pitfall two: even when he has the race at his mercy – whether or not this was premeditated, it is what happened – the Badger cannot restrain himself. There is a consensus here – Alain Vigneron: 'Hinault fell on his face due to his own pride and excess of zeal.' Jean-François Bernard: '[He] should have won the 1986 Tour, the problem was he wanted to add more to what he had.' Jean-René Bernaudeau: 'Hinault was beaten by Hinault, not by LeMond. He has the jersey, he has a big lead, and he attacks again. LeMond picks up the body.' In Guimard's view, Hinault should have won that Tour, 'against all logic'.

Delgado agrees: 'He had the Tour in his pocket but he

was determined to win with panache. Due to his determination to win the Tour *a lo grande* his attacks backfired completely. And from [Superbagnères], LeMond just had to watch him. I always liked Hinault and his vision of epic cycling, sometimes he got it right, sometimes he messed it up. I had the feeling, always, that he wanted to win the Tour. LeMond's only objective was to sit on Hinault's wheel and he didn't do anything for himself to win that first Tour.'

In the 1986 Tour, two different visions of cycling came head-to-head and neither truly understood the other. On the one hand, there was the newcomer, Anglo-Saxon, for whom the Tour was an ideal, tinged with romance. The Tour was one of four objectives that the young LeMond had written in his training diary and for Anglo-Saxons, cycling could be what Abt terms 'a thing of beauty'. The Europeans didn't see it that way. Hinault was a man bred into cycling from a locale steeped in the sport, a pragmatist for whom winning the Tour de France was the climax to a game that you played rather than mangle metal in a factory, for which you were lucky enough to be given a salary which dwarfed what metal-bashing would bring in.

Hinault says now, of that attack on the Tourmalet descent, 'I enjoyed myself like a little loonie, like a schoolboy.' In 1986, for the first time in a decade, he had *carte blanche* to play as he wanted; unlike on many occasions since 1982, his body was cooperating fully by making all its potential available to him. And in a couple of months the game was going to be over for good; he was demob happy. LeMond never showed Hinault's basic aggression on a bike; nor had he figured out that the game Hinault liked to play was one in which he was the dominant party, like the older boy in the playground who has to decide who goes in goal and who is referee, even if he hasn't got as certain a touch as the centre forward.

After eight years of being at the heart of events, how could Hinault see things otherwise and revert to being a mere bit-part player? As he explained afterwards, 'I said at the start of the year, "I'll pull the strings in the Tour. I'll play with the others." This Tour has been an enormous pleasure for me because everything revolved around me.' In that sentence is the key to the way Hinault rode in the 1986 Tour: it was his game and he would play it how he wanted. If LeMond didn't understand, *tant pis*.

In this crowded Tour, with its three stars, there were two winners, and neither was the man who wore the yellow jersey into Paris. The race was a triumph for the two Bernards, Tapie and Hinault. Tapie's (unauthorised) biographer Airy Routier states that the Alpe d'Huez triumph was 'exactly what the French were wanting. Tapie had devised it a few hours earlier ...' For Philippe Crepel the 1986 race was 'the apotheosis of the scenario that Tapie had created'. How could he top 1985, when Hinault won Tour No. 5 and clinched the Giro–Tour double? Here's how, in Crepel's view: 'The climactic moment of the story: two massive champions cohabiting. And he was already looking elsewhere, he already had his eyes on the next stage.' Tapie's career would reach its zenith – his entry into politics and football – shortly after the 1986 Tour; his fall would follow later, but that is another story.

As for the other Bernard, whatever LeMond and the US media may have felt about him at the time, Hinault had forged a scenario in which he could not lose. Faced with the onset of age, and an opponent who was his superior in form, he still had certain cards in his hand: the fearsome 'Badger' persona, LeMond's combination of passivity and paranoia, his ability to bluff and double-bluff. He had a trump up his sleeve in the fact that he did not *need* to win. But he played what he had been dealt with nous worthy of Poulidor beating his teammates at poker to pay for a training camp.

'By serving as mentor to the American, Hinault proved his perfect knowledge of the button that unleashes public fervour. He wins either way. If he wins the Tour he is a hero. If he loses it, he's an idol,' wrote Jean Amadou in *L'Équipe*. LeMond might not buy the 'mentor' notion, but he would not argue with the fact that Hinault won either way: if he happened to win the Tour he would have all that went with it. If LeMond won the Tour and Hinault looked as if he might have won it, the home fans and media would love him just as much, perhaps even more. 'Even if he didn't win, this was his greatest Tour de France,' said Jacques Anquetil.

What's certain is that LeMond had mixed feelings about that Tour for several years afterwards. 'It was good – at the time I was bitter – but it would have sucked if he had only towed me along. I'm glad it happened in that way because I know I beat a real Hinault, probably one of the best Hinaults.' LeMond had become completely fed up of the implication that Hinault had given him the Tour. 'You've dreamed about winning the Tour since you were sixteen years old, you finally do it, and everyone's saying, "Hinault gave it to you, he could have won if he'd wanted." I was sick inside.

'Part of the Tour is having that team feeling, having everybody around you support you, and that was not the case and that is what really bummed me out,' he told me. 'The fact everyone said Hinault could have blown me away – I mean come on! It burned me out of cycling. That winter [1986–7] I was real down on Europe. I hated every journalist I saw because it was the same old question. I have bad memories of that whole Tour.'

Philippe Bouvet's view is that the 1986 Tour ended Hinault's career on an unanswerable question: 'Could he have won the sixth Tour or not? The 1986 Tour will be ambiguous. What can be said is that he was very clever in how he handled it. He made a mistake in attacking on the Tourmalet but fell on his feet.' Crucially for Bouvet, it provided the perfect ending to Hinault's career, making him 'the only cycling champion to emerge unbeaten from his various defeats'.

In their study of the Tour de France, Hugh Dauncey and Geoff Hare reached a similar conclusion, but with the view that Hinault knew what he was doing that July.

'Dominating a race totally with complete athletic superiority or a masterfully calculating limitation of risk is
unlikely to produce enthusiastic fervour, but a champion
who wins in a mix of "uncertainty" over the final result
and by demonstrating "panache" in his manner of winning,
combines success in... sport,' write Dauncey and Hare.
'Thus... Hinault "manufactured" the final element of his
public image by bowing out of cycling as an *heroic* "failure"
who had missed out on a sixth Tour win despite riding
with aggression, style and panache because he had to
honour his agreement of 1985.' In this context, Hinault's
attacking that July makes perfect sense: every time he
demonstrated his strength, he underlined that he could
have won the Tour, were it not for the fact that he had
given his word to another. And if the attacks failed, he
had lost nothing.

Millar believes that Hinault was on a charm offensive
that year, related in part to the fact that the previous year,
there had been a clear sense that LeMond had helped
him to win. 'Nineteen eighty-five shocked Hinault a little,
the perception that his public didn't like him. In the '86
Tour there was definitely a change in his attitude, a definite softening in how he felt he had to go about his job.'
Here was, after all, a man who was celebrated for his
dislike of the crushes of photographers, television cameras
and reporters that was the hallmark of a Tour stage finish,
and who had had his share of run-ins with the media.

'Before that he didn't care what anyone thought of how
he raced and what he said. Before that he didn't set out

to elicit any sympathy from any one. Everyone knew he was on a charm offensive – he didn't show the same level of anger towards everything, just towards a few vital things, like kicking the crap out of the climbers and playing with Greg's head.' Like Raymond Poulidor, Hinault had learned – just in time in his case – which buttons to press to get the public on his side. Writing in *L'Équipe*, Jean Amadou concluded: 'The fearsome beast became a cuddly toy.'

CHAPTER 14

THIS IS NOT AU REVOIR, IT'S GOODBYE

I was in the same position as Poulidor. But before being Poulidor I learned to win and built a palmarès. *I learned to win, and then later I learned to lose.*

– Bernard Hinault

Bernard Hinault's retirement was in marked contrast with other greats' exits from the sport. Eddy Merckx struggled for eighteen months before accepting the inevitable. Rik Van Looy set out from home for a race one day in 1970 and simply decided to call it a day there and then. Jacques Anquetil rode an interminable series of lesser events to milk his market value to the maximum before quitting at thirty-six in a similar style to Van Looy, while Fausto Coppi was so far past his sell-by date in his final years that many wished he would stop for his own sake. The end of Hinault's racing career was *lucide*, as he liked to put it: a clear-headed, almost cold-blooded decision.

The Badger ceremonially hung up his bike on a date that had been public knowledge for several years: 14 November 1986, his thirty-second birthday. The occasion was marked by an immense celebration in the town of Quessoy, just inland from Yffiniac, where he and his wife Martine had made their home. The festivities had taken a year to organise, and included a cyclo-sportif for 3,600 riders, a concert, fireworks and an invitation cyclo-cross race on a half-mile course lined with 15,000 fans. They were all invited into a massive marquee (the second biggest in France, it was said) for slices of the Badger's birthday cake. The guests filed through the tent, which had been fitted out like a museum full of Hinault's jerseys bikes and trophies. Among the gifts was a hundred-year-old bottle of Paul Ricard pastis, said to be one of just three in the world. Afterwards, Hinault was photographed for the now defunct magazine *Sprint 2000* on a podium next to a waxwork wearing a La Vie Claire jersey and clutching a stuffed badger snarling as viciously as could be imagined.

'It was a total love-fest and he deserved it,' recalled Sam Abt, one of the few non-French reporters to attend the Blexit. 'I remember I was astonished to see all the jerseys. Even though I knew his record, when I suddenly saw all of them, it was overwhelming. I was very impressed by him – so many riders say they are going to stop but want to do one more year. It wasn't as if he hated what he was doing. He loved it and there wasn't really anything else he could do. He kept his word, which counted for a lot.'

Hinault had won his last race, a criterium in Angers on 19 September. His goal had been to win the world championships in Colorado a few weeks earlier and then stop racing in what would have been dramatic style, just as he would probably have quit if he had won the Tour. Having won the Coors Classic stage race on LeMond's home turf, he was in fine form for the World's, but he attacked too early, an error he had made before. Moreno Argentin bridged to him accompanied by two strong Frenchmen, Laurent Fignon and Charly Mottet, and Hinault preferred to let his national teammates have their chance rather than permit the peloton to bring them all back. Fignon blew; Mottet won the silver medal behind Argentin with Hinault fifty-ninth.

The one truly major feat missing from Hinault's *palmarès* was the world hour record, which Coppi, Anquetil and Merckx had broken before him. His early background as a track pursuiter and his subsequent dominance in time trials on the road gave him at least as good a chance as Moser, who took the record in 1984. He and Guimard had looked into a possible attempt in 1978–79, when Hinault had only recently stopped pursuiting, and they had concluded that the best method would be to take to the track shortly after completing the Tour de France. This had been Merckx's approach and it would work for Chris Boardman in 1996, but it wasn't right for Hinault. As he pointed out, 'At that time [of the year], you don't think about an hour record. Everything was ready for it, apart from me.' Merckx's suffering en route to beating the record in 1972 had been legendary, which may have dissuaded the Badger; but in addition a post-Tour record attempt would cut across racing the criterium circuit, as well as the world road race championship. So the record remained unchallenged.

Hinault's exit wasn't universally acclaimed. The writer Olivier Dazat felt that there was romance in the sight of a fallen cycling champion dragging himself through races on willpower alone. For Dazat, the descent to the realms of the mere mortals that marked the end of the careers of Merckx, Anquetil and Coppi was a crucial way of emphasising what had been, of expiating their previous dominance. 'The fall is part of the destiny of an exceptional creature, the ultimate show of pride, a masochistic stubbornness that makes them go ever lower.'

That was, however, at odds with the feelings of many of those who watched Merckx's travails in late 1977 and early 1978, and who had observed Coppi's drawn-out end. Hinault clearly didn't share that romantic view: 'I'd watched two champions who I admired a great deal, Anquetil and Merckx ... At thirty they were still performing at a high level, at thirty-two or thirty-four less so. I said that I owed it to myself to avoid going the same way – if at thirty-two I couldn't perform as well, I wouldn't be better at thirty-four or thirty-five.' Among the greats of cycling, his was one of the shortest careers: two years less than Merckx, five less than Anquetil, who spent thirteen and sixteen seasons as pros respectively. Miguel Indurain's career would be shorter; Lance Armstrong's longer.

There are those who feel that perhaps Hinault should have continued to race for longer, that it was his utter determination not to go back on his word that made him stick to his guns and quit while the going was good. There was a definite parallel with the promise he made to Greg LeMond in 1985. 'He never takes a step backwards,' his soigneur Joel Marteil told *L'Équipe*. 'It's his way of functioning, "I've said something, I'm not going back on it." With LeMond, he dug a trap for himself. The same thing with his retirement. He stuck to it. Even though I heard him say later, "Who knows what would have happened if I'd pushed it back?"' As Maurice Le Guilloux said: 'All he wanted was to achieve a beautiful end to his career, but with the potential he had, he could have done one or two more years without any problems.'

Some thought Hinault could have won more in his twelve seasons as a pro, notably his old mentor Robert Le Roux, who was echoed by the Badger's confidant and *directeur sportif* Maurice Le Guilloux. 'In his head, Bernard was a rider three months out of twelve,' said Le Guilloux. 'With a different approach he would have been unbeatable twelve months out of twelve. But he needed to relax and freewheel occasionally.'

At the retirement celebration, one reporter asked the Badger if he was sure he wouldn't be coming out of retirement for Paris–Nice. The reply was joyously sarky: 'You can't catch me out with that one. Everyone knows I won't be making my comeback until the Critérium International.'

Twenty-seven and a half years later, Jean-François Bernard walks almost sheepishly into the press centre at the Tour de France in Leeds. There is no fanfare, no sense of importance about him. While Bernard Hinault or Stephen Roche still exude self-belief in their body language and are immediately recognisable, only a hard-core student of cycling in the 1980s would know that the shy-looking man, round-faced, greying, sitting anonymously among a group of radio reporters, was once the Next Big Thing in French cycling. Nowadays, in between work as a radio consultant, Bernard leads hunting parties in search of 'big game': deer, wild boar, wild goats, through the Parc du Morvan near his home in central France. For a few years, however, 1986 to 1989, Jean-François Bernard was Bernard Hinault's anointed heir, until it all went horribly wrong.

French cycling has had a thirty-year succession crisis since the Badger quit and Bernard's experiences mark the start of the story. In 1986, Hinault's last year, Bernard scored a solo victory in the Tour de France stage to Gap and finished twelfth overall in his first attempt at the race. With Fignon failing to return from his operation and *Le Blaireau* on the retirement trail, the French media and the race organisers were looking for a new star, and Bernard was named by Hinault as a possible successor. 'I ended up being projected to centre stage very rapidly,' says Bernard. In 1986, he was also the *mascotte* of Jacques Chancel's daily post-stage television chat show, the new professional selected to come on each day to give his view. This gave him a far higher media profile than Hinault or others had enjoyed early in their careers but that in turn proved counter-productive.

In the 1987 Tour de France, LeMond was expected to lead La Vie Claire, which was now backed by Toshiba, another of Tapie's companies. With the American absent due to his near-fatal shooting accident that April, Bernard headed the team, finishing third, winning two time-trial stages and wearing the yellow jersey after a dominant ride in the epic test up Mont Ventoux. This victory prompted Pierre Chany to write in *L'Équipe*, 'He has demonstrated that he [has] the perfect combination of innate talent and animal energy which characterises all exceptional champions.' However, the day after Ventoux he fell victim to an alliance between the other leading riders, prompted by Guimard's Système-U team in what was clearly a backlash against La Vie Claire's monopoly on the race in 1985 and 1986.

On that day, Bernard lost over four minutes in one fell swoop; he now believes his career may have hinged on that episode. 'I did not lose the Tour by very much – I won two time trials, could have won overall for sure. It basically came down to a puncture at the wrong time in the stage across the Vercors. Everyone wanted Koechli's skin, so I could find no one in the field to help me – and they got my hide as well. It was a big war between Guimard and the others and Koechli. Koechli wasn't from within the milieu, he worked in different ways, we'd had that [very successful] Tour the year before, so no one was going to help. If I had won the Tour in 1987, that would have changed a lot of things. If you win a Tour, it's not the same game at all; the rest of your career has a totally different complexion.'

The 1988 Tour was billed as a straight *franco–français* battle between Fignon and Bernard. Fignon's form was on the up; Bernard had won three stages in the Giro and had been well placed until he was put out by an unfortunate crash in an unlit tunnel. 'It's delivery time for Bernard; a brilliant attacker, he enjoys incontestable popularity,' wrote Maurice Vidal in *Miroir du Cyclisme*. 'To fully merit and retain that popularity, he *must* win the Tour de France this year.' Vidal made the point that Tapie's patience was liable to run out and described Bernard as having 'a reputation which has come before his *palmarès*, a mediatic hero'. The writer was correct, as Bernard now acknowledges: the young rider's profile was greater than his achievements merited. Two years into his career, Hinault had barely got round to buying his first car; Bernard already had a Porsche, which Tapie had given to him after his stage win at Gap.

Bernard started the 1988 Tour with lingering tendinitis in his knee, struggled through the Alps and quit in the final week. And that was pretty much that: he missed the 1989 Tour due to an operation on his knee and was a busted flush by 1990, although he made a brief return to his best in 1992 after joining Miguel Indurain at Banesto. He reflects now: 'I've always had the image of a rider with a long list of victories, even if I haven't won much. Everybody thinks of me as Hinault's successor. That's who I am.'

Bernard was not the first man to be saddled with the status of 'the next Hinault'. The question had first arisen in 1983 after the Badger's second knee operation. After that year's Tour, the answer looked obvious, particularly in Cyrille Guimard's view: Laurent Fignon. There seemed little doubt once the Parisian had dominated the old master in the 1984 Tour. By November 1986, however, the waters had muddied. Like Hinault, Fignon had had a knee operation, but his struggle to regain form was proving more difficult than his former leader's; the injury had been more severe, the surgery more radical. Marc Madiot had won Paris–Roubaix for Guimard, but did not have the climbing ability needed for the Tour. Bernard was expected to fill the gap.

   'Fignon never fulfilled the promise he showed in 1984,' says Philippe Bouvet. 'But Bernard never had the career he looked as if he might. That meant for the first time since the war, we had no champions in French cycling. After Fignon and Bernard it was a poor generation and it all got mixed up with the doping question.' By 1990, when I reported on the Tour for the first time, French fortunes were already on the slide. Fignon's time as a Tour contender came to an end that year on a rainy roadside in

Normandy; Bernard was anonymous until he abandoned. Bernard Tapie's involvement in cycling came to an end in 1991; in Toshiba's last season, the bulk of their results came from a Swiss cyclist, Tony Rominger. It was clear by then that no immediate French successor to Hinault or Fignon was going to emerge. And as Bouvet observes – and as Guimard has also pointed out – once the 1990s got under way, with the emergence of the blood booster erythropoietin – commonly known as EPO – it became impossible to read the quality of a cyclist in any case.

French cycling found new heroes through the 1990s – Laurent Jalabert, Richard Virenque, Laurent Brochard, Luc Leblanc – but it was a rapidly changing and more complex world than the one that bred Hinault and his brethren. Brochard and Virenque fell foul of the Festina doping scandal in 1998, while Jalabert's status was always ambiguous: the most successful French champion post Fignon – thanks to a dominant 1995 – he spent the bulk of his career with teams outside France and never seemed that interested in his homeland until retirement beckoned. The decline was such that in 1999 no Frenchman was able to win a stage in the Tour. French one-day Classic wins had always been rare; now they were like hens' teeth.

The fact that French cycling was experiencing the same phenomenon as Belgium post Merckx or Italy in the era after Coppi was already a puzzle when I met Hinault in 1993. 'Logically, if you have a super-champion in the sport, it should bring young riders in, riders who want to emulate that super-champion,' he mused. 'But super-champions are difficult entities. You don't get many of them, perhaps ten in a century. You don't just build them. You start with someone who is gifted by nature, who has certain capacities. Others have less quality and make do with what they have.'

His old teammate Marc Madiot came back into the sport as a team manager in 1996 and was still running the Française des Jeux squad, sponsored by the French national lottery, nearly twenty years later. He agrees that the issue of the Hinault succession had clouded minds, in much the same way as the search for a new Merckx had haunted Belgian cycling for a generation. 'I'm not certain about a Hinault complex. People always wait for the new messiah. What Guimard said was [a great champion] was either born or he was not. He either exists or he doesn't. People were always seeing the new Hinault – it's a bit like believing in miracles, it's the same kind of logic.'

When Bernard is asked about the poisoned chalice, his first point is that it wasn't handed only to him. 'It was a great generation,' he says. That is absolutely the case. France was seething with talented cyclists in the 1980s. While my boss at Livarot was nurturing Thierry Marie and François Lemarchand to more than decent pro careers, just down the road in Rouen the brightest prospect of all, Philippe Bouvatier, was being groomed in his turn – like Bernard and Marie he would race at the Los Angeles Olympics before turning professional. Normandy turned out an amateur world champion, Richard Vivien, in those years as well; like Bouvatier he ended up in obscurity.

Those that did make it to the top of cycling from Bernard's generation included Charly Mottet – another Guimard discovery who wore the yellow jersey in the 1987 Tour, and finished fourth that year as well as in 1991; the Breton Ronan Pensec, who finished sixth in the Tour at the age of twenty-three; Marc Madiot and his brother Yvon; Luc Leblanc, who shone in the 1991 Tour and won the 1994 world road championship – but who has since admitted using EPO; one-day racer Martial Gayant; and Gilles Delion, a Koechli protégé who won the 1990 Tour of Lombardy. 'We were parachuted into being champions much too fast,' summarises Bernard. 'If Hinault had done another year that would have changed a lot of things.' He feels that LeMond and Fignon's injury travails meant too much was expected of their immediate successors before they were ready.

'It was a tricky time; we were a good generation with a lot of potential – the crop after Fignon. There was the end of Hinault's career, and the problems Fignon had – he was there without being there. I had a very good Tour in 1986, in 1987 Hinault was no longer there and I ended up leading. I was very young – only twenty-three or twenty-four [but] I was thrust forward as Hinault's successor very quickly. I was third in the 1987 Tour and won two stages, after that in 1988 I was very strong – I won three stages in the Giro, fell and couldn't finish, started the Tour and abandoned. That was a break in my career. I struggled to get back…It was complicated because it just went too quick.'

Bernard says that the expectations proved too much for him, and believes it was true of his contemporaries. 'There was enormous pressure – no more Hinault, no Fignon, no past French winner of the Tour. Everyone was used to seeing Frenchmen winning the Tour because of those two; that meant the press absolutely wanted a French winner and it just went too fast for us. I had a lot of difficulty taking the pressure. Too much was asked of me, and too soon. It was everything – sponsors, public, media – the moment you made a faux pas, or you stopped getting results, you were left exposed, broken. It's complicated when you are young and don't have experience. No one understood psychology at the time. It wasn't structured. We could all go well in races like Liège, the Dauphiné, the Tour, but we were given no time to grow.'

Bernard feels that French cycling is returning to something like the years he knew when he turned professional for La Vie Claire, but he acknowledges that the country still lacks the true all-rounder it needs to win the Tour de France. 'Jalabert was good but not a high mountain climber – Virenque was a climber but couldn't time trial. Take Pierre Rolland' – one of the finest of the current generation – 'he's often with the best in the mountains but if you have two time trials in a Tour, one fifty kilometres, the other forty kilometres, he ends up with a handicap of eight minutes. How can you gain eight minutes in the mountains in today's cycling? It's impossible. We haven't had that complete rider – no Contador, no Wiggins.

'We haven't had an athlete since Fignon and Hinault with the right qualities to win the Tour. The two last French Tour winners were very good time triallists. For many years, we have had no riders who are capable of winning time trials in the Tour. We have super climbers, no problem there, but no time triallists. Who's the last French rider to win a long time trial in the Tour?' There's a little pause, for dramatic effect. 'It's me'. And then he mutters, 'hallucinant'... beyond belief.

As he had planned, once the last glass of champagne had been drained, Hinault took up breeding dairy cows on a forty-eight-hectare farm outside Calorguen, ten kilometres south of Dinan, which he had bought in 1983. His cousin René – who had himself moved into agricultural engineering – was hired to help him out. It was the classic dream of a lad brought up on a small peasant holding: a big farm of his own. It was the road that Jacques Anquetil had travelled before him, but Master Jacques had ended up on an estate outside Rouen, which was four times the size of the Hinault domain. He was also involved in Ouest Levure, a business supplying bakers' materials to boulangeries.

Within two weeks of his retirement, the Tour de France organisers were in touch through the former national trainer Richard Marillier, who had directed Les Bleus as

Hinault won the rainbow jersey at Sallanches in 1980. This was neatly ironic given his first major impact on the Tour had been at the head of the strike against those same organisers in 1978. 'Félix [Lévitan] didn't appreciate Hinault leading the strike, but he was anything but stupid,' said Jean-Marie Leblanc, who had Hinault on his management team when his tenure at ASO started in 1989. 'He had understood that Hinault was a leader and it was better to have him with him than against. It may have seemed like a cynical calculation, but it made sense.'

Early on, Hinault was a race regulator, directing the various motorbikes and official cars that circulate around the riders. Then he advised on routing. Not long after Leblanc took over at the end of 1988, he appointed the five-times winner 'ambassador' as part of his campaign to take the race back to his roots. In Leblanc's view, having the five-times winner running affairs on the podium after each stage of the Tour lent greater gravitas to the protocol of pulling on jerseys, shaking hands with men in suits, and making sure the riders kissed the correct girls in short skirts. Some of Hinault's former rivals and friends found his ceremonial role beneath him; Zoetemelk says, 'Given what he had shown on the road, I wouldn't have expected him to take up such an ancillary function.'

Abt had expected Hinault to go into politics. 'It's difficult to say that he had limited ambitions, but the French had so few heroes at the time and he was an authentic hero. He was a good-looking guy, articulate enough not to trip over what he was saying, his name was known to everyone and there were no skeletons in the cupboard. That's almost the definition of a successful French politician. He could do no wrong as far as the French were concerned – here's a guy who wades into a bunch of strikers, in a country with a highly developed union system, and comes out with no retribution. The thing with LeMond made him popular as well – there was no blowback from that at all.' Ironically, it was Martine Hinault who became the local mayor, prompting Calorguen natives to make the slightly heavy joke that the village had only two celebrities, 'Madame the mayor and her other half.'

Perhaps wisely, Hinault never became a *directeur sportif* although he was the French national team selector from 1988 to 1993. There were two bids to put him at the head of a team, one for French telecoms company Bouygues, which proved abortive because it was mounted too late in the season and the riders they needed had already been signed elsewhere. The other was with a Chinese company – 'about ten years ago' – in which he was proposed as a technical consultant. 'I was interested because it would have been starting from nothing.' Generally, however, he feels he would have been too hard on the riders. 'I think the riders are scared of me. With me, you wouldn't hear French riders saying before they've turned a pedal, "I'm paid this much and this is what I want to win." I would be the one who made the rules: "Win races and then you will win this much." You only become a champion if you are hungry.'

There is now a gently nostalgic side to Hinault, which
seems to have developed as his racing days have receded.
In the 1989 Tour, Joël Pelier – who had received a
tongue-lashing from Hinault in the Tour only four years
earlier – found the Badger encouraging him from an
official car as he attempted successfully to win the Tour
stage at Futuroscope. In 1995, Robert Millar's last year
as a pro, the Scot was in a similar situation when he got
into a break in Flèche Wallonne: his old adversary
appeared alongside in a red Tour de France Fiat. 'He
came up and shouted, "*Allez mon petit*," which is a term
of endearment in French. It wasn't the Bernard Hinault
I knew. I was quite shocked that he could say something
encouraging, something that wasn't aggressive. I suspect
it took him a fair while to make the shift from thinking,
"I could beat these guys the way they are riding," to,
"Bloody hell, he's actually human."'

In 1993, Hinault clearly didn't like discussing the past;
now, however, reliving the great races – particularly those
that have been forgotten – is something he embraces. He
has recently rediscovered some of his earliest bikes. The
machine on which he won the Tour of Lombardy in 1979
was given to *Vélo* magazine, who used it in a reader's
competition at the end of that season. It was discovered
in the collection of a hard-core cycling fan who lived
seventy kilometres from Hinault – and when he died, it
was auctioned off for charity; it is now on show in the
Hinault bike shop in Saint-Malo. Hinault's first bike –
the one that belonged to his brother – was found near

his home; it had been given away, but it still had his brother's initials on it. 'I put it in the boot of my car and took it home.' One of his time-trial machines – a Look low-profile from 1985 to 1986 – had been given to the town of Saint-Brieuc and was unearthed in a cupboard in the town hall. 'It's good to see how these things evolved, and they need to be shown to people – it's important to make them dream.'

The Badger has become almost cuddly. He has the aura of a national treasure, a reminder of a bygone golden age. 'Hinault is like Gérard Depardieu,' said his former team-mate Marc Madiot. 'He can say what he wants and can allow himself to do anything.' He likes to retreat to the farm in Calorguen when not on duty for ASO; he likes country life, riding his bike, popping into his son's bike shop outside Saint-Malo. As a little exchange regarding a pheasant implies ('I could shoot that, pluck and gut it and then cook it with a good red wine'), there is an epicurean side to him. Mostly, he exudes positive optimism – there's not a lot of soul-searching about him. He's also pretty cold-blooded about racing – 'You totally forget the bad moments, especially when you're racing. Real memories are – for example – the death of someone close to you.'

It became a cliché among journalists that whenever Hinault was asked what the riders in the race should do in a given situation, he had one answer: 'Attack'. It was as if he knew what was expected of him and was happy to provide it. Occasionally, there has been a whiff of controversy, particularly when he backflipped over Lance

Armstrong as the Texan morphed from the Tour's greatest champion to its ultimate black sheep. However, coping with the vagaries of who is a great champion in the last twenty years of cycling has proved beyond many of us; for those who are employed by the Tour de France organisers, it has proved virtually impossible to maintain a consistent position as one by one the best riders in the sport have shone, been presumed innocent until proven guilty, and then been proven guilty. At times, Hinault has seemed incongruously hard on his successors, coming out with statements like, 'The French don't go training, no one slaps them in the face to move them forwards. They earn too much money and don't make enough effort. You have to put a knife to their throat to get results.' There might have been a grain of truth in it, but in the years of 'two-speed cycling' it didn't sit well.

Where his own past is concerned, Hinault seems happy in his skin without being sentimental. 'In terms of the blend between their careers and their lives, I've said for a long time that the two most intelligent champions I've known in cycling are Raymond Poulidor and a bit later Bernard Hinault,' wrote Guimard in his memoirs. 'What's the ultimate aim in life? To be happy and to feel happy in what you do every day. Poulidor stopped cycling and since then has only done things that he likes to do. Hinault is pretty much the same.' Hinault stopped farming in 2005 and now rents the land out. 'I have two children who don't want to follow me into it. I don't see why I should bust my ass if they don't want to pick it up from me.' Recently he has expanded his activities for ASO to about 120–130 days a year and got back on his bike, on the grounds that having given up working around the farm, he needed to keep fit somehow. Typically, or perhaps to propagate the legend of the Badger a bit more, he simply asked his wife to stop the car and let him ride home in the rain one day in 2007.

Some things haven't changed, however mellow the Badger may seem. On his visit to Yorkshire in 2014, Hinault rode steadily enough up the long climb out of Cragg Vale at the head of a large group of locals, but coming back down with British professional Russell Downing, Downing was taken aback when the five-times Tour de France winner couldn't resist attacking him at full pelt on the sinuous descent. In similar vein, Stephen Roche rode a criterium in Brittany for former professionals with the Badger in 2013 and noted, 'He was still getting annoyed with everyone.' Roche also recalled riding a sportive with the former *patron*. 'We were in the second row [of riders] and a rider ahead kept touching wheels. Hinault shouted at him, "Keep your bike straight"; he did it again, so he yelled, "Keep your fucking bike straight." The guy said, "I'm not used to riding in a *peloton*," so Hinault answered, "You'd better get used to it or this could be your last time."'

CHAPTER 15

REBIRTH

'Of course I want to see a Frenchman win the Tour – I hope it happens in my lifetime.'

– Bernard Hinault

In the meeting room, a huddle of nervous-looking men in suits and six casually dressed journalists sit around the projector looking at the whiteboard as Olivier Quéguiner, the managing director of the French Cycling Federation, explains why we are here. We know already: this is the launch of the FFC's project to found its own professional cycling team with the goal of winning the Tour de France with a French cyclist. Thirty years after the last *franco–français* Tour of 1984, it has come to this. It feels surreal. France has more top-class professional cycling teams and a bigger pool of cyclists in the top tier of the sport than any nation on earth, but if you want a measure of how keenly the lack of a successor to Bernard Hinault is felt, here it is.

Outside the fresh-smelling rooms, diggers are still finishing the car parks that surround the velodrome-office-rider-accommodation-BMX-track complex in Saint-Quentin-en-Yvelines, thirty-five kilometres south of Paris, the FFC's new home. Further inside the building, the velodrome has that unique aroma of fresh-sawn pine. The previous evening, the €68-million complex, the only vestige of Paris's bid for the 2012 Olympics, had been formally opened in a blur of champagne and canapés – the foie gras wrapped in dark chocolate particularly French and particularly inedible – and a longueur of interminable speeches by a succession of civic dignitaries, all presented, inevitably, by the breathless speaker Daniel Mangeas.

The press pack handed out the next morning is a hastily stapled together set of A4 sheets dotted with phrases such as 'iconic platform', 'through the line channel marketing' and 'corporate social responsibility', but missing one fact: if they want this project up and running for 2015, the men in suits have just a few months to find tens of millions of euros. New beginnings always have an awkward feel to them. Five years earlier, I'd shared a croissant with a bevy of nervous men in suits and casually dressed journalists in London's Lanesborough Hotel, where, over breakfast, Dave Brailsford had told us of his aim to win the Tour de France within five years with a British cyclist. It had been met with the same slightly sceptical and knowing response that had greeted the French project. Brailsford had his big money backer in place *before* getting

the press in. On the other hand, the FFC croissants were
better. But there were so many similarities: the forced
optimism, the slightly rushed press pack, the sense of not
quite knowing where this would lead, but amid all that,
the feeling that the trek to such a lofty goal had to start
somewhere and this might as well be it.

What drew the ironic smile here, for an Englishman,
was the complete lack of any ambiguity: in its attempts
to recreate the golden past, the French governing body
was turning to the British model. The hope was that the
Saint-Quentin velodrome would turn into a centre of
national Olympic excellence, uniting national coaches and
the best national talent, that would eventually match
Manchester, where the British project to win the Tour de
France had its roots. Like Brailsford's Sky, the FFC team
would be based at the velodrome. The presentation of the
national professional team project used images of Team
Sky's iconic bus with its list of international names. The
centrepiece of the velodrome launch – among the streamer
climbers, BMX stunt riders and Irina, a chanteuse with a
guitar – was an exhibition match between France's
sprinters and a selection from, inevitably, Great Britain.

Thirty years earlier almost to the day, I'd written to
cycling clubs in Brittany and Normandy – including
Hinault's old club in Saint-Brieuc – to find a place to
race. That was driven by the reality of the time. In the
early 1980s, France was one of cycling's promised lands,
a destination of choice for a young British cyclist with
nothing but enthusiasm to recommend him. My cycling

mate Andy and I knew that the sport in Britain had nothing to offer us in terms of racing, prize money, gaining experience. To make any progress, we had to get to France. By 2014, *la terre promise* was now on our side of the Channel, where the racing calendar was growing at every level, team numbers expanding, participation in youth and women's cycling thrusting forwards. Two Tour de France wins for the world's leading professional team in the last two years had capped it off. 'Team Sky could be a benchmark for us,' admitted Quéguiner. Of the six journalists invited to the launch, not one was French: we were all English-speaking, as the goal for marketing agency Sportfive and the FFC was to get the message to potential backers outside French borders, tacit acceptance that this was not a concept for the *hexagone*.

By happy coincidence, three days later I was headed for Majorca, to drop in on Team Sky and its Sirs Wiggins and Brailsford. Brailsford – who, like me, had headed to France in his youth with his bike and his kitbag and his hopes – picked up on the parallels at once when we spoke about how the French were trying to emulate what he and Sky and Wiggins had achieved. 'Good luck to them,' he said. Would it be a project for him? 'You'd have to go for it, imagine the scale of finding a French winner of the Tour. It's the ultimate goal in cycling.' Later in 2014 he repeated the same sentiments in an interview with *L'Équipe*; winning the Tour with a Frenchman just might be the next big project. It was a statement that former Cofidis manager Eric Boyer, for one, had found 'very pretentious and very disrespectful, as if French managers aren't capable and competent enough to do it'.

The FFC's project intrigued, but so did the bigger questions behind it: what was the future for French cycling and where did it lie? That reflected a lengthy crisis of confidence that could be traced back to the moment in November 1986 when Hinault placed his bike on the ceremonial peg. The collapse had its origins in the struggles of Fignon and Bernard in the late 1980s. The decline had been so precipitous that by 2004 the imminent death of French cycling was being proclaimed. 'Cycling is in a trough across France,' said the writer Jean Bobet, brother of Louison, noting that his and Hinault's homeland had been hard hit. 'As Breton cycling has been so powerful for so long, its fading is the more apparent.'

The paradox could not be missed. As the Tour de France grew ever more popular and profitable – and ever more hyped around the ephemeral appeal of Lance Armstrong – you could talk to bike-shop owners who bemoaned the lack of young cyclists entering the sport, and you could see signs on the Tour's roadsides complaining that regional cycling was dying. The French calendar thinned out as a variety of races, some with lengthy histories and evocative names, were closed down: the Tour de l'Aude (1987), Bordeaux–Paris (1988), the Tour d'Armorique (1994), Tour du Vaucluse (1998), the Midi Libre, Grand Prix des Nations, and Classique des Alpes (all in 2004). Major events such as the Dauphiné Libéré and Paris–Nice struggled before being taken over by the Tour de France organisers ASO.

That was just the top of the pyramid: '[Road] cycling [in France] is dying a lingering death with events disappearing each year,' wrote Pierre Ballester in *Fin De Cycle*, his apocalyptic view of the sport after Armstrong. 'The after-Tour criteriums are down to a mere handful, new licence holders are turning to BMX and mountain biking rather than the road, the group that remains interested in cycling is an ageing one, but the Tour is living very healthily.' Ballester quoted several figures: a decline in mid-level races, Pro Route – open to top-level amateurs and some professionals – of 36 per cent (172 races) between 1998 and 2008. The post-Tour criteriums had almost halved in number from thirty-seven in 1997 to eighteen in 2011 – many organisers could not afford the fees asked by the senior riders in an era of high wages. There had been a drop of 11,000 road-racing licences between 1998 and 2011, although a rise in BMX and mountain-bike licence holders meant that the French Cycling Federation's member base still increased.

In his memoirs, Laurent Fignon was equally pessimistic if more restrained. 'Initially the problem was the fallout from the Festina scandal. Several generations of kids were turned off cycling and the sport that profited was football, crowned by the legends of France '98 [and Euro 2000].' Fignon noted that soccer and rugby appeared to appeal to a far broader racial and socio-economic spectrum. He added: 'There were clumsy mistakes made by the governing body... [a] focus on major clubs that developed young riders. That decision reduced the base of the pyramid... ignoring the fact that the clubs that are best at recruiting are the little provincial set-ups in villages and often supported by local sponsors. They had the chance to bring on champions of their own and were able to hang on to them for a few years. Then, thanks to regional and national squads, those at the base gradually worked their way up to the top, without the small squads suffering. All this was wrecked. The young riders move on too quickly without having the chance to be toughened up and to nourish the spine of the sport as they develop. The base doesn't radiate out as widely as before. Cutting off growth at the lowest level means the top ends up in a state of drought.'

The soul-searching was understandable, but it was an open question whether French cycling was dying or merely mutating. It is certain that the prolific grass-roots calendar that produced Anquetil, Hinault and the golden generation of the 1980s – and which I experienced in Normandy – is no more. Many local races have died due to increased organising costs, particularly policing due to the upsurge in other road traffic, ageing club officials, traffic calming in town centres, and social changes in the sport's rural power base.

Even so, the sport has begun to produce a new wave of promising young riders in the last four or five years. The journalist and club official Noel Nilly feels the reforms Fignon criticises, which were made in the 2000s, have borne fruit. 'At the time of Hinault there was no structure in the sport but there were big numbers of competitors. Now, the numbers are not the same, but it's better structured. The clubs form a pyramid, it's very clear how it's organised and the riders can move up and down. The restructuring was inevitable because French cycling was average – there were no Frenchmen capable of winning Classics or the Tour de France.' It's partly down to structure: the best professional teams – FDJ, Europcar, Ag2R – have amateur feeder clubs that feed into the professional teams – CC Etupes, Vendée-U – and in these, only the riders are amateurs. The staff are full-time. The upshot is that while the pool of local races is smaller and the pool of cyclists has shrunk, the process of feeding them through to professional teams is more closely managed.

The crisis in terms of professional team numbers came relatively early, in 1993 and 1994, when there were just two squads of note. Since then, France has consistently fielded four or five top-level professional squads, in spite of the pressures on sponsorship after the 1998 Festina doping scandal, and the relative lack of results internationally since then. What's clear is that in spite of continual forecasts of doom since 1998 – some of them written by me – the sport has not died. It has changed, but that is true across Europe.

The decline in the level of French performances in its showcase home event is what has made the headlines, but it has been a complex business. If you look at the Tour de France statistics, and do not ignore the known drug-takers in the 1990s – Laurent Jalabert, Richard Virenque, Luc Leblanc – on the grounds that they were competing on equal terms with other drug-takers, reports of the home riders' eclipse were actually premature in some senses. In the twenty-five Tours since 1989, the French have usually had at least two stage wins – one in ten – and regularly up to four or five. This can look dire given that in some Tours – 1979 or 1984 – the home riders might win up to a dozen stages, but it might be viewed as acceptable for a race in which the rest of the world is now competing, rather than the more parochial event the Tour was until the 1980s. Also, France has tended to lack a specialist bunch sprinter who can win two or more stages in a given Tour.[22]

The French have been less successful in terms of placing riders in the top ten overall in the Tour: they have failed to do so on nine occasions since 1989. Against that, they have managed to place two riders in the top ten in seven Tours over the same period. Here, however, another element has to be considered: the history of doping. Between 1986 and 1998, the year of the Festina scandal, there were only two years in which no Frenchman was either on the podium or within reach of it. Between 1999 and 2010, there was only one year, 2000, when a French cyclist was remotely near the podium; in five of those

---

[22] Since 1989, the French have recorded one or no stage wins in seven out of twenty-five Tours, and four or more in six. See Appendix Two for more details.

Tours, no French cyclist was even in the top ten. That roughly coincides with what is termed the era of 'two-speed cycling', the years between the Festina scandal of 1998 and the inception of the UCI's biological passport in 2009. This was the time, when, many French commentators claim, most French cyclists were riding 'clean' after the French teams responded in the wake of Festina, while blood doping in its various forms remained rife in some squads from outside France at least until the biological passport began to bite in 2009–10. The results of French cyclists were distorted, believed observers such as Laurent Fignon, who wrote, 'A lot of the best French riders lived through the worst years of "total doping". From the point where France decided to "wash whiter than white" our riders were completely left behind. That is what has happened since 1998. That was the price that had to be paid.'

Since 1999, while positive tests and police investigations have nailed many of the non-French riders who have finished in the top ten of the Tour as blood dopers, the French cyclists to have figured prominently in the Tour have been immune.[23]A detailed examination of lists of riders banned for blood boosting as a result of police inquiries or positive tests backs up the 'two-speed' thesis. Particularly given their large numbers, French riders and teams are very much in a minority, and there is absolutely no reason to suggest that this might be because they

---

[23] For details, see Appendix Three.

were experts at evading tests. Including the US Postal Service and Operación Puerto investigations, there were approximately 150 bans handed down for doping offences related to blood boosting in cycling between 1999 and 2010. Of these just six involved French cyclists or cyclists in French teams.

By July 2014, the question of where the next French Tour de France winner might come from looked a little clearer, and it didn't look likely to be the FFC and Sportfive's project. Nor did it look as if Brailsford would be needed unless he got the Murdoch chequebook out and hired a Frenchman or two. The scenes at the end of the 2014 Tour de France in Périgueux after Jean-Christophe Péraud and Thibaut Pinot clinched second and third overall were astonishing: Pinot's boss Marc Madiot giving a double high-five to his brother Yvon; Péraud prostrate on the tarmac, unable to speak, and doing something unprecedented on the Tour – refusing to talk to television because he was too emotional.

Usually at the Tour it is only the overall winner who comes into the press room to give one concluding interview after the final time trial. At Périgueux, Péraud and Pinot turned up as well, as if the French were saying to the international media: 'Look at us!' It was too early to tell if this marked the end of thirty years of hurt, but it was a tangible reward for fifteen years of effort, sometimes bordering on humiliation, as Philippe Bouvet underlined for *L'Équipe*. 'There was so much that had been lived through coming to the surface, all those years when they had been trodden underfoot.'

The year 2014 was not a repeat of the Hinault–Fignon Tour of thirty years earlier, although it was the first time since then that two Frenchmen had finished on the podium of the Tour. The national euphoria was such that you could be forgiven for thinking Péraud and Pinot and Romain Bardet, who had finished sixth, had been hotly contesting the overall win. In fact, they had been riding on the coat-tails of the overall winner Vincenzo Nibali, and had never looked likely to shake him. The last French winner of the Tour looked on with avuncular amusement. 'What I like about Pinot is that he doesn't always do what he is told,' was Hinault's verdict. 'As for Bardet, even in the final time trial [where he finished twenty-sixth], we saw that he has balls. I think we're heading for one hell of a rivalry between those two. Perhaps even on the level of the one between Anquetil and Poulidor, or the one that existed between Laurent [Fignon] and me.'

The euphoria in French cycling circles was partly down to the years of 'two-speed cycling'. The national trainer Bernard Bourreau was just one voice paying homage to what was termed a 'lost generation'. 'They weren't less good than the riders of today, but they happened to be there at a bad time in a bad era. We were made to look like fools.' One of those riders, Nicolas Fritsch, who was strong enough to finish third in the Tour of Switzerland in 2002, but called time on his career at twenty-eight, explained how it had felt to race in those days: 'What was difficult a few years ago was that doping was organised among certain teams so all the riders in those teams were stronger. There was more than one team doing this so half the peloton were using EPO and making the races crazily fast. Physically and mentally it wore you out.'

'We were really blocked by [two-speed cycling], because the French teams were relatively clean,' said the FDJ trainer Fred Grappe. 'Fritsch was an exceptional athlete; today he would be in the top ten in Grand Tours. [David] Moncoutié could have had a different *palmarès* altogether. I take my hat off to Sandy Casar who finished sixth in the Giro in 2006. I never heard him say "fucking druggies", but I can understand the bitterness that he could have felt. We looked useless but we had riders of that calibre.'

'The differences [today] are less extreme,' Madiot told me. 'I can't say everything is perfect [but] it's more manageable than in the period we unfortunately lived through.' Madiot felt that the period of 'two-speed cycling' had led to a mindset that had been hard to change. 'You live with the hope that it will get better...at the time when things actually happen you don't know what's going on. For example, if we had known the entire truth about Lance Armstrong, it would have been even harder than it was. It was better that way...you always hope you might get better. You adapt to events. Where you once dreamed of winning the Tour de France, the world championship or Paris–Roubaix, you dream of Paris–Camembert, Cholet, the French Cup. In cycling you can always focus on something that is achievable. Before, you would go to the Tour to achieve something big, then when we had the difficulties we did, you would say that winning a stage would be a really good Tour. If you had said that at the time of Renault it would have been laughable.'

A more level playing field meant that riders like Pinot and Bardet had none of the crises of confidence that had afflicted the generation before them. Success gave them greater appetite leading to more success. 'Before, when French riders turned pro, they were heartbroken,' was the view of Europcar *directeur sportif* Dominique Arnould. 'There was a huge gap.' Meanwhile, trainers like Grappe and Madiot's brother Yvon were keen to underline that other factors contributed to the improvement in French fortunes: the move to bigger squads after the inception of the UCI's World Tour calendar meant there were more French riders in pro teams; the development of a network of trainers within several of the higher-level French amateur teams as well as the professional squads; the flourishing feeder teams linked to pro squads, and a new confidence at under-23 and junior level on the international stage, which meant new professionals expected success early in their careers and knew more than the rudiments of training. 'Now that the fight against doping is more efficient, talented youngsters get results immediately and have no complexes,' said Arnould.

French cycling again looked complete. The years of 'two-speed cycling' had seen the emergence of a group of riders who were best described as '*baroudeurs*', talented,

courageous and clever individuals who specialised in picking up occasional stage wins in hillier stages of the Tour:
Thomas Voeckler, Pierrick Fédrigo, Casar. But by 2014
France had pure climbers with all-round ability in Bardet,
Péraud, Pierre Rolland and Pinot, and sprinters in Arnaud
Démare, Nacer Bouhanni and Bryan Coquard, while
baroudeurs were still going strong: the evergreen Voeckler
and the other Tour hero of 2014, Tony Gallopin. One
thing was still lacking, however: a champion of the mag-
nitude of Louison Bobet, Jacques Anquetil, Hinault or
Fignon to act as a figurehead, to contend for the overall
win in the Tour and to be a constant presence in the
biggest one-day Classics and push for victory in the Giro
d'Italia and Vuelta.

On this, Madiot, Guimard and Hinault spoke with one
voice: champions are born, not made. This is supported
by the fact that nations well outside the cycling heartland
have produced some of the greatest champions in recent
years – Sean Kelly, Greg LeMond, Cadel Evans, Thor
Hushovd – and that at the same time other 'historic'
cycling nations such as Belgium and Italy have struggled
in the same way as France to produce successors to Eddy
Merckx and Fausto Coppi. If the formation of the greatest
cycling champions was purely down to the best environment, a new Merckx or Coppi would have emerged, as
would a new Hinault.

This prompts another thought: if French cycling is still
producing a consistent number of half-decent cyclists, as
it clearly is, and a super-champion of the Hinault ilk is

a matter of random genetics (and sadly, in the 2000s, the right blood doping programme), there might be another way of looking at the Hinault succession crisis. It may sound like sacrilege but was France ever truly a power in world cycling?

Before the rapid expansion of cycling in the 1980s, French cyclists were massively successful at home in their domestic events, just as Italian cyclists shone in their calendar and the Flemish ruled Flanders. French victories in the one-day Classics and world road race championships have always been rare: Hinault was an aberration here, as was Louison Bobet. Jacques Anquetil, for example, won only two Classics (he shone in the Grand Prix des Nations time trial) and no world road title. In the relatively parochial 1950s, 1960s and 1970s, it was more straightforward for the second-string French champions – Bernard Thévenet, Roger Pingeon, Roger Walkowiak, Raymond Poulidor – to paper over the gaps between the years of the French super-champions by performing strongly in the Tour de France, their home event, which just happened to be the most important race on the calendar. Their successors have faced a far stiffer task across the board due to increased international competition since the 1980s, and life became even tougher for them in the 2000s due to 'two-speed cycling'.

As Marc Madiot saw it, by 2014 French cycling was finally reaping the benefit of a balance between past and present, coupled with a healthy reality check after 1998. But whereas many had wondered if hosting the Tour was that beneficial due to the annual pressure of competing in the biggest race in the world on home soil, the FDJ manager believed that the Tour had saved the day. 'The good fortune of French cycling is that it is still alive after the difficult period post-1998. The [professional] calendar is pretty much the same, the teams have evolved a little bit, the Federation has been stable. That's allowed us to get through the tricky years. In a natural way, thanks to the miracle of genetics, we have a good generation, but they are there today because we had the capacity to conserve our roots...We restructured...put in place the *suivi longitudinal*[24] – we were the only country to have it and every one laughed in our faces – that's what has allowed this new generation to come through.

'In the difficult time the riders knew it was hard to get results, so they just took what pleasure they could in racing. Today, they put results first. [The young riders] have all got into this *logique du resultat*. It's all been possible because there was this capacity, willpower...it was good luck that we have the Tour in France. We were lucky to have old-school cycling, almost a century of lived history. The Tour goes back to 1903, all the village races go back fifty or sixty years to around the [time of] the war – luckily all that hasn't gone. There are fewer races now of course but there are places where I raced as a

---

[24] A system of health checks brought in in France from 1999 which worked in a similar way to today's biological passport, but did not carry anti-doping sanctions.

boy where there are still races now. We aren't at the end of the long road yet – the important bit now is not necessarily to have a Tour winner but to have charismatic French riders who are known and recognised by the wider public, not just in the world of cycling.'

Perhaps the most interesting aspect of the home riders' triumph in the 2014 Tour de France was the fact that France's hottest cycling prospect wasn't even at the race. That spring, I sat in the bar of a small countryside hotel, lost at the end of a back road in the Ardennes south of Liège, and couldn't help wondering if the young man sitting opposite me might be the next Bernard Hinault.

The things that Warren Barguil has in common with his illustrious counterpart are impossible to ignore. Like the Badger he comes from deepest Brittany – his home is in Inzinzac, just inland from Lorient on the peninsula's south-west coast. Camors, where Bernard Hinault made such an impression in the criterium at Easter 1975, is twenty-five kilometres to the east. Fifteen kilometres to the north is Plouay, home of the Grand Prix Ouest France, where young Warren was taken to see the world road race championships at the age of eight. As with so many Bretons, cycling ran in the family – it was Barguil's father who was the early inspiration rather than his cousin, and like the Hinault cousins, father and son raced together – and as with the Badger, Barguil was a precocious talent: a French junior national champion, and a winner of the Tour de l'Avenir.

Being Breton, Barguil has the inevitable reputation for being stubborn. Like his antecedent, he had a reputation for attacking without restraint, when he was younger at least. Like Hinault, he's *taiseux* – not a man who gives a lot away. He seems quiet, restrained as he talks, but there is one other coincidence: Barguil made his major Tour debut in the Vuelta a España, albeit at the age of twenty-one, and it was a winning one: he took two mountain stages. But the similarities with the Badger end there. Barguil began cycling as a BMX rider, he turned professional for a Dutch team, Argos-Shimano (from 2015 Alpecin-Giant), and he has relished the fact that they have kept him under wraps in a way that would have been tough for any French team to do. Then again, he was less than happy when he was left out of the 2014 Tour so that they could focus fully on their sprinter Marcel Kittel.

Like all the new generation of French cyclists – Pinot, Bardet, Bryan Coquard et al – Barguil knows his cycling history, and he knows about the pressure to find a new Hinault. 'As soon as somebody sticks out, immediately [they are told] you're the best, you're the one. Then when they make a few mistakes, there is an overreaction. The wait has gone on a long time, that's why people have lost patience.' Like Jean-François Bernard, he wishes the hype would die down. He says he 'can't wait' to discover the Tour, to win one-day Classics, but he wants to do so in his own time, at his own pace.

Barguil refers to the Badger with a dispassionate

distance that might seem surprising until you recall that he was born five years after Hinault had retired. When he began cycling the golden era was already twenty years distant, as far removed from him as the years of Coppi must have seemed to the young *Blaireau*. 'Who doesn't know Bernard Hinault? He's a legend. I remember going up Mur de Bretagne' – a famously steep ascent in the heart of Brittany, halfway between Saint-Brieuc and Lorient – 'and seeing his face on a huge poster. I know the story about his fingers getting frozen at Liège, about his abandon in the 1980 Tour. We would go on training camps with [national trainer] Bernard Bourreau, and he would tell us his anecdotes – Hinault at Sallanches and so on.'

Admiration for the Badger aside – what young French cyclist is going to denigrate their greatest champion? – Barguil shows a welcome reluctance to discuss Hinault. He certainly does not embrace the notion that he might be the next Hinault. It is an attitude summed up by his liking for a famous anecdote: when Lance Armstrong won his first Tour stage in 1993 and was asked if he was the next Greg LeMond, he replied that in fact he wanted to be the first Lance Armstrong. Barguil recalls Marc Madiot making the inevitable Badger comparisons during the 2012 Tour de l'Avenir, to which he would reply, 'I want to be like myself.' He tells me: 'You have to think of being yourself. You shouldn't wipe out the past. You can't erase it [but] I want to create my own place [in cycling]. I don't want to be an imitation of Hinault.'

Given the history of other cyclists thrust into the role, it is probably just as well he feels that way. As well as a desire to avoid the obvious headlines and consequent pressure, that is a reflection of reality: it is almost twenty years since a Frenchman could be realistically tipped as a possible to win the Tour. And Barguil himself has not even started the Tour de France. But as I sup my coffee in that bar in that small hotel, I simply have to trace the connections between the small quiet figure in the Giant-branded tracksuit and the snarling face in the black and yellow diagonal stripes. Whatever the cyclists themselves may say, whatever reality informs us in our more cold-blooded moments, however much we may know we shouldn't, therein lies the point: we cannot help ourselves. None of us.

Just as Italians constantly refer back to Coppi and Belgians to Merckx, the search for another Bernard Hinault among the French – among all cycling fans – is bound to go on, however misplaced that may be. If there is a disconnect from reality there, that is simply countered: fans and sports media do not connect with sport for pragmatic reasons. This is not just a cycling phenomenon: look at England football followers constantly wondering if the next World Cup will be the new 1966, British tennis commentators hoping on behalf of Tim Henman, or Welsh rugby lovers watching this year's sensation at fly-half. We can't help making the connections to the past, because nostalgia is part of what ties us emotionally to sport. An endless source of interest for sport lovers lies in how the links are maintained, the latest twists in the old, old stories. Barguil has every right to want to see the Badger buried; those who line the roadsides of France every July will all be thinking: long live the next New Hinault.

BERNARD HINAULT
MAJOR VICTORIES

1972: (amateur) national junior road race championships; Breton championship; Grand Elan Breton.

1974: (amateur) national pursuit championship; Breton pursuit and one-kilometre championships; stage, Route de France; stage, Tour of Tarragon.

Professional from October 1974.

1975: (Gitane-Campagnolo) national pursuit championship; overall, Circuit de la Sarthe. Season-long awards: Promotion Pernod.

1976: (Gitane-Campagnolo) national pursuit championship; overall + one stage, Tour du Limousin; overall + one stage, Tour d'Indre-et-Loire; overall + one stage, Tour de l'Aude; overall + one stage, Circuit de la Sarthe;

Paris–Camembert; stage, Étoile des Espoirs; criteriums: Chardonnay, Schellenberg, Wohlen, Brugg, Cléguerec. Season-long awards: Prestige Pernod.

1977: (Gitane-Campagnolo) Gent-Wevelgem; Liège–Bastogne–Liège; Grand Prix des Nations; overall + two stages, Dauphiné Libéré; overall + stage, Tour du Limousin; stages, Étoile des Espoirs, Tour d'Indre-et-Loire; criteriums: Hénon, Plaintel, Callac. Season-long awards: Prestige Pernod.

1978: overall + three stages, Tour de France; overall + prologue + four stages, Tour of Spain; overall + stage, Critérium National; national road race championship; Grand Prix des Nations; criteriums: Ronde des Korrigans, Circuit de l'Aulne, Henon, Lannion, Maël-Pestiven, Maurs, Neufchâtel-en-Bray, Plancoët, Pontoise, Roanne, Saint-Gilles-Croix de Vie, Callac, Plessala. Season-long awards: Challenge Sédis; Prestige Pernod.

1979: overall + points + seven stages, Tour de France; overall + four stages, Dauphiné Libéré; Tour of Lombardy; Flèche Wallonne; Grand Prix des Nations; overall + stage Tour de l'Oise; Circuit de l'Indre; stage, Critérium International; two stages, Étoile des Espoirs; stage, Tour of Luxembourg; criteriums: Bourges, Circuit de l'Aulne, Concarneau, Fontenay, Fontenay-sous-Bois, Fougères, des Herbiers, Hénon, Ploërdut, Saint-Marie-sur-Mer, Saint-Macaire-en-Mauges, Callac. Season-long awards: Challenge Sédis; Prestige and Super Prestige Pernod.

1980: gold medal, world road race championship; prologue + two stages, Tour de France; overall + one stage, Giro d'Italia; Liège–Bastogn–Liège; overall, Tour de Romandie; stage, Tour Midi-Pyrenees; prologue + stage, Tour de l'Aude; stage, Tour du Limousin; stage, Critérium International; criteriums: Bain-de-Bretagne, Brasschaat, Landivisiau, Maël–Pestiven, Plessala, Fougères, Changé, Redon, Plelan-le-Petit. Season-long awards: Super Prestige Pernod, Challenge Sédis.

1981: overall + prologue + four stages, Tour de France; overall + four stages, Dauphiné Libéré; Paris–Roubaix; Amstel Gold Race; bronze medal, world road race championship; overall + three stages, Critérium International; stage, Red Zinger Classic; stage, Tour of the Mediterranean; criteriums: Aix-en-Provence, Circuit de l'Aulne, Josselin, Lannion, Nogent-sur-Oise, Olivet, Palermo, Paris, Quimper, Saint-Claud, Toulouse, Lamballe, Plessala, Château-Chinon. Season-long awards: Super Prestige Pernod, Challenge Sédis.

1982: overall + prologue + three stages, Tour de France; overall + five stages, Giro d'Italia; Grand Prix des Nations; overall + stage Tour of Corsica; overall + prologue, Tour d'Armorique; overall + stage, Tour of Luxembourg; stage, Tour de Romandie; Grand Prix La Marseillaise; criteriums: Bol d'Or des Monédières, Critérium des As, Lorient, Callac, Cluses, Polynormande. Season-long awards: Super Prestige Pernod, Challenge Sédis.

1983: overall + two stages, Tour of Spain; Flèche Wallonne; stage, Tour Midi-Pyrenees; Grand Prix Pino Cerami.

1984: prologue, Tour de France; Grand Prix des Nations; Tour of Lombardy; Baracchi Trophy (with Francesco Moser); overall, Four Days of Dunkirk; stage, Tour of Valencia; criteriums: Lisieux, Calais, Tours, Callac, Lamballe, Regenboogkoers.

1985: overall + prologue + two stages, Tour de France; overall + one stage, Giro d'Italia; stage, Red Zinger Race; criteriums: Bussières, Saussignac, Lamballe, Circuit de l'Aulne.

1986: three stages + King of the Mountains jersey, Tour de France; overall + two stages, Coors Classic; overall, Vuelta Valenciana; prologue, Four Days of Dunkirk; stage, Tour Midi-Pyrenees; stage, Clásico RCN; Luis Puig Trophy; criteriums: Angers, Calais, Joué-les-Tours, Toulouse, Pongy, Callac, Chateau-Chinon.

HINAULT AND THE GREAT TOURS

TOUR DE FRANCE
8 starts.
5 overall wins, one second place, one abandon.
28 stage wins.
71 days in *maillot jaune*.

GIRO D'ITALIA

3 starts.

3 overall wins.

6 stage wins.

28 days in the *maglia rosa*.

VUELTA A ESPAÑA

2 starts.

2 overall wins.

7 stage wins.

12 days in the *maillot amarillo*.

French performances in Tours de France in the post-Hinault era: best rider overall, number of home stage wins

1987: Jean-François Bernard 3rd, Charly Mottet 4th, Laurent Fignon 7th, seven French stage wins

1988: Eric Boyer 5th, Ronan Pensec 7th, Denis Roux 10th, two stage wins

1989: Fignon 2nd, Mottet 6th, four stage wins

1990: Fabrice Philipot 14th, three stage wins

1991: Mottet 4th, Luc Leblanc 5th, Fignon 6th, Gérard Rué 10th, five stage wins

1992: Pascal Lino 5th, six stage wins

1993: Jean-Philippe Dojwa 15th, one stage win

1994: Leblanc 4th, Richard Virenque 5th, three stage wins

1995: Laurent Jalabert 4th, three stage wins

1996: Virenque 3rd, Leblanc 6th, three stage wins

1997: Virenque 2nd, six stage wins

1998: Christophe Rinero 4th, Jean-Cyril Robin 6th, one stage win

1999: Virenque 8th, no stage wins

2000: Christophe Moreau 4th, two stage wins

2001: François Simon 6th, four stage wins

2002: David Moncoutié 13th, one stage win

2003: Moreau 8th, two stage wins

2004: Moreau 12th, three stage wins

2005: Moreau 14th, one stage win

2006: Moreau 7th, three stage wins

2007: Stéphane Goubert 27th, two stage wins

2008: Sandy Casar 14th, three stage wins

2009: Casar 10th, one stage win

2010: John Gadret 18th, five stage wins

2011: Thomas Voeckler 4th, Jean-Christophe Péraud 9th, Pierre Rolland 10th, one stage win

2012: Rolland 8th, Thibaut Pinot 10th, four stage wins

2013: Romain Bardet 13th, one stage win

2014: Péraud 2nd, Pinot 3rd, Bardet 6th, two stage wins

APPENDIX 3

The era of 'two-speed cycling': positive tests/riders implicated in police inquiries for haemoglobin boosters such as
EPO or blood doping post-Festina

Year	Overall total	Total French riders or French teams
1999	8	1 (Laurent Roux)
2000	1	0
2001	10	1 (Pascal Hervé)
2002	5	0
2003	9	0
2004	16	5 (Cofidis inquiry = including David Millar, Philippe Gaumont, Frank Vandenbroucke)
2005	8	0
2006	35[25]	1
2007	4	0
2008	6	0
2009	10	0
2010	17	1 (Mickael Larpe)
2011	4	0
2012	24[26]	2 (Bobby Julich, Steve Houanard)

[25] Operación Puerto

[26] US Postal inquiry

This is a relatively crude way of testing the thesis that French cyclists were victims of 'two-speed cycling' in the era immediately post-Festina: a look at how many French riders or French team members were among those who tested positive for haemoglobin-boosting drugs or methods on the premise that these were the most effective forms of doping to achieve high overall placings in the Tour de France.

The facts are that only the Cofidis scandal of 2004 implicated more than one rider in a French team, and even then the evidence suggested that these were three small groups operating independently rather than a system within the team. There is certainly nothing to resemble the methodical doping at teams such as US Postal Service, Rabobank and T-Mobile or the networks that existed around Dr Michele Ferrari.

Given the disproportionately high numbers of French cyclists within the sport, one would expect the numbers of positive tests for blood boosters to be far greater if they had been engaging in blood doping on any scale. To that extent, the figures bear out the 'two-speed' thesis.

GREATS OF BRETON CYCLING

Lucien Petit-Breton (1882–1917) Winner Tour de France 1907 and 1908, Hour Record holder 1904, winner Paris–Tours, Milan–San Remo. 'The Argentine' was an early French hero in what is now known as cycling's heroic era. Born Lucien Mazan, raised in Argentina, Petit-Breton died near the First World War front in eastern France.

Jean-Marie Goasmat (1913–2001) The 'Leprechaun of Pluvigner' was a diminutive, puckish-looking rider, massively popular in Brittany in spite of the fact that, in modern terms, he didn't win a great deal on the international stage. His career lasted from 1935 to 1951, and included one top-ten placing in the Tour de France, plus what should have been a podium place in 1938, had he not fallen foul to internal politics in the France squad. He was a fine all-rounder capable of winning one-day events such as Paris–Vimoutiers and Grand Prix Plouay, time trials such as the Grand Prix des Nations and stage races such as the Circuit de l'Ouest and Critérium National.

Jean Robic (1921–1980). Winner of the 1947 Tour de France, he was a curious-looking little cyclist variously nicknamed '*Biquet*' (the little goat) or '*tête de cuir*' (leather-head) because of his penchant for wearing a cumbersome crash hat. He was actually born in the Ardennes to a Breton family who returned to the region when he was seven. Other than winning six stages in the ten Tours de France he started, he landed the cyclo-cross world title in 1950. He was legendary for being handed bottles containing lead at the top of mountain climbs so that his light weight would be less of a disadvantage when going downhill.

André Mahé (1919–2010) Winner of Paris–Roubaix in 1949, *ex aequo* with Fausto Coppi's brother Serse after a controversial finish where he was misdirected by officials and no one was sure who had really won. Also took Paris–Tours in 1950.

Louison Bobet (1925–1983) The baker's son from Saint-Méen-le-Grand near Rennes was the first rider to win the Tour de France three years running, from 1953 to 1955. Hinault's direct forerunner in his all-round ability on the international stage: he also won Milan–San Remo (1951), Giro di Lombardia (1951), Critérium International (1951–52), Grand Prix des Nations (1952), world road race championship (1954), Tour of Flanders (1955), Dauphiné Libéré (1955), Paris–Roubaix (1956) and Bordeaux–Paris (1959). He was variously described as 'private', 'moody' and was surprisingly fussy, precipitating a minor crisis by turning down his first yellow jersey in the Tour because it was made of artificial fibre not pure wool. His brother Jean also raced, less successfully, before becoming a leading writer and broadcaster.

Albert Bouvet (b. 1930). 'The Bulldog of Fougères', winner of Paris–Tours in 1956, a former stonemason who was largely responsible, after retirement, for devising the modern route of Paris–Roubaix.

Joseph Groussard (b. 1934). A prolific sprint winner on the French circuit whose major victories were in Milan–San Remo in 1963 and the final stage of the Tour de France at the Parc des Princes in 1959. His younger brother Georges enjoyed a shorter career that included a long spell in the 1964 Tour's yellow jersey and fifth overall. Joseph's son-in-law Philippe Dalibard had a brief professional career before becoming a prolific winner of amateur events in the 1980s.

Cyrille Guimard (b. 1947). Best known for managing Bernard Hinault and Laurent Fignon at Renault, Guimard was a successful road sprinter who shone on the track and in cyclo-cross. Guimard's major victories include: seven stage wins in the Tour de France and two in the Vuelta, plus a host of stages in French events such as Paris–Nice,

Dauphiné Libéré, and two bronze medals in the world road race championships (1971 and 1972). He is also known for fighting Eddy Merckx almost all the way to Paris in the 1972 Tour, pulling out with a day to go due to the knee injury that would end his career.

Marc Gomez (b. 1954). Surprise winner of Milan–San Remo in 1982 – a rare French win in the event – and French national champion the same year.

Frederic Guesdon (b. 1971). The last French winner of Paris–Roubaix, in 1997, born in Louison and Jean Bobet's home town of Saint-Méen-le-Grand. Also took Paris–Tours in 2006, a rare French Classic winner in the era of 'two-speed cycling'.

For those who want to know more about Breton cycling, I can recommend *Les Grands Cyclistes Bretons* by Georges Cadiou (Alan Sutton, 2005) and *l'Aventure du Cyclisme en Bretagne* by Jean-Paul Ollivier (Editions Palantines, 2007).

BIBLIOGRAPHY

Books

Abt, Samuel, *Greg LeMond: The Incredible Comeback*, London: Stanley Paul, 1991

Abt, Samuel, *In High Gear: The World of Professional Bicycle Racing*, San Francisco: Bicycle Books, 1989

Ballester, Pierre, *Fin de Cycle*, Paris: Editions de la Martinière, 2013

Bordas, Philippe, *Forcenés*, Librairie Arthème Fayard, 2008

Brunel, Philippe, *Bernard Hinault*, Paris: Solar, 2014

Dauncey, Hugh & Hare, Geoff (eds), *The Tour de France 1903–2003: A Century of Sporting Structures, Meanings and Values*, London: Frank Cass & Co Ltd, 2003

Dazat, Olivier, *Seigneurs et Forcats du Vélo*, Paris: Calmann-Lévy, 1987

René Deruyk and Jean-Yves Herbeuval, *Les Secrets du Sorcier Jean Stablinski*, Lille: La Voix du Nord, 1994

Fignon, Laurent, Fotheringham, William (trans), *We Were Young and Carefree*, London: Yellow Jersey, 2010

Fotheringham, William, *Roule Britannia, Great Britain and the Tour de France*, London: Yellow Jersey 2005

Guimard, Cyrille, *Dans les secrets du Tour de France*, Paris: Grasset, 2012

Hinault, Bernard, *Moi, Paris*: Calmann-Lévy, 1978

Kelly, Sean, *Hunger*, Redbourn UK: Peloton Publishing, 2013

Le Roux, Robert, *Coureur Cycliste, ce que tu dois savoir*, Conde-sur-Noireau: Score 1976

Penot, Christophe, *Jean-Marie Leblanc: Gardien du Tour de France*, Saint-Malo: Éditions Cristel, 1999

Magowan, Robin, *Tour de France, 75th Anniversay Race*, Boulder: Velopress, 1979

Marchand, Jacques, *Vélodrame*, Paris: Calmann-Lévy, 2008

Maso, Benjo, Horn, Michiel (trans), *The Sweat of the Gods*, Norwich: Mousehold Press, 2005

Moore, Richard, *Étape*, London: HarperSport, 2014

Ollivier, Jean-Paul, Hinault, Bernard (preface), *L'Aventure du Cyclisme en Bretagne*, Quimper: Éditions Palantines 2007

Ollivier, Jean-Paul, *Un peu de memoires, beaucoup de souvenirs, Jean-Paul Ollivier*, Quimper: Éditions Palantines, 2014

Roche, Stephen, *Born to Ride*, London: Yellow Jersey 2013

Routier, Airy, *Le Phenix, Le Retour de Bernard Tapie*, Paris: Editions Grasset, 2008

Sergeant, Pascal and Hinault, Bernard, *Bernard Hinault: l'Abecedaire*, Paris: Éditions Jacob-Duvernet, 2012

Magazines, newspapers and internet articles

Author interview with Greg LeMond, *Cycle Sport*, February 1994

Author interview with Hinault, *Cycle Sport*, August 1993.

Author interviews with Hinault and Paul Sherwen, *Cycle Sport*, July 1995

Philippe Bouvet, 1981 Paris Roubaix piece, *Vélo*, April 2001

Philippe Bouvet's review of the 1984 Tour in *l'Équipe* throughout July 2014 was also a valuable resource

Roger de Vlaeminck interview, *Vélo*, April 2014

Alasdair Fotheringham's account of the 1983 Vuelta on www.cyclingnews.com, August 2014

Benoît Heimermann's profiles of Bernard Hinault, *l'Équipe* 5, 12, 19, 26 July 2014

Hinault interview, *l'Équipe*, 21 June 2003

Hinault interview, *L'Express*, 2011

Hinault interview, *Vélo*, September 2012

L'Équipe's coverage of Hinault on his sixtieth birthday in November 2014 provided valuable insights. So too the celebration copy of *Vélo* magazine dated December 2014.

Serge Laget's feature on the 1978 Vuelta a España, *Vélo*, September 2010

'Made in France', *Vélo* special edition April 2013

Miroir du Cyclisme, various, 1978–1988

JB Wadley, 'Way Out West In Brittany', *Sporting Cyclist*, April 1960

Jacky Hardy's special edition of *Sport 2000* magazine published on Hinault's retirement

The website www.bikeraceinfo.com proved the best source of accurate results for the Tour de France in particular

Bernard Tapie's discography can be sampled on the website www.bode-et-musique.com

The films *Slaying the Badger* (John Dower, 2014) and *LeMond vs Hinault: Parole de Blaireau* (Patrick Chène 2014) offered valuable material from Jean-François Bernard, Paul Koechli and others.

INDEX